Klaus Herrmann

Self-Organizing Ambient Intelligence

Klaus Herrmann

Self-Organizing Ambient Intelligence

Principles, Algorithms, and Protocols

VDM Verlag Dr. Müller

Imprint

Bibliographic information by the German National Library: The German National Library lists this publication at the German National Bibliography; detailed bibliographic information is available on the Internet at http://dnb.d-nb.de.

Cover image: www.purestockx.com

Publisher:
VDM Verlag Dr. Müller Aktiengesellschaft & Co. KG, Dudweiler Landstr. 125 a, 66123 Saarbrücken, Germany,
Phone +49 681 9100-698, Fax +49 681 9100-988,
Email: info@vdm-verlag.de

Produced in USA and UK by:
Lightning Source Inc., La Vergne, Tennessee, USA
Lightning Source UK Ltd., Milton Keynes, UK
BookSurge LLC, 5341 Dorchester Road, Suite 16, North Charleston, SC 29418, USA

ISBN: 978-3-8364-9896-8

Abstract

In the last two decades, the advent of wireless networking technology and the achievements in the miniaturization of electronic devices have set new trends in distributed computing. This ultimately enables a new paradigm for embedding mobile users in intelligent environments that support them in their interactions with their local physical surrounding. This vision is called *Ambient Intelligence* (AmI). There are still many challenges ahead on the way towards the realization of AmI. One question that is central to the entire concept is: *How can we render AmI systems self-organizing such that they can indeed disappear in our environment without creating a massive administrative problem?*

In this book, we propose a model for a dedicated AmI infrastructure that supports the user in his interaction with his physical environment and with external entities. This infrastructure is called *Ad hoc Service Grid* (ASG) and provides wireless services in a decentralized and self-organizing fashion. We identify three distinct problems associated with self-organized service provisioning in the ASG model and propose algorithms and protocols that solve them. The problem that is at the center of our work is the *self-organized replication and distribution of arbitrary services* in an ASG. A set of algorithms is presented that solves this problem in a completely distributed way. The two other problems we tackle are the *discovery and lookup* of dynamically distributed service replicas and the *reconciliation* among a dynamic group of replicas. Together, the mechanisms we propose lay the foundation for a general AmI software platform. We will derive the architecture of such a *Serviceware* from these mechanisms. Detailed experimental results are presented that show the validity of our concepts and identify ways for tailoring our algorithms and protocols to the requirements of specific applications. Furthermore, we propose a new general model and a classification methodology for self-organizing software systems. We employ this model to evaluate our own solutions.

The focus of the research work presented in this book is on the global-scale interactions in an AmI system. We call this the *macro-level of interactions* to separate it from the focus of most current research projects. These projects concentrate more on adaptations at the *micro-level*, pertaining to the *internal* structures of specific applications and services. Our work complements these efforts by providing solutions for structuring AmI systems *externally*, for example by distributing a group of service replicas within an ASG network.

Acknowledgements

I would like to thank my colleagues Dr. Matthias Werner, Dr. Gero Mühl, Michael Jaeger, Dr. Torben Weiß, and Andreas Ulbrich for uncountable fruitful discussions that have inspired me. Furthermore, I would like to express my sincere gratitude to Prof. Dr. Kurt Geihs and Prof. Dr. Hans-Ulrich Heiß for their generous support and for giving me the chance to complete the scientific work documented in this book. I would also like to thank the *Deutsche Telekom AG* for funding my position at the Berlin University of Technology. The resources that were made available to my colleagues and me through this funding were excellent.

I would like to express my apologies to all of my colleagues for my constant effort to acquire as much computing power as possible in order to complete my simulations and generate the results displayed in this book. This may not have been the most pleasant experience for all them. My tendency to formulate requests for CPU cycles with a certain touch of inevitability may have appeared somewhat impertinent at times. Thank you for approving them.

It has been a long journey with a number of dead ends before this manuscript finally *emerged*. Along the way, I had to appreciate the fact that not everything tends to *self-organize*. However, it is rewarding to find that, if enough *non-specific pressure* is applied to a certain subject, all *the little components* finally fall into the right places to form *the whole* thing.

Contents

List of Figures

List of Tables

Part I

Introduction

Chapter 1

Motivation

In the last two decades, two trends have dominated the computer industry and computer science: the advent of wireless networking technology and the achievements in the field of miniaturization of electronic devices. The wireless revolution frees us from the burden of requiring a physically wired infrastructure for communication while the advances in miniaturization enable us to carry powerful electronic devices with us that are able to exploit this *wireless freedom*. The two most notable and commercially most relevant products, that have been created as a result, are cellular phones and wireless hotspots. Cellular phone networks are primarily targeted towards global, mobile voice communication. Wireless hotspots enable broadband Internet access at specific locations, e.g. at airports, hotels, and also at an ever-increasing number of private homes. Both represent wireless extensions of established communication technologies: the phone and the Internet.

However, the ability to carry small wireless devices for communication and computation also enables a paradigm that may soon complement the mentioned technologies and, eventually, merge with them: *Ambient Intelligence*. Ambient Intelligence (AmI) is more than an access or communication technology. While mobile phones and hotspots enable the user to communicate with any person and to access any information available on the world-wide Internet, AmI technologies can enhance his *interaction with his current physical environment*. AmI is not explicitly limited to this local environment, though. In fact, in the AmI visions, all three technologies (mobile phones, mobile Internet access, and the interaction with the local environment) are merged into an all-encompassing communication technology that the user is constantly embedded in. However, the direct interaction with the physical environment via appropriate wireless services is a feature that is not present in the other two technologies, at least not to a similar extent. This concept is different, for example, from location-based services that are being offered by mobile phone providers. Classical location-based services are provided in a centralized fashion. The provider can acquire the mobile phone's coordinates and send information pertaining to these coordinates to the phone. Thus, such services are not provided *by* but *on behalf of* the environment and by a central authority via a global communication infrastructure. While this model may be one part of AmI in general, the truly new concept of AmI is that the services and the hardware necessary for providing these services is embedded in the user's physical environment and distributed in nature. It enables local interactions with people, objects, and services in the local surrounding. There is no central authority that is controlling such an infrastructure, and it does not rely on any global communication network. As a consequence, anyone may, in principle, setup a local infrastructure and provide specific *Ambient Services* that enable the user to interact with the local provider's facilities.

Long before the European Commission's *Information Society Technologies Advisory Group* (ISTAG) has formulated its Ambient Intelligence vision [48], similar ideas have originally been proposed by Mark Weiser. Weiser's concept of *Ubiquitous Computing* (UbiComp) envisions a world where computing devices are not any longer perceived as distinct objects that have to be operated explicitly. Instead, computing technology recedes into the background of our every-day lives. Wireless networking and the miniaturization of computing devices are enabling technological trends for this new paradigm.

While the research on UbiComp has primarily been focused on the development of appropriate devices, the AmI vision abstracts from this problem and formulates more explicitly how the technology should change our lives to the better. At the center of this vision lies the demand for a technology that is offering services in a user-friendly and unobstructive way. The interaction between human users and between humans and their environment shall be enhanced. Today, this interaction is an explicit act. For example, if somebody enters a shopping mall on his weekly shopping trip, he needs to manage his shopping list, find all products, find the right way through the mall, calculate the overall price, take decisions concerning the trade-off between price and quality, and a plethora of other things. Essentially, people need to take care of all the little details themselves. This could change if AmI becomes reality. In the future, the shopping mall may be enhanced with diverse services that facilitate many aspects of a shopping trip in order to render the trip more comfortable and more efficient. A *navigation service* may guide the user through the mall. A *product finder service* may automatically investigate the items on the customer's electronic shopping list and offer a list of products that satisfies a set of constraints (overall price, quality, etc.). A *personalized recommendation service* may review the customer's long-term habits and his current objectives and propose some complementary products (e.g. the right wine for the menu that is most likely composed of the ingredients in the customer's shopping cart). The possibilities one may envision are endless. However, the challenges ahead on the way towards the realization of this vision are manifold, too.

Chapter 2

Focus and Contribution

The research objectives laid out by the ISTAG along the vision of AmI are targeting a broad range of technological fields concerning hardware and software, as well as "socio-technical" factors and legal issues. All of which shall be resolved in a pan-European research effort. In this book, we focus on a set of questions involved with the setup and the operation of a local Ambient Service infrastructure. The problem that is at the center of these issues is that *manual management is prohibitive* and must be reduced as much as possible. This has the following reasons:

- The *massive distribution of hardware and software* complicates the problems of explicitly taking management decisions and manually enforcing respective actions.

- The *high degree of dynamics* leads to a situation where the cycle of problem detection, the decision about appropriate actions, and the enforcement of these actions takes too long. In the meantime, the situation that triggered this manual process is likely to have transited to yet another situation that requires different actions. Under these conditions, manual management may not only be ineffective but even counterproductive.

- *Anyone may become a service provider.* This is one of the great strengths of the AmI paradigm as we interpret it. However, this also means that the personnel that is responsible for the services does not consist of trained IT experts with a background in network and systems management.

As a consequence, AmI systems have to have the ability to self-organize. They have to create and maintain useful structures by themselves, ensuring that the system operates acceptably well. We focus on three central problems:

1. *What would be the fitting model for a dedicated hardware platform that could be deployed explicitly to offer Ambient Services?* Until now, the diverse visions in the field of AmI implicitly assume that some hardware is already present in the environment. However, what if some local provider decides to offer Ambient Services without already having the necessary hardware platform? We propose a model for such a platform that is easy to install and flexibly scalable at

moderate costs. Moreover, the proposed hardware platform enables diverse business models that range from centrally installed infrastructures, to the rental of devices in changing numbers, and to the contribution of individual hardware devices for the benefit of a whole community of small service providers.

2. *What would be the core functionalities and services of a software platform that would be required for the basic self-organizing operation of Ambient Services?* In particular, we propose a Serviceware model that fits the dynamics and the distributed nature of Ambient Intelligence. Furthermore, we identify three core requirements for the operation of Ambient Services: the replication and distribution of services such that Quality of Service constraints are met, the discovery and lookup of such dynamically distributed services, and consistency models for handling dynamic stateful services adequately. We focus on self-organized mechanisms for each of these fundamental AmI problems and propose specific solutions.

3. *What would be a fitting model of self-organizing software systems that could enable us to evaluate different self-organizing solutions in the area of AmI?* We introduce a new model that is general enough to enable the evaluation of any self-organizing software system. In particular, we employ it to reason about the protocols and algorithms proposed in this book. This model is accompanied by a classification methodology that allows researchers to argue about the self-organization ability of their respective systems.

Thus, the contribution of this book encompasses more than a specific self-organizing solution. It takes a step towards a common understanding of self-organizing software systems. This understanding and the resulting design approaches are of central importance for the realization of the AmI visions. These visions clearly target at a complete shift of intelligence from the user side *and* the operator side into the specific AmI infrastructure. We conclude that the ability of such an infrastructure to self-organize diverse aspects of configuring, running, and managing Ambient Services is the key to its realization.

2.1   Methodology

Our infrastructure for Ambient Services is a special case of a mobile ad hoc network (MANET) [60]. It employs wireless ad hoc networking technology to establish a spontaneous network among the hardware nodes and the mobile devices of users. At the date of this writing, appropriate ad hoc networking technology is still not commercially available for building large-scale networks. The two most prominent technologies are IEEE 802.11 (WLAN) and Bluetooth. In its current version, WLAN does not provide a mode that easily enables multi-hop ad hoc networks due to a lack of proper MAC support. Bluetooth, on the other hand, promises to enable so-called *scatter networks* which, in theory, represent multi-hop ad hoc networks. However, most commercially available Bluetooth products do not support this mode. Therefore, at the moment, it proves difficult to build a real-world testbed for testing the concepts developed in this book. Moreover, the algorithms and protocols proposed here require the network to have a certain scale. The self-organization effects are difficult to observe with a network of about 10 nodes only. They require a network size that is one order of magnitude larger. Finally, each of the quantitative results presented throughout this book is based on a large number of measurements with the same basic setup but randomly generated starting conditions (network topology, client behavior etc.). This guarantees that the results are statistically relevant, which is impossible to achieve in a real-world environment.

For these reasons, the concepts are developed and evaluated using a simulation framework. This opens the possibility to perform a high number of detailed experiments and record various system parameters. It also makes experiments reproducible under different conditions to test the influence of specific changes on the performance of algorithms and protocols. We use the RePast agent-based simulation toolkit for our experiments. RePast provides support for implementing discrete event-based simulations.

The focus of this book is clearly on self-organization principles above the networking layer. We may have used a simulator like *ns-2* that also considers the problems involved with the interactions on the physical and data link layers (e.g. radio transmission and medium access). However, we decided to abstract from these issues since the self-organization mechanism under investigation are quite complex by themselves. The effects may be rather subtle and are sometimes hard to analyze. Therefore, we decided to keep the simulation as simple as possible. Aspects below the networking layer would have introduced a plethora of additional system parameters that would have been hard to factor out. However, the next step after having established stable higher-level concepts should clearly be the transition to a simulation environment that explicitly models the physical aspects of mobile wireless communication, to see if the corresponding effects affect our algorithms and protocols. This would be the first reality check by which we could adapt the systems proposed in this book in order to make them work in real networks.

2.2 Structure of the Book

The book has four major parts. In Part I, the problem domain of Ambient Intelligence is introduced. We present a general overview of the state-of-the-art in the related areas. In particular, we investigate the key concept of self-organization.

Part II presents the models we rely on in the rest of this book. Most notably, in Chapter 4, we introduce our model of self-organizing software systems (SOSS) and a classification methodology that builds on that model. The SOSS model can be used in general to classify any software system (and possibly also systems outside the software domain) into self-organizing and non-self-organizing ones. In particular, we use this general model to reason about the systems that we propose in the remaining part of the book and to show that they are indeed self-organizing. Chapter 5 presents the *Ad hoc Service Grid* (ASG) model. An ASG maybe deployed specifically for the provision of Ambient Services at some concrete location. We discuss the concepts concerning the ASG infrastructure, the underlying network, and its usage by clients. Furthermore, we give several application scenarios to establish an intuition for the range of application domains that are covered by this model.

Part III represents the main part of the book. Here, we develop the three core mechanisms that are required for the basic operation of an ASG. After a short introduction, we describe which basic middleware mechanisms the respective algorithms and protocols build on in Chapter 7. Subsequently, in Chapter 8, a set of algorithms is developed that deals with the fundamental problem of dynamic replication and placement of arbitrary Ambient Services in an ASG. The concept of self-organized dynamic replica placement occupies the largest part of this book since it is at the center of the self-organizing infrastructure as we envision it. Chapter 9 presents a system for the discovery and the lookup of service replicas. The task of finding a service replica becomes especially tough due to the dynamic nature of the replica placement system. We demonstrate that an efficient and yet effective lookup is still possible. The self-organization features of the lookup system allow it to deal with a set of possible failures while still maintaining its basic function. Finally, in Chapter 10 we propose an optimistic consistency model, and we develop corresponding algorithms and protocols that enable dynamically replicated stateful Ambient Services to maintain an acceptable level of consistency. This is achieved, even though there is no single entity that has a global view on the overall group of replicas.

Part IV concludes this book. We summarize the major results, review and analyze their applicability to the area of Ambient Intelligence, and present our conclusions. At the end, we give an outlook on open problems that have to be addressed in future research.

2.2.1   Remarks on the General Structuring

The concepts discussed in the three major algorithmic chapters in Part III are quite diverse. Therefore, we present the fundamental concepts and reviews of related work locally, in the respective chapter. Experimental results and evaluations are, likewise, presented at the end of each chapter. We do this to improve readability and make each core chapter as self-contained as possible.

Chapter 3

Background

Contents

In our attempt to provide a self-organizing infrastructure for Ambient Services, we have to deal with several fields of distributed systems research either explicitly or implicitly. In this section, we give an overview over the most important ones among these fields. First, we review the current state of the art in AmI research. An analysis of the existing approaches in this area is made to clarify the major research directions and the differences to our work. We will show that the results presented in the remaining parts of this book are original since they tackle questions that are complementary to those studied thus far.

Subsequently, we give short introductions on the concepts of Mobile Ad hoc Networks as well as the related approach of Wireless Mesh Networks. As a communication infrastructure, the ASG is situated in this area. We will show that it is quite close to the concept of Wireless Mesh Networks. However, we will not delve too deeply into the various issues involved with this kind of networking technology. The respective sections should only give a general understanding of these problems as we do not provide answers to networking issues in this book.

Finally, we take a close look at the concept of self-organization towards the end of this background section. We discuss the general properties observed in naturally occurring self-organizing systems and investigate their practical relevance to distributed computer systems. Furthermore, we give a detailed state-of-the-art analysis of existing approaches to rendering distributed systems self-organizing. This includes several top-down approaches envisioned by some major industrial as well as academic initiatives, and a number of bottom-up approaches proposed by concrete research projects.

3.1 Ambient Intelligence

The AmI visions laid out in Chapter 1 are rather abstract. The dynamic and flexible provisioning of wireless Ambient Services poses questions concerning networking technologies, location-based service frameworks, security and privacy concerns, context-awareness etc. Each of these areas represents a major research domain, and the results that have to be produced by each field have to be put together to eventually realize AmI. This book is dedicated to questions concerning the structure of an AmI infrastructure and investigates the algorithmic aspects of a software platform that allows the self-organized operation of AmI systems. Therefore, we limit this background section to issues related to AmI architectures and focus on middleware approaches that have been proposed to support AmI.

There are essentially two major strands of research in this area at the moment. The first one deals with question of what an appropriate middleware could look like. The research in the middleware area has been active for many years and is always quick in conquering new domains. Thus, a plethora of systems has been and continues to be proposed here. The second strand originates from the area of *Service-Oriented Architectures* (SOA) and copes with the numerous problems involved with finding, matching, and composing services in an AmI environment. There is a set of tools, most notably from the Web Services domain, of which some variations are being deployed.

3.1.1 Multi-Agent-Based Middleware Systems

An interesting fact that becomes apparent during a review of the current state-of-the-art in AmI-related middleware systems is that most of these systems are agent-based, relying on mobile agents, intelligent agents or a mixture of both. This technology promises to provide a means for the flexible construction of applications that are supposed to consist of dynamic groups of agents. They can be composed at runtime, and they may adapt to changes, for example by migrating among the computers in a network. However, some criticism is appropriate here. In most publications, the above-mentioned properties are readily assigned to any system that is based on agent technology. Very few authors substantiate their claim that the use of multi-agent system (MAS) solves the problems found in AmI. This seems to be a myth rather than reality.

Cabri et al. propose their LAICA system as an agent-based middleware for AmI [25]. They claim that agents "can naturally deal with dynamism, heterogeneity and unpredictability". However, this is not an inherent feature present in any agent-based system. Instead, mechanisms that enable such abilities must be carefully designed and implemented explicitly. The authors do not report how this is done in the LAICA system. It remains unclear, as to why LAICA supports AmI applications particularly well. The work presented by Vallée et al. [172] seeks to combine *multi-agent techniques* with *semantic web services* to create a system that can adapt to the user's current context. The authors propose that groups of agents may join in a context-aware service composition process. O'Hare et al. advocate the use of "agile agents" as a design principle for AmI [122]. These mobile agents are based on the *Beliefs Desires Intentions* (BDI) model that is well-known in intelligent agent research. The authors present three software systems that are based on such agents and that bear some relation to the concept of Ambient Intelligence. However, apart from rather general statements, no real motivation is given as to why this particular technology should be ideal. Rodríguez et al. present their agent-based SALSA middleware which is specifically targeted at healthcare applications [143]. The SALSA architecture equals that of many systems that already exist. The authors do not motivate why SALSA is specifically adequate for healthcare applications or AmI in general. An interesting middleware system that is based on mobile agents is presented by Satoh [151]. This system enables objects or humans to be "tagged" with mobile agents that implement some functionality pertaining to the object. The agents exploit their mobility to stay close to the objects (or humans) they function for. The linkage between agents and real-world objects is achieved by using RFID tags. This is one of the few agent-based AmI approaches for which a clear motivation is conceivable.

3.1.2 Service Matching and Composition

The problem of finding an appropriate service to match a user's current demand has been investigated for at least a decade. It moved to the center of attention as systems like CORBA (Common Object Request Broker) became popular in the early to mid 1990s. Since then, one can potentially provide a large set of services that is easily accessible by a client via the Internet. Such a service market creates diversity which raises the problem of connecting to the *right* service. Since interface descriptions are very precise but also very specific, the usage of semantic information about services and AI technologies have been proposed [134, 135]. The advent of *Service Oriented Architectures* (SOA) and the Web Service technologies has caused researchers to revisit this problem using similar concepts like ontologies and topic maps. Additionally, the SOA introduces the idea of service composition which means that what is perceived as a single service by the user can in reality be combined of a number of individual services running distributed over the Internet.

The area of AmI raises similar questions: How can the best service be found that matches the demands of a mobile user in an AmI environment? How can this selection be made based on fuzzy semantic information, and how can a service be composed *on-the-fly* from other services in a way that is transparent for the user?

Omnisphere is an architecture that supports the discovery of service components and the binding of such components to create a composed service [147]. Constructs that the authors call *typed data flows* are used for service composition. A matching mechanism is proposed that employs user preferences, devices capabilities, and the user's context to select a set of matching service components. Subsequently, Omnisphere connects these components using typed data flows. Hellenschmidt et al. propose the SodaPop system that allows the composition of higher-level services from the components available on individual user devices [67, 68]. The users participate in a temporary coalition such that each of them can benefit from the higher-level service. Such a coalition of devices is called a *device ensemble* by the authors. They claim that their system enables devices to self-organize in order to collectively provide a service. No explanation is given by the authors as to why this system is called self-organizing. Hellenschmidt et al. as well as Vallée et al. advocate the use of multi-agent systems to realize service composition as agents are largely autonomous and flexibly composable.

A different approach is taken by Issarny et al., who suggest using a declarative language for specifying AmI systems [86]. The *Web Service Ambient Intelligence* WSAMI language allows the specification of composed services. The concrete service instances are retrieved at runtime from the specific environment using a core middleware that is based on Web Services technologies like SOAP. In this approach, the composition is largely specified at the design stage rather than leaving it completely to decisions taken at runtime.

3.1.3 Micro Adaptation

Most systems presented above enable a specific form of *micro adaptation*: They concentrate on adaptations within applications, for example, by allowing them to be composed of a dynamic group of agents. This is usually triggered by the demand and the context of individual users. Thus, a single application or service may restructure internally by exchanging certain components (sub-services, communication channels etc.) in order to react to changes in the individual user's context. This context may change, for example, if the user demands different services, different service characteristics (e.g. QoS), or if he moves physically. Thus, such adaptations are internal to applications or services and they are user-centric.

The means for achieving this form of adaptation can be quite diverse. In some projects, agents are used as flexible building blocks for applications [25, 172, 122, 67, 68, 143]. Other researchers use more traditional component-based frameworks like the BASE micro-broker middleware by Becker et al. [18] or the MADAM approach presented by Geihs et al. [56]. These approaches are complemented by systems that put a bigger emphasis on the design time and the software engineering side. For example, Fuentes et al. propose AOPAmI, a system based on *Aspect-Oriented Programming* (AOP) [53] to enable adaptation within applications.

3.1.4 Discussion

From the analysis of the existing approaches in the area of AmI, it becomes evident that, at the moment, the overwhelming majority of the efforts are focused on the technical issues at the *micro level* of interactions. By "micro level", we mean the level at which individual users, devices, clients, and services interact. At this level, issues like communication channels, service descriptions, and service interfaces are important, and explicit technologies are proposed, for example, for enabling the interaction of a user with a service. The adaptations at this level mostly take place within applications and services or in the interaction between individual users and services.

Another property of the current approaches is that, in most cases, they have a *user-*

centric view. The question that is implicitly at the center of the respective research is: How can the user be supported in the best way if he enters an AmI system?

Of course, these issues are very important since they concern the immediate interfaces presented to the user. However, complementary infrastructure-centric questions about the macro-level behavior of AmI systems have not been tackled thus far:

- How is an AmI infrastructure organized at large?

- How can the different interactions at the micro level stimulate the creation of appropriate global (macro) structures?

This is the area of research that we cover in this book. Our view is clearly set on the macro-level infrastructural aspects of AmI systems. We argue that both the *micro-level, user-centric* and the *macro-level, infrastructure-centric* issues need to be researched, and that especially the latter aspects have not received the attention they deserve.

3.2 Mobile Ad hoc Networks

The miniaturization of electronic devices and the advent of wireless networking technology have enabled the invention of small portable computers (e.g. PDAs or mobile phones) that are able to connect to each other using a wireless networking technology. Classical computer networks consist of stationary computers (servers, desktops, workstations etc.) that are connected via fixed-wired infrastructures (e.g. Ethernet-based LANs). The new breed of portable wireless devices may be used to create wireless networks consisting of numerous devices that connect spontaneously when they are in close proximity and detect each other. These *Mobile Ad hoc Networks* (MANETs) pose fundamentally different problems than classical networks [32]:

- Devices are powered by batteries. Thus, energy-conserving communication mechanisms are of major importance [21]. This concerns all layers from the application layer down to the physical signal transmission. A MANET can only survive if the individual devices do not exhaust their energy in a short time span. This is especially true in specific subcategories of MANETs like sensor networks [3]. The devices in these networks have only very limited battery capacities.

- The wireless communication medium is not as reliable as a fixed-wired network. Connectivity may be weak or intermittent due to user mobility and interference effects in the radio signals [87].

- The substrate on which a MANET is typically built consists of the personal devices of individual users. This raises the question as to why a user should provide his scarce resources (e.g. battery power or communication bandwidth) for the sake of the community (e.g. by routing foreign traffic).

- The topological maintenance of a MANET is basically not possible. Users do not have an overview of what happens if they move. They usually do not consider the consequences of their own mobility on the overall MANET. Thus, the MANET is subject to unpredictable dynamics. This has to be compensated, for example, by appropriate routing protocols.

All of these issues have been very actively researched over the last decade. Especially the problem of setting up a reliable multi-hop routing infrastructure within MANETs has stimulated the creation of a wide variety of different ad hoc routing protocols. However, the problems present in MANETs cannot be made transparent by introducing some networking layer alone. Instead, they range all the way up to the application layer, where the intermittent connectivity must be accounted for by introducing new middleware systems that enable asynchronous communication among applications.

3.3 Wireless Mesh Networks

In recent years, a special class of wireless networks has emerged that involves stationary computers as well as mobile devices. These communication infrastructures are called *Wireless Mesh Networks* (WMN) [4]. A WMN commonly consists of a backbone network made up of stationary computers that are connected using a wireless networking technology. In principle, this is very similar to conventional MANETs in that computers connect to other computers that are within their transmission range. However, these network nodes are not mobile and they have unlimited power supplies as well as extended computational capacity. Within this wireless backbone network, mobile clients may exist that connect to the backbone and to each other in order to communicate. Such networks are beginning to be deployed as an access infrastructure to the Internet or as a local communication network with limited coverage. They are easy to install and they may be scaled up or down in size as needed without major configuration efforts. The wireless multi-hop infrastructure provided by the WMN backbone is much more reliable and efficient than a MANET due to the lack of dynamics (device mobility). The ASG network that we propose is in fact nothing else than a WMN extended by service provisioning capabilities.

3.4 Self-Organization

Self-organization is a concept that is pervasive in most naturally occurring complex systems. Numerous examples can be found in physical, biological, social, and economical systems whose components are living creatures, inanimate physical objects, or a mixture of both. These examples include the well-organized dynamics in heated fluids and the behavior of sand piles as well as the activities in a colony of social insects, the intelligence arising from the seemingly amorphous substrate of the brain, and the complex economic structures created by people selling and buying goods on a global market. Unfortunately, many of the concepts and mechanisms that are working in a self-organizing system can only be defined in a relatively fuzzy way. Today, science is able to understand the behavior of many of these systems by identifying such concepts and by explaining how they interact in each concrete system. However, we are still far away from a general model of self-organization that may be transformed into an engineering approach in a straight-forward way. Thus, there is no simple construction plan for building a self-organizing system for a specific task. This would be the ultimate goal of complex systems research.

We do not claim to tackle this problem in this book. Instead, we model a system consisting of several algorithms and protocols that enables an Ad hoc Service Grid to organize certain aspects of its overall function without external intervention. Subsequently, we claim that the overall system exhibits self-organization features. In order to enable the reader to validate this claim, we give an overview of the state of the art in self-organizing systems research, here. In Chapter 4, we give an explicit model of a *self-organizing software system* that is in line with the set of commonly stated definitions. In the rest of this book, we evaluate our algorithms and protocols against this very model to substantiate our claim.

Most researchers tend to formulate their definitions in slightly different terms, depending on their specific scientific discipline. There is a plethora of definitions in the area of self-organizing systems formulated by biologists [26], psychiatrists [10, 11], physicists [126, 62], chemists [119], and complex system researchers [78], just to name a few. Most of these definitions have some key aspects in common, and the differences are to a large extent only very subtle. A good overview over some popular definitions is presented by Carl Anderson [7]. For our purposes, we choose the following definition given by Scott Camazine et al. that was motivated by their view on self-organization in biological systems [26]:

Definition 3.1. *Self-organization is a process in which pattern at the global level of a system emerges solely from numerous interactions among the lower-level components of the system. Moreover, the rules specifying interactions among the system's components are executed using only local information, without reference to the global pattern.*

For this introductory section on the concept of self-organization, we will stick to this informal definition. In Chapter 4, we build a more formal model on this definition that allows us to present a coherent line of argument in order to prove the claim that a given software system is self-organizing.

3.4.1 General Concepts

Naturally occurring self-organizing systems seem to have one important, unifying property: They are complex. The term *complex system* is often used informally to express that a system is not easily understandable. However, complex system research has a more formal way of defining what a complex system is. Moreover, there is a very clear difference between a *complicated system* and a *complex system*. A classical example for a complicated system is a car. A car is composed of a large number of parts that interact to create an automobile. Typically, each part is present only once and has a dedicated purpose (there is only one drive shaft and this drive shaft cannot take over the role of the clutch). If one part breaks down, usually the whole system fails to work properly. With a certain level of knowledge in automobile technology, one can understand how the whole (the car) serves its purpose by decomposing the car into its constituent parts and analyzing them in isolation. This is the fact, because all parts interact with other parts in a straight-forward (i.e. linear) way.

A complex system is completely different. Well-known examples are colonies of social insects (e.g. ants and termites) or the human brain. Such a system is typically composed of a large number of identical, or at least very similar, components. This creates a massive redundancy and, therefore, a high degree of robustness as the loss of a single component does not affect the overall system. In the brain, for example, thousands of neurons die every day without an immediate impact on our cognitive capabilities. Typically, the components of a complex system are comparably simple. A single neuron and an individual ant do not possess a great complexity by themselves. Instead, the *interaction* between these components plays the central role in a complex system. In many cases, this interaction is non-linear: The actions of one component stimulate other components to execute similar actions. This process reinforces itself and leads to a very quick, exponential build-up of structure (positive feedback). Usually, such a feedback process is slowly stopped as some resource that it consumed is depleted (negative feedback). Such an interaction between positive and negative feedback seems to be characteristic for many self-organization processes: Structures are built up quickly until the controlling effect of negative feedback sets in and steers the organizational process into some sensible direction and towards stability.

A simple example of such a process is the foraging behavior of ants (see for example [26]). If an ant discovers a food source and carries food back to the nest, it deposits a chemical substance (called pheromone) that attracts other ants. These ants, in turn, deposit additional pheromone as they follow an existing pheromone trail. Thus, the pheromone attracts more ants which produce more pheromone. This feedback process quickly recruits all ants that are available in the vicinity. As the number of ants that do not yet participate in the foraging quickly shrinks, a negative feedback sets in. At some point there are no additional ants that may be recruited. This simple mechanism does not only enable the ant colony to exploit a food source very quickly and efficiently. It also selects the most profitable and, at the same time, the closest food source available. Thus, a sufficiently large number of very simple creatures solves a difficult optimization task in a short time by applying only a very simple set of rules. Moreover, they only communicate indirectly and by a very simple mechanism.

This observation has stimulated researchers to create a whole new breed of optimization algorithms called Ant Colony Optimization (ACO) [47], and a number of approaches to the management of telecommunication networks [93]. More importantly, it demonstrates that a complex system like an ant colony cannot be understood simply by decomposing it and by analyzing the constituting components like in the car example. This classical reductionist approach that has been popular in science for hundreds of years fails because the properties of a complex system are only present if the system acts as a whole: "The whole is more than the sum of its parts." (Aristotle, *Metaphysics*) Properties that occur from the interactions in a system rather than from the components themselves are commonly called "emergent". This leads us to a simple and very abstract model of a complex self-organizing system in which two levels exist:

- The *component level* is the level at which the actions of individual components are investigated. The ant itself has some interesting features at this level. For example, biologists would be interested in an ant's mechanisms for producing and depositing pheromones.

- At the *group level*, the collective behavior of the interacting components bears specific emergent properties. The foraging behavior of an ant colony is a feature of the group level. An individual ant's ability to deposit pheromones is a necessary requirement for this behavior, but it cannot explain it.

In summary, the following properties are typical of naturally occurring, complex self-organizing systems:

- They consist of a **large number of redundant components,** which makes them very robust. Even if a number of components fail to function, the whole system continues to work fine and degrades only slowly as the number of failed components increases.

- Their components usually display a **certain degree of randomness** in their behavior which helps them explore possible actions and new states. This randomness quickly converges to a coordinated and goal-directed behavior if an appropriate stimulus is present. For example, before any food is detected, individual ants essentially move randomly searching for such a food source. After food has been found, the pheromone-driven recruitment mechanism quickly creates the shortest possible trail between the nest and the food source.

- They have **no central coordinator** whose failure may cause a total breakdown of the system. Instead, they control themselves in a decentralized fashion.

- They apply a **combination of positive and negative feedback** to build up and maintain useful structures. This non-linearity prevents us from applying a classical reductionist approach for analyzing them.

- They produce **complex global behavior from numerous local interactions** that is directed towards a specific goal. The interactions at the component level are often only indirect. Foraging ants manipulate their environment by depositing pheromones. They do not communicate directly with their fellow ants. This concept of indirect communication and the coordination of work through the subject of the work itself has been termed "stigmergy" by the French biologist Pierre-Paul Grassé [61, 46].

- They display a **high degree of adaptivity** in their behavior. They may quickly react to changes in their environment in order to restore an acceptable mode of operation.

- They often exhibit **multistability**. The system may switch between different semi-stable global patterns, but without any changes in the lower-level interactions. This may be caused by fluctuations in the system itself (intrinsic) or in the environment (extrinsic). For example, Sole et al. modeled and studied the raid patterns observed in ant colonies and found that qualitatively different patterns emerge as two different model parameters are manipulated [157]. Thus, a quantitative change in the model often stimulates qualitatively different stable states.

3.4.2   Relevance to IT Systems

Obviously, many of the properties mentioned above are highly desirable in modern IT infrastructures. In recent years, the explosive growth of modern computing infrastructures has created its own negative feedback effect [74]: The numerous interactions among the lower-level components in a natural complex system render such a system highly interwoven. Complex dependencies between the components develop that typically span several indirections. Analyzing which consequences a small change to a single component may have, is almost impossible. Modern computer systems that consist of numerous hardware and software components pose similar problems. The number of interdependencies tends to grow in a non-linear fashion since adding component $(n + 1)$ to the already existing n components may potentially create n new dependencies. Therefore, the complexity of the overall system can get out of hand very quickly. This alone represents a severe problem for the administrative personnel. Moreover, each single component may have a large number of tunable parameters that makes it hard to even optimize the component in isolation. Additional trends that increase the complexity of modern IT infrastructures include the increasing heterogeneity of hardware and software, the extension of communication network with wireless components, and the increasing mobility of the employees that work within such infrastructures. Finally, the accelerated development of new technological trends forces companies to restructure their IT systems more frequently. The complexity that arises from these developments, has reached a level at which the manageability of IT systems is severely degraded. As a result, larger systems tend to operate suboptimally and less reliable since the task of managing them overwhelms the administrative personnel. This introduces a limiting factor in the growth of such systems resulting in their stagnation, a phenomenon that has been termed "complexity crisis" [95].

Major companies like IBM [82], Intel [163], Sun, and Microsoft [111] have realized this trend and are in the process of introducing new concepts and stimulating researchers to find solutions. Ideally, a complex IT infrastructure should be able to self-organize in the same way as a complex biological organism does. Most notable among these efforts is IBM's Autonomic Computing Initiative (ACI) [82, 95].

However, while natural self-organizing systems possess desirable properties like robustness, adaptivity, and graceful degradation, other properties are problematic in the IT domain. For example, the inherent randomness is something that users and operators would rather not want from their computing infrastructure. Instead, the system is expected to be *dependable*. The impreciseness usually exhibited by natural systems and their tendency to learn from mistakes are other aspects that are quite problematic in IT systems. Imagine a system that may only defend itself from attacks that were successful at least once, like the immune system of the human body. Similarly, think of an operating system that manages to copy your files *almost correctly* in *most cases*. Such a mechanism creates diversity in biological reproduction systems. However, it creates sheer confusion in a computer system. The basic problem is that we would like to copy the positive features of naturally occurring self-organizing systems, but at the same time we would like to avoid the other features that do not fit the idea of a dependable computer system. Unfortunately, there is no easy way to separate them since in most cases the desirable features vanish as we eliminate the unwanted ones.

Another important aspect in the integration of self-organization principles into the management of IT systems is *selection*: All naturally occurring self-organizing systems have become what they are today by going through a long and rigorous process of adaptation and selection. Successful features were reproduced, other features simply died out [77]. The systems that we observe today have developed over millions of years and generations. Nature was able to experiment with an overwhelming number of different *versions* and the only measure for selection was their fitness for survival[1]. The shaping of similar systems in the IT domain faces a different form of selection. A software development process that bears several improved versions of the same product is not comparable to the process of natural selection. If we want to map different software components onto what a single ant represents in an ant colony, and if we expect the overall software system to exhibit emergent features like the overall ant colony does, we might have to adapt the software development processes.

3.4.3 Top-Down Approaches

The last two decades have seen the development of sophisticated tools for managing IT infrastructures more or less manually. Of course, many procedures within the overall management process are automated nowadays. However, there is still a human in the control loop who takes crucial decisions and executes maintenance tasks. The new vision that system developers, integrators, and operators pursue is called "Self-Management". A self-managing system is supposed to organize all aspects of its own management without human intervention.

The current state of the art in self-managing computer systems is characterized by two different levels of abstraction between which a large gap exists. This resembles the two-level model of self-organization itself (see page 16): At the higher level, abstract concepts and far-reaching visions are discussed. It comprises initiatives like Autonomic Computing [82, 95], Proactive Computing [163, 179], Soft Computing [186], Homeostasis [156], and Organic Computing [115, 173]. All of the publications that we just cited are non-technical and present visions that, according to the respective authors, shall become reality within the next 5 to 10 years. They state requirements, abstract concepts, and generic architectures. At the lower level, a diverse set of radically different technical approaches exist. These approaches include self-optimizing software systems [43, 171, 64], rejuvenation (the controlled and well-timed restart of software components) [106], self-stabilization [44, 45], swarm intelligence [108, 42, 41, 181, 182], basic self-assembly mechanisms [117], programming paradigms based on the chemical reactions and self-healing capabilities of living cells [58], and security systems that mimic the immune system [51]. Most of these approaches employ mechanisms borrowed from very specific biological systems. It is difficult to find common concepts that may be abstracted to form a more general model that fills the gap to the abstract higher level. Thus, these remain largely isolated, special-purpose solutions.

The gap between the high-level visionary concepts and the low-level isolated solutions is the biggest problem that self-management faces at the moment. No common conceptual framework is available that could guide the coordinated development of cooperating solutions to implement the visions. There is hope, however, that the

---

[1] I assume an evolutionist view, without meaning to offend any religious belief.

structure and the mechanisms of the human body may provide such a conceptual framework: *Autonomic Computing* and *Organic Computing* build on the idea that complex organisms (e.g. the human autonomic nervous system) provide blueprints for technical solutions that shall have similar properties. However, the original *biological blueprints* themselves are still not completely understood. In the following, we will briefly review the main principles and goals of the most notable initiatives in the area of self-management.

Autonomic Computing

IBM's Autonomic Computing Initiative (ACI) [84, 82, 95, 158] sketches an abstract architecture for self-managing systems consisting of *autonomic elements* (AEs) that manage their own internal state and the interaction with other elements using *autonomic managers*. Autonomic managers shall control autonomic elements using some form of *closed control loop*, a concept that has been known from control theory for several decades, based on higher-level policies. An autonomic system shall be an interactive collection of autonomic elements [95], and AEs are supposed to function at many levels, from individual hardware components to global enterprises. The inspiration for the ACI has been drawn from the human autonomic nervous system that controls many bodily functions like breathing and respiration without conscious intervention by the mind. The general concept of self-management has been divided into four sub-categories:

- **Self-configuration:** Automatic configuration of components to adapt them to different environments

- **Self-optimization:** Automatic monitoring and adaptation of resources to ensure the optimal functioning with respect to the defined requirements

- **Self-healing:** Automatic discovery, diagnosis, and correction of faults

- **Self-protection:** Anticipation, identification, and protection from arbitrary attacks

These four aspects of self-management are now commonly accepted as so-called *Self-* Properties*, and they are also used in other contexts apart from the ACI.

Organic Computing

The ACI has a clear focus on solving current problems in the management of large-scale IT systems by introducing self-management in existing systems. It also defines a road map for the evolution of today's system into self-managing systems. In contrast to that, Organic Computing (OC) [153, 115, 173] does not aim at evolving existing systems, its goal is to shape a new IT world from scratch, in which "self-organization with all its facets will determine all components of the organic computer" (translated from [173]). All aspects of the hardware architecture and the software infrastructures on top of this hardware shall be shaped after the concepts found in organismic life. According to [173] this shall be realized by the year 2010. However, at the moment there is no coherent set of concepts observable behind this set of ambitious visions.

Proactive Computing

Proactive Computing (PC) [163] is an initiative started by Intel to overcome the complexity crisis. PC presents some visions and features that overlap with Autonomic Computing [179]. However, Intel puts a bigger emphasis on interconnecting the computer world with the physical world in order to enable computers to aid humans in their every-day life. A computer system shall be a closed loop such that the human user is not bothered with controlling or managing it. Furthermore, it shall be proactive in assisting users. This requires the ability to anticipate by employing context-awareness and statistical reasoning about the environment.

3.4.4 Bottom-Up Approaches

The collection of industrial initiatives aimed at rendering computing systems self-managing (autonomic, proactive, or organic) may best be characterized as *top-down approaches*: They formulate high-level concepts, goals, and visions and present a set of requirements and properties for systems. What would be the next step in the implementation of these concepts? In a valid software development process, an engineer would try to refine the concepts until he gets some lower-level models that may be implemented. However, for the class of systems that is targeted in this case, this presents a major problem. In some sense or another, all of these initiatives strive towards the *emergence* of some global collective behavior that exhibits sufficient intelligence such that systems are able to take care of themselves. While this intelligent behavior may be specified, it remains unclear what lower-level principles are that must be implemented to realize them. After all, the emergent properties are not present in the lower-level components. So how shall they be programmed to create the desired global behavior? Currently, this is the barrier we face [110]: No development process is known that leads from the specification of emergent properties to their implementation at the lower level. There are some initial steps towards a solution to this problem [184, 59]. However, such approaches tend to be "rather philosophical" (cited from [59]). More detailed considerations about the challenge of engineering complex systems have been stated by J. M. Ottino [124] and William B. Rouse [146].

On the other side, there is an overwhelming number of different projects that apply a *bottom-up approach* to solve diverse problems in computer science using self-organization concepts. Most of them draw their inspiration and large parts of the actual solution from specific biological systems. Most notable among these systems are colonies of social insects (e.g. ants, termites, and wasps). Until the advent of computers that enabled simulations, the principles employed by biological self-organizing systems were largely unexplored. Only the ability to build computer models of living systems to simulate them and to study their validity allowed a deeper insight into the nature of self-organization processes. This simulative research has provided models, for example, of the foraging behavior of ants, the nest building of termites, and the flocking behavior of birds. These also represent the most commonly adopted bio-inspired models used in computer science. In the following paragraphs, we try to categorize the mainstream of this research and give a brief overview of the activities in this area. Of course, in the face of the sheer number of such systems that have been created in the last few years, this overview is far from being complete.

However, it provides insight into the diversity of the different approaches in the area of self-organizing software systems. This diversity represents the main difficulty in generalizing them.

Middleware Approaches

An important area in the research of distributed computer systems is the design of middleware platforms that simplify the development, the deployment, the operation, and the maintenance of distributed applications. Since the mentioned social insect colonies, in a sense, also represent distributed systems with collaborating components, it appears to be beneficial to transfer some of the principles found in insect colonies to the design of middleware systems. The purposeful adaptive behavior of systems that consist of a large quantity of simple, interacting entities has been termed *swarm intelligence* [23]. The principle of *stigmergic communication*, that is, the indirect communication between collaborating individuals via the subject of their work [46], is closely related to swarm intelligence. Especially the concept of mobile agents seems to fit that of moving insects very well. Furthermore, stigmergy presents an attractive means for decentralized coordination.

This has inspired a large number of projects that propose very similar systems [69, 102, 68, 107, 161, 145, 12, 116]. Some of these systems regard the new concepts for middleware design more from the classical perspective of computer science and try to make them accessible for distributed application development [69, 116, 107]. This may further decoupled operation and enable mobile applications. Moreover, it stimulates the design of new communication paradigms that may render distributed applications less rigid and more flexible. Some projects implicitly advocate the view that the introduction of bio-inspired concepts alone makes the application running on top of the middleware self-organizing [102, 67, 68, 161, 118, 145, 12]. Of course, one cannot capture the self-organizing behavior of biological systems simply by copying some of their structural properties in a very coarse-grained way.

The general concept of such middleware systems builds on the implementation of applications as loosely coupled groups of relatively simple entities. In some cases, they may be mobile in that they can move between nodes at runtime. These entities communicate indirectly by some blackboard mechanism or using communication infrastructures like tuple spaces [57]. The latter mechanism also allows for the dissemination of (anonymous) messages via some sort of diffusion mechanism [69, 107] to model processes that are similar to those found in nature.

Object Classification, Clustering, and Communities

In some cases, natural systems show amazing abilities to cluster, collect, or even classify different physical objects. For example, certain ant species pile up the corpses of dead nest mates in certain locations [23]. Other insects sort their brood according to the stage of their development [40] and, thus, perform complex classification tasks. Models of these systems have been developed that enable very simple entities with a small set of simple rules to perform this task in a computer system. Other researchers have adopted this to cluster and classify documents (e.g. web pages) according to certain properties [140, 80].

Similar objectives have been achieved in clustering communities of websites according to the similarity of their contents [50, 22] and in clustering users into communities according to their interests [176, 167]. These approaches rely on the concept of complex social networks. This is not directly inspired by insects. However, it also demonstrates the inherent ability of natural (in this case social) systems to perform clustering tasks.

Ant Colony Optimization

One specific ability of ant colonies has attracted a particularly high volume of interest: The ability of ants to find the shortest path between their nest and a food source can be applied in a plethora of different optimization and network management tasks. Especially the optimization community among the computer scientists has adopted the principles that steer this natural process to design new, more robust and efficient algorithms for classical optimization problems. The new discipline in the area of optimization algorithms is called *Ant Colony Optimization* (ACO) [47, 23]. For example, the well-known Traveling Salesman Problem (TSP) can be solved by a group of virtual ants using artificial pheromones to mark routes, similar to real ants that mark their path between a food source and the nest. The TSP is informally defined as follows: a traveling salesman has to visit a number of cities and return to his starting city at the end such that the overall route he traveled is as short as possible. This problem is NP complete. In the ACO algorithm, a number of ants travel among the cities choosing their next hops randomly but favoring nearby locations. At the end of each tour, an ant deposits an amount of pheromone on each of the links it traversed. This amount is inversely proportional to the overall length of the ant's path. After all ants have completed their tours, shorter paths have a higher concentration of pheromone. In the second phase, the ants are started again, but this time they are guided by the pheromone laid down in the first pass in addition to the inter-location distance. Eventually, this leads to a solution that is very close to the optimum in a relatively short time. This optimization algorithm has also been applied to other problems.

Swarm-based Approaches to Network Management and Control

The same general principles of foraging ants used in ACO, is also applied to various management and control problems in telecommunication systems. Network routing, for example, deals with the same general problem of finding an optimal path between two locations (computers in a network). In this context, optimal may have different meanings that may be mapped to some cost function. The routing algorithm is faced with the problem of finding the path with the lowest cost. It has been shown that an ant-based approach yields good results when it is applied to the network routing problem [41, 113, 93]. It has also been employed for distributed fault location [182] and load balancing [154] in communication networks. A general ant-based framework for solving diverse problems in telecommunication networks has been presented by White et al. [181] and a similar system called AntNet was proposed by Di Caro and Dorigo [42]. Numerous ant-based routing systems have also been proposed for mobile ad hoc networks [28, 27, 123].

Robotics

In the field of robotics, coordination mechanisms are investigated that are perceivable, for example, in flocks of birds or schools of fish [142, 169]. These animals move in a coherent way as a unit in order to optimize foraging or evade predators. Each individual follows simple rules based on the behavior of its immediate neighbors in the swarm. Essentially, each individual tries to stay at a certain distance from its neighbors (separation), it steers towards the average heading of its flock mates (alignment), and it tries to stay in contact with the flock (cohesion). These principles are being applied to control the autonomous collective movement of groups of robots that may be employed, for example, in warfare and rescue operations [49, 141].

Another example of biological emergent behavior mimicked by robots is shown by Holland et al. [81]. In a classical experiment, a group of autonomous agents used the principles of stigmergy to collect a number of scattered frisbees on one pile. The robots managed to achieve their goal despite the fact that they were only equipped with a set of simple sensors and without the ability to communicate. Similar approaches are described by other researchers [178, 40]. The mechanism used in these applications is the same used in the document clustering approaches presented above.

Complex Networks

Complex networks represent a more general self-organizing phenomenon. In 1967, the renowned psychiatrist Stanley Milgram conducted an experiment that led the way towards a new understanding of networked structures three decades later. Milgram's experiment indicated that any two people in the United States are connected by a chain of about 6 acquaintances. This is surprising if we consider the overall size of the network of acquaintances. This phenomenon has been termed "six degrees of separation", and a network that has the property of connecting its nodes with short paths is called a *small-world network*. Three decades later, a new science has developed from this initial experiment. It has been shown that a large number of very diverse networks possess the small-world property. This includes networks of reactions between chemicals in the human body, social networks, and even the Internet and the World Wide Web [6]. The sociologist Duncan Watts and the mathematician Steve Strogatz proposed a *small-world network model* that gave insight to the structure of these networks [180]. Later, the physicist Albert-László Barabási published the *scale-free network model* that also explained how such networks evolve [16, 6]. The creation of such a network is a self-organizing process in which new nodes join the network and follow very simple rules. In essence, each new node prefers to attach to a node that is already highly connected. This universal principle of network evolution is called *preferential attachment*.

In computer science, these models are very important since they also apply to the Internet and the World Wide Web. These networks are man-made. However, there is no central control in the process that creates them. The structure of the World Wide Web, for example, emerges from the individual decisions made by the people that put hyperlinks on their web pages. The tendency to link a personal page to big, popular sites introduces preferential attachment and creates a small world. This structural property is exploited, for instance, to improve web search engines [1]. It also led to new advances in the search technology used in peer-to-peer networks like Freenet [188]. The fact that social networks (in which people are perceived as nodes and their acquaintances are modeled as edges) form scale-free networks, too, has also inspired new ways of modeling user mobility in ad hoc networks [70]. This approach simply exploits the fact that the users' mobility is largely dictated by their social relations which has not been considered in classical mobility models before. In general, the discovery of the ability of networks to self-organize and create specific structures leads to many new technological innovations that improve communication within computer networks.

Part II

Models and Assumptions

In the following chapters, we introduce and discuss various models that constitute the foundation for the algorithms and protocols introduced in Part III. We start off by developing a model for self-organizing software systems which we view as one of the major contributions of our work. Such a model for classifying software systems did not exist before.

Afterwards, we introduce the general concepts of the Ad hoc Service Grid model as far as the hardware side, the networking, and the characteristic properties are concerned. This includes the network model we assume, basic network functions like clustering, as well as usage models and a number of application scenarios.

Chapter 4

Self-Organization Model

Contents

In Section 3.4, we gave an informal overview of self-organization and summarized commonly observed properties of self-organizing systems using examples wherever possible. This creates an intuitive understanding of the general concept. However, in order to be able to express as precisely as possible *why* and *how* our algorithms and protocols are self-organizing, we need to provide a more precise definition. In this section, we propose a *practical* model for *self-organizing software systems* (SOSS) [76]. The properties assigned to an SOSS according to our model are such that one can offer objective and more formal evidence that a given system is an SOSS. Albeit, they still comply with the commonly stated properties of self-organizing systems.

Software industry and computer science are currently facing a dilemma: The complexity crisis creates an increasing demand for self-organizing software systems. However, there is no design process or any recipe for the construction of such systems. Moreover, there is not even a model for self-organizing software systems that enables a classification of existing systems into self-organizing and non-self-organizing ones. Nevertheless, an increasing number of publications in computer science claim that a specific algorithm, protocol, or system is self-organizing. The overwhelming majority of these publications do not state any definition of self-organization, or they rely on a rather vague and blurred definition. Furthermore, there is no common ground on which one may evaluate these systems in this respect. In many cases, the definition and the interpretation of the concrete system within the boundaries of such a definition are completely left to the reader. From a scientific standpoint, this is a rather unsatisfactory situation as it prevents any comparison between systems.

At first glance, such a comparison and a methodology for classification seem academic and irrelevant in practice. After all, the important aspect is a system's performance and not whether it is inside some theoretical system class of self-organizing software systems. However, with the plethora of existing systems in this domain, a classification may be of great value in finding the *common design features* among these systems. This, in turn, can ultimately yield new approaches to a general design methodology for such systems. Thus, in the face of the difficulty of finding a top-down approach for such a design process, a classification may pave the way towards a bottom-up approach: We may study existing software systems empirically and classify them to isolate their common design features and try to generalize them. The immediate consequence of a classification methodology is an increase of order among the existing systems. This is desirable as it increases clarity and provides a framework for discussion. Moreover, it provides a way to substantiate the claim that a given system is self-organizing.

The general task of categorizing systems into self-organizing and non-self-organizing systems is hard to accomplish based on the existing knowledge about self-organization. Therefore, we confine our model to software systems. We do not claim that the model presented in the following sections can be used to categorize *all* existing systems (biological, physical etc.). This allows us to make some assumptions that may not be valid in general and, thus, reduce the complexity of the model. However, it could well serve as a starting point for more general models.

4.1   Towards a Model for SOSS

The definition of Camazine et al. (Definition 3.1 on page 15) has most key ingredients: It states that a self-organizing system has a "global level" and "lower-level components", and that the interactions among these components let a global "pattern" emerge. Moreover, it stresses that the components act in a decentralized fashion ("using local information") and that none of them has the overall plan ("reference to the global pattern") for the creation of the pattern. That is, the pattern at the global level is not explicitly encoded into the behavior or the interactions of the components.

We will stick to this definition and refine it in several ways in the following sections. Our definition is based on a small number of properties of SOSSs that can be quantified or even proven. In the remaining part of this chapter, we will discuss each of these properties in detail, and will present methods for quantifying and proving them.

4.1.1 The Difficulty of Deduction

There is one property that is commonly assigned to self-organization and the related concept of emergence[1] that is rather unscientific and of great destructive power when it comes to defining these terms: It is usually assumed that, for a system to be self-organizing or for its properties to be emergent, it must not be *easy to deduce its global behavior* from the behavior of its components. This assumption stems from the belief that self-organizing systems are complex and, thus, cannot be analyzed with the means of the classical reductionist approach. This means that the system's properties arise from the interactions among the components, not from the components themselves (see Section 3.4.1).

We do not dare to comment on the general validity of this chain of implications. However, we dispute that the *difficulty of deduction* should be regarded as a defining property of self-organization and emergence as this essentially removes any possibility of stating a scientific definition. First of all, if the difficulty of deduction was a defining property, then we would need a metric for measuring this difficulty. This, by itself, is an awkward thing to define. Ronald et al. tried to devise an emergence test [144] that is inspired by the famous Turing test for detecting intelligence. This emergence test is based on the *surprise* felt by the observer as he analyzes the system's description and its behavior. Apart from the fact that "surprise" is hard to quantify, it is also depending on the observer's capabilities. An observer A may be *smart enough* to be able to deduce the system's global properties from its components, while another observer B may consider this task to be very difficult. Therefore, the same system possesses emergent properties when viewed by observer B and does not possess such properties when perceived by A. Even worse, though, is the fact that as soon as B has discovered the relation between the lower-level components and the global-level behavior, the system also loses the attribute "emergent" from B's point of view. Therefore, according to such a definition, emergence would be relative to the observer and to some cognitive process within the observer. Thus, it is observer-dependent and time-dependent. Such a concept does not seem to be useful for classifying systems as it is highly subjective. There is no way of proving that any statement such as "system S possesses an emergent property" is false under this theory of emergence. Therefore, according to Karl Popper's widely accepted *concept of falsifiability* [133], it is outside the set of scientific theories.

For this reason, we leave the concept of *difficulty* or *surprise* completely out of our definition.

4.1.2 The Concept of Emergence

In the spirit of the above argument about the difficulty of deduction, we prefer a rather simple definition of emergence:

---

[1]For the sake of simplicity, we do not differentiate the terms "self-organization" and "emergence" any further at this point. This is obviously not appropriate in general. We will come back to this point later on.

Definition 4.1 (Emergence). *A property of a system is called "emergent", if it is not present in any of the system's components and results solely from the composition of the system.*

Such an *emergent property* vanishes if we decompose the system into its components. Note that this is also true for properties whose emergence was obvious before the composition process. Under this definition, most composed systems have emergent properties since the sole purpose of composing systems from components is the creation (emergence) of some new (emergent) properties. Any definition that explicitly involves the factor of unexpectedness may be more intriguing, but is certainly less useful. Our simple definition captures the unexpected properties as well as the expected ones and is, thus, more general.

The concept of "emergence" seems to be closely related to that of "self-organization". More specifically, any self-organizing system seems to exhibit emergent properties since it creates structures (organization) that are not present in its components. It is clear, however, that the reverse implication is not valid: A system that exhibits an emergent property does not necessarily *organize itself*. A bicycle, for example, is a composition of a number of components that enables cycling. The property of enabling cycling is emergent. However, a bicycle does not build or restructure itself.

In summary, we can say that, from our point of view, the only scientifically useful definition of emergence that is possible thus far is a rather simple and general one. It possesses no great power of discriminating between self-organizing and non-self-organizing systems since more or less any system possesses emergent properties. For that reason, emergence has no central role in our model.

4.1.3 Properties of a Self-Organizing Software System

The goal of our model is to provide a definition with a concise list of features that are necessary for a software system to be self-organizing. Secondly, we aim at providing the tools for proving that a given system has all of these features and, thus, is self-organizing. We make one assumption about SOSS that may not be valid for general self-organizing systems: We assume that an SOSS organizes itself *in order to adapt to its environment*. Thus, an SOSS is also an adaptive system. Please note that there may well be software systems that organize themselves according to some structure just for the sake of creating structure, independently of any adaptation purpose. We do not dispute this fact. One may, for example, create a distributed system in a communication network that arranges its global communication scheme such that the communication paths between the processes form the shape of a flower when viewed from high above. This structure may not be useful at all with respect to the application. Although such a system may be self-organizing, it is not in the class of SOSS as we define it. We think that this represents a useful restriction since we are interested in systems that create *useful* structures.

Based on the general definition of Camazie et al. and on this restriction to adaptive systems we state our basic definition of SOSS as follows:

Definition 4.2. *A self-organizing system is an adaptive system that adapts to fit its environment by changing its structure. This structure at the global level arises solely from numerous interactions among the lower-level components of the system. More-*

over, the rules specifying interactions among the system's components are executed using only local information, without reference to the global structure.

This definition does not really support us in proving anything. It is merely informal. To make a step towards provability, we must extract the core features of the definition, and we need to define them in more formal terms. These features and the questions that need to be answered on the way towards a classification framework are presented in the following list:

- An SOSS organizes itself. That is, it **creates structure**. How can we identify structures in a system?

- An SOSS is an **adaptive system**. Are there any models for adaptive systems that allow us to show that a given system is adaptive?

- The structuring (or organizational) process is executed **without centralized control** and without explicit reference to the global structure. How can we determine if a system runs under centralized control?

Our premise can be stated as follows: To classify a given system as belonging to the class of SOSSs, we need to identify its structure, prove that the system is adaptive by changing this very structure, and show that this structural adaptation is executed in a decentralized fashion. In the following sections, we investigate these properties and the possibilities for proving them in greater detail.

4.2 The Concept of "Structure"

The term "pattern" is used by Camazine et al. since many biological systems display the result of their self-organization visually as colorful spatial patterns. Typically, the terms "pattern", "structure", and "organization" are used as synonyms. The structures created by self-organization might be spatial, temporal, spatiotemporal, or functional in nature [62, 13]. Thus, the definition of structure may vary widely depending on the specific system we observe. Intuitively, we would define the term "structure" as follows:

Definition 4.3 (Structure). *Structure is the property of a system by which it constrains the degrees of freedom of its components.*

For example, an ant colony that is not currently building trails may be viewed as being *unstructured* in the sense that the individual ants are free to adopt any arbitrary movement pattern. This results in the absence of any visible structure since the ants essentially move randomly across the available space. However, if they form trails, the ants are largely constrained to the movement along the pheromone paths. Thus, the trail structure constrains each ant in the way it behaves compared to the unstructured case.

How can we capture this abstract notion such that we can offer prove that a given system is structured? The concept of *entropy*, known from thermodynamics and also from Shannon's theory of information [155] is of great help here. Entropy is a measure for the degree of disorder in a system. One may also say that entropy measures the uncertainty we have about the state of a system. If a given system is free to be in any of its possible states, the entropy is at its maximum. For such a system, we cannot predict what its state will be at any point in time, and we would describe such a system as completely disordered and random. If, however, the system is by some means constrained to a subset of all possible states, the uncertainty about its state decreases and, conversely, the degree of order in the system increases. Thus, entropy can be used to find out whether the degrees of freedom of a system's components are constrained and, thus, whether that system exhibits structure.

The idea to detect structure using entropy is not new. In 1956, eight years after Shannon's original publication about the application of entropy to information theory, Garner and McGill proposed a more general application of Shannon's concept to measure the variance or uncertainty of some random process [55]. Their uncertainty analysis was then taken up by Ross Ashby. Ashby was a British psychiatrist, neuroscientist, and mathematician, whose article *"Principles of the Self-Organizing Dynamic System"* [10] (published in 1947) is frequently cited as the first publication that used the term "self-organization". Ashby discusses the nature of "organization" (what we call structure) in great detail and introduces the term "conditionality" to describe structure [11]. Conditionality is present if the relations between components are conditional on other components. He goes on to state that uncertainty analysis would be the means of choice to analyze conditionality and, therefore, structure.

Claude E. Shannon defines information entropy as follows [155]:

$$H(P) = -K \sum_{s \in S} P(s) \cdot \log P(s) \tag{4.1}$$

The constant K decides about the measurement unit. In the following, we will simply set $K = 1$. S is the *state space* of the system and $s \in S$ is one possible state. $P(s)$ is the probability for the system being in state s according to the probability distribution P. In order to apply Shannon's entropy to a given system, we first need to define the state space S for that system. Here, we assume that this space consists of a finite number of discrete states the system can be in.

To detect a trail structure in an ant system, for example, we may define a 2-dimensional state space. As the first dimension, we use the average pair-wise distance d between ants. Obviously, ants are much closer together when they build a trail as opposed to the unstructured case where they may move freely. However, the closeness does not really capture the trail-building as ants may simply clump together to reduce their pairwise distance. Hence, we use a second dimension for our state space that captures the fact that ants show coherent movement in the trail. Each ant moves in one of two general directions: Either from the nest to the food source our vice versa. In the unstructured case with random movement, the directions of movement are also random. To capture the coherent movement of all ants, we assume that each ant has a heading expressed as an angle in a global coordinate system. One can easily see that two ants move into the same or in opposite directions if and only if the absolute values of the sinus of their headings are equal. Thus, we may use the standard deviation of that absolute sinus value over all ants in the system to get a scalar value that describes the global degree of coherence c in ant movement at any point in time. Our state space now consists of two dimensions, and at any point in time, the system has a pair of values $s = (d, c)$ identifying a unique point s in that space that describes its state. Depending on the nature of the system, d and c may be continuous. If this is the case, the state space can be easily discretized by dividing the continuous scales into subranges. The indication for a trail structure is given if the system *prefers* small values for d and c.

For other systems, the state space can be defined in a completely different way, reflecting the nature of the structures that shall be investigated. The question that can be answered using Shannon's entropy can be formulated as follows: Is there a smaller subset S' of S in which the system resides preferably? If this is the case, then the system's components are constrained in their degree of freedom as they may not explore the whole state space. This is equivalent to the statement that our uncertainty about the system's state is reduced, which, in turn, is indicated by a small entropy value.

If the ant system structures into a trail, it obviously resides in a subset of the state space that is characterized by comparably small values of d and c. To decide if this is the case, we have to observe the system and record its states. That is, we simply count how many times the system has been in which state. After k observations, we can convert these counters into a probability distribution by dividing each counter by k. This yields the probabilities $P(s_i)$ with which the system was in the state s_i over the observation period.

Now, we can easily apply Shannon's entropy measure to this probability distribution. The entropy is maximal with a value of $H(P) = \log |S|$, if all states in S are equally probable. $H(P)$ is minimal with $H(P) = 0$ if one state $s_0 \in S$ has probability $P(s_0) = 1$. Thus, the system has always been in state s_0 during the observation period. If the system has been observed to reside in a subspace $S' \subset S$ with $|S'| > 1$, then $H(P)$ takes an intermediate value.

We conclude that we can prove that a given system is structured by applying the well-known entropy measure. The nature of this structure can be captured by a careful design of the system's state space. Thus, if we have an intuitive idea about what comprises a system's structure, which we usually have, we can investigate this specific structuring process by designing the state space accordingly. Based on this specific design, we can observe the system and precisely quantify its structures using the concept of statistical entropy.

4.2.1 Some Remarks

It should be emphasized that the design of the state space is critical. There is no canonical definition with respect to a specific system. Designing the state space in a way that does not capture the structuring process properly may yield confusing results. It may be argued that, by explicitly designing the state space, we define something into the system that we would like to measure, and that this is not an objective process. Indeed, one may find a definition for the state space that emphasizes the *wrong* aspects of the system and shows structures that are not really of interest. This should be avoided by clearly stating the motivation for choosing a specific state space design. However, it is clear that the observer's view on the system has a large influence on the detection of structures. We will deal with this general problem later in this text.

Moreover, it is important to recognize, that according to the uncertainty analysis based on statistical entropy, a system that remains static over the observation period, is always found to be maximally structured. The absence of dynamics removes any uncertainty about the systems state as it always resides in the same static state. Thus, it makes no sense to apply this concept to static systems.

Statistical entropy does not enable us to detect structural changes. That is, if a system transits from one structure to another (e.g. in order to adapt), this does not necessarily change its statistical entropy, unless the transition is coupled with a phase of disorder or loss of structure. Statistical entropy merely allows us to recognize *if* a system is structured but not *how* it is structured. The same entropy value may occur for widely different structures as long as these structures occupy subsets of the system's state space that have the same size.

4.3 Defining Adaptivity

Ashby states that something might be organized but that the important question is whether this organization is "good" or "bad":

> "If we have half a dozen lenses, for instance, that can be assembled this way to make a telescope or that way to make a microscope, the goodness of an assembly obviously depends on whether one wants to look at the moon or a cheese mite." ([11], p. 112)

If we apply this statement to software systems, we can say that such a system might build structure in some sense, but that the really interesting question is: What is this structure good for? More specifically, we are only interested in self-organization processes that build structure in order to adapt to their environment. Today, this adaptation process is mostly executed manually, and we call it administration or IT management. By introducing self-organizing software systems, we would like to reduce or even remove this explicit manual management. Thus, the purpose of the self-organizational process is to adapt to a changing or unforeseen environment.

Therefore, we identified adaptivity as a necessary condition for a software system to be called self-organizing. Now, we are faced with the question: What is the definition of an adaptive system? So far, we have relied on an intuitive understanding of what adaptivity means. We stated that a system changes to fit its environment. In the following, we define this intuition more formally by adopting a definition of adaptivity given by Lotfi A. Zadeh in 1963 [185]. In this definition, Zadeh takes a black-box approach in that he simply states how an adaptive system should behave and not how this behavior should be achieved internally. This allows us to take any existing system and test whether it is adaptive or not:

Let $\mathfrak{S}$ be the system, and let $\{S_\gamma\}$ be a family of all possible time-dependent input functions for $\mathfrak{S}$, where γ specifies the concrete input function for $\mathfrak{S}$. Let $P(\gamma)$ be a function that measures the performance of $\mathfrak{S}$ under the input function S_γ. We say that $\mathfrak{S}$ *performs acceptably well under* S_γ if $P(\gamma)$ is in a prescribed class W of performance functions: $P(\gamma) \in W$. W defines a *criterion of acceptability* for $\mathfrak{S}$. For example, if $P(\gamma)$ is real-valued, then W could be the set of all performance functions whose values exceed a prescribed number. Thus, we may think of $P(\gamma)$ as a fitness function for the system $\mathfrak{S}$ and W would be the set of all functions that exceed a certain fitness threshold. Zadeh states that "a primary characteristic of an adaptive system is its ability to perform acceptably well in a changing and/or incompletely known environment". He defines this environment by a relation $\gamma \in \Gamma$, where Γ represents a subset of functions from $\{S_\gamma\}$ that $\mathfrak{S}$ may be subjected to. Based on this terminology, Zadeh defines an adaptive system as follows:

Definition 4.4. *A system* $\mathfrak{S}$ *is adaptive with respect to* $\{S_\gamma\}$ *and* W *if it performs acceptably well (i.e.* $P(\gamma) \in W$), *with every source in the family* $\{S_\gamma\}$, $\gamma \in \Gamma$. *More compactly,* $\mathfrak{S}$ *is adaptive with respect to* Γ *and* W *if it maps* Γ *into* W.

To prove that some system is adaptive, one has to map the system to this definition. That is, one has to define the family of input functions $\{S_\gamma\}$, the performance function $P(\gamma)$, the acceptability criterion W, and the environment Γ. Subsequently, one has to show that the system really maps Γ into W.

In the preceding section, we emphasized that the definition of the state space is critical as we may design it in vastly different ways. Some of these designs may capture the structuring process, while others do not. The same is true for adaptivity. Zadeh himself states that

> "[...] our premise is that all systems are adaptive, and that the real question is what are they adaptive to and to what extent." [185]

In designing a description ($\{S_\gamma\}$, $P(\gamma)$, W, and Γ) for the adaptive system, we may choose these elements such that the system appears to be highly adaptive. The question that has to be asked as a part of the design process and, later on, of the verification process is: Does this specific definition make sense?

4.4 Decentralized Control

The third necessary condition for an SOSS, besides the creation of structure and adaptivity, is that it does not use some central controller to achieve this. But why is this part of the definition necessary? Why can the system not have one subcomponent that is central within the system, which controls the organizational process? From the biological standpoint that motivated the definition by Camazine et al., the reason may simply be that (most) biological self-organizing systems function without central control. However, there is also a more general explanation. Heylighen et al. put it like this:

> "The control needed to achieve this [self-organization] must be distributed over all participating components. If it was centralized in a subsystem or module, then this module could in principle be removed and the system would lose its organization." [79]

Consider a system $\mathfrak{S}$ that can be decomposed into a subsystem $\mathfrak{C}$ and a set of subsystems $\mathfrak{S}' = \mathfrak{S} \setminus \mathfrak{C}$ such that $\mathfrak{S}'$ loses its ability to self-organize. Then, $\mathfrak{C}$ obviously functioned as a central controller within $\mathfrak{S}$, and the original definition of what comprises our self-organizing system would actually abuse the meaning of "self" in "self-organizing". $\mathfrak{S}$ does not organize *itself*, it rather consists of a distinct subsystem $\mathfrak{C}$ that organizes the rest of the system $\mathfrak{S}'$. If the definition of a self-organizing system would include $\mathfrak{S}$, then it would lose its discriminating power completely since it would include any system that creates organization in one way or the other. One could always extend any system's definition until the controller is inside to make it self-organizing.

However, this argument is problematic since it heavily relies on what we define as the system's components. For example, an ant-based system that uses pheromone-based trail-laying behavior to find shortest paths can be decomposed in at least two ways:

1. We may define that the system is composed of a number of individual ants, or

2. we may claim that it is composed of the trail-following behavior of ants and the trail-laying behavior that consists of the pheromone deposition mechanism.

Under the first definition, the ant system can clearly not be decomposed in the above-mentioned way. The second definition, however, allows us to remove any of the two components such that the system loses its ability to self-organize. Which of the two definitions is more valid, then? The first one clearly matches the concept of numerous interacting entities much better. The second one is somewhat artificial since it uses a different dimension to decompose the system such that each of the two subcomponents is visibly composed of a number of subcomponents (individual ants) itself. However, in general, the same problem of finding the right description that we found in the state space design and in the proof of adaptivity also exists here. We have to be careful in finding a useful and valid definition of the system's components.

Since we would like to be able to provide evidence that a given system is in the class of SOSSs, we have to state more formally what decentralization means. To define the term "decentralized system", first, we have to state what our definition of the term "system" is. This will actually not add anything new or surprising to our informal understanding of the term. It just clarifies things for the succeeding discussion:

Definition 4.5 (Software System). *A software system $\mathfrak{S}$ consists of a set of well-defined interacting components. We identify $\mathfrak{S}$ with the set of its components and call any subset of $\mathfrak{S}$ a subsystem. Furthermore, every software system $\mathfrak{S}$ has a well-defined function $f_{\mathfrak{S}}$.*

A system's components may be heterogeneous or homogeneous. In our context, we may identify the system's function as its adaptation to the environment, but in general, the function of $\mathfrak{S}$ may be any useful computation. A software system may have several independent functions. For our discussion on decentralized control, however, we must specify the exact function that is subject to the control process. This is simply a restriction of the view on a specific system: We ignore all aspects of the system that are not relevant for our purpose and, thus, simplify any related discussion. Based on Definition 4.5, we first define what a *central controller* is:

Definition 4.6 (Central Controller). *A central controller $\mathfrak{C}$ of a system $\mathfrak{S}$ with respect to $f_{\mathfrak{S}}$ is a subsystem of $\mathfrak{S}$ that controls the actions of the remaining subsystem $\mathfrak{S}' = \mathfrak{S} \backslash \mathfrak{C}$ such that $\mathfrak{S}$ is able to perform $f_{\mathfrak{S}}$ but $\mathfrak{C}$ is unable to perform $f_{\mathfrak{S}}$ in isolation (without $\mathfrak{S}'$).*

The reader may object that $\mathfrak{C}$ may control the actions of $\mathfrak{S}'$ and still be able to perform $f_\mathfrak{S}$ on its own, without $\mathfrak{S}'$. Why does the definition not allow this case? If $\mathfrak{C}$ is able to perform $f_\mathfrak{S}$ in isolation, then one of the following two statements must hold:

1. $\mathfrak{C}$ can be reduced further by removing (controlled) components from $\mathfrak{C}$ and adding them to $\mathfrak{S}'$. Thus, $\mathfrak{C}$ contains an equivalent smaller central controller that complies to the definition and, therefore, the original decomposition did not succeed in isolating the controller.

2. If that is not the case, $\mathfrak{C}$ is simply a more condensed decentralized version of $\mathfrak{S}$. What is the contribution of $\mathfrak{S}'$ to the execution of $f_\mathfrak{S}$, then? $\mathfrak{S}'$ could simply be removed from $\mathfrak{S}$ without destroying its functionality. This implies that $\mathfrak{S}'$ is redundant in the definition of $\mathfrak{S}$, and we would prefer the functionally equivalent but simpler decentralized system $\mathfrak{C}$ instead of $\mathfrak{S}$.

The first case is indicative of an insufficient decomposition while the second shows that the system was not defined properly.

The following *Decomposition Theorem* simply follows from Definition 4.6.

Theorem 4.1 (Decomposition Theorem). *If a software system $\mathfrak{S}$ possesses a central controller, then $\mathfrak{S}$ can be decomposed into two subsystems $\mathfrak{C}$ and $\mathfrak{S}' = \mathfrak{S} \setminus \mathfrak{C}$, such that neither $\mathfrak{C}$ nor $\mathfrak{S}'$ can perform the original function $f_\mathfrak{S}$ of $\mathfrak{S}$. We call this kind of decomposition a* destructive decomposition.

A colloquial way of expressing the essence of Theorem 4.1 is the following: If a system is controlled centrally, then it has a central point of failure. Accordingly, our way of proving that a system works in a decentralized fashion, is to show that it has no central point of failure.

The reverse implication is not true: A system may be decomposed destructively without having a central controller. If one removes the database tier from a system that was constructed following a classical three-tier architectural approach, the whole system inevitably breaks down. Thus, its functionality is lost. However, the database is clearly not a central controller in this system. It is simply a critical system. Similarly, consider our ant colony example. There is a critical mass (number of ants) below which the colony is unable to create trails. This critical mass is depending on several environmental conditions. A colony with a critical mass can be decomposed destructively, for example, by dividing it in half. This division would render each of the two groups of ants unable to form a trail. However, one cannot dispute the fact that the ant system uses decentralized control mechanisms only.

4.4.1 Proving Decentralization

In order to prove that a given system is decentralized, we need to show that it is impossible to decompose it destructively. According to Theorem 4.1, this impossibility implies the absence of a central controller. Based on the description of the system, one may not necessarily have to investigate any possible decomposition. A thought experiment in which one iteratively removes one component at a time may suffice in many cases. After each hypothetical component removal, one has to show that the system still fulfills its function. For systems with a homogeneous structure (e.g. those comparable to the ant colony), it may be shown that for a sufficiently large number of components (exceeding the system's critical mass), it is not possible to divide the system into two subsystems such that both are unable to fulfill the function.

4.5 Global Knowledge and Local Interactions

It is generally assumed that self-organizing systems produce global patterns from local interactions. That is, the components of the system do not use any blueprint, template, or recipe; nor do they have a leader amongst them [26]. While the occurrence of a leader corresponds to a centralization of control which we explicitly dealt with in Section 4.4, blueprints, templates, and recipes have not been discussed yet. A blueprint is an abstract plan present in the components of the system, similar to the way in which buildings are constructed following the blueprints made by architects. A template is a physically existing prototype of a structure that may be (more or less) copied to reproduce the structure. Finally, a recipe is a step-wise behavior that is hard-coded into the system's components. If each component follows this recipe, the desired structure is generated. Camazine et al. deal with these alternatives to self-organization in great detail in their book on *Self-Organization in Biological Systems*.

It is rather obvious that none of these three alternatives is coherent with our understanding of self-organization. After all, each of the three means for building structure is in some way imposed on the system from the outside. Thus, the system does not create structure *by itself*. Instead, it gets explicit instructions for the construction process from outside the system.

Each of these alternatives also represents global knowledge in one way or the other. However, there are also more subtle forms of global knowledge and one may dispute as to whether the use of global knowledge must be rigorously excluded from a definition of self-organization. Carl Anderson discusses this issue stating the example of thermo regulation in a honey bee comb [7]. He claims that the air temperature the bees use to decide whether they start ventilating fresh air into the hive or whether they start shivering to produce heat, is some form of global knowledge. Nevertheless, this process would be referred to as being self-organizing. Another example from computer science is the popular interior gateway routing protocol OSPF (Open Shortest Path First) [114]. In this protocol, each router runs a process that holds the entire network topology in order to apply Dijkstra's shortest path algorithm for calculating network routes. The topology information is exchanged among routers using broadcasts. Is this system self-organizing? Each component has global knowledge and the interactions are also global. However, it definitely creates structure (network routes) and it is adaptive to topology changes. Moreover, it has no central controller. But, is the globally replicated topology information a blueprint or maybe a template? Note that it is not imposed from the outside. It is produced by interactions among the components. However, it represents an existing structure outside the system.

At this point of our discussion, we simply lack the necessary formal methods for getting a better grasp on this problem. Thus, any argument in this respect must, for the moment, rely on informal reasoning. We would need a much better way of expressing what exactly is "global" and, opposed to this, when is some action "local"? When does "implicit" become "explicit"? These are questions that rely more on assessment than on formal definition and classification.

In any case, we would argue that OSPF is not self-organizing, simply because there is a *reference to the global pattern* which we explicitly ruled out in definition 4.2.

4.6 The System's Definition

As we have seen in the previous sections on the proof of the creation of structure, adaptivity, and decentralized control, the system's definition always takes a central role. The same system may be defined in one way such that these proofs succeed, or in another way such that at least one proof fails. This seems to be a true statement irrespective of the system under investigation. The core problem in this respect is that there never is a single canonical description of a system that is more valid than any other description. We have seen an example in Section 4.4 where we defined an ant colony in two completely different ways. Most people would object to the claim that the second description does a good job at capturing the essence of an ant colony. Nevertheless, it is possible to define the system in this particular way. In this case, it is obvious that the first description should be preferred over the second one since it is much better at displaying our intuition. However, this choice may not be that obvious for all existing systems. Things get even more complicated when different levels of abstraction are considered. Camazine et al. make the following statement:

> "In discussing the brain for instance, the neurons and their local interactions (synaptic signaling) may be considered the source of the emergent self-organized property of thought; at a different level of analysis, however, the brain may be viewed as a centralized leader with external control over the outputs of motor nerves." ([26], p. 47)

While we cannot give general advice on how to define a system properly, we can at least state which elements should be included in a valid description. A description should be structured such that anyone who studies it, is enabled to evaluate its validity. We will take a closer look at such an evaluation later on.

4.6.1 The Elements of a Description

For a valid classification of a specific system under our model, it is necessary to define the following elements of the system's description in greater detail:

- **The system itself:** We stated that a self-organizing system organizes itself in order to adapt to its environment. Therefore, we need to describe which elements belong to the system and which lie outside its boundaries. In particular, a proper definition is required of what comprises the system's components.

- **The environment:** Since the system shall adapt to its environment, we need to define the exact border that separates the system from the environment. Moreover, the way in which the environment interacts with the system needs to be described. Note that, with respect to Definition 4.4 the environment then defines $\{S_\gamma\}$ and Γ.

- **The system's internal structure:** As we stated in Definition 4.2, a self-organizing system changes its internal structure (or organization) to achieve adaptation. Thus, we need a precise definition of what comprises this structure. This definition should capture the structural aspects of the system whose change causes the adaptation.

- **Good versus bad structure:** To judge whether an established structure is useful under the specified constraints, we require a classification of good and bad structures. Note that with respect to the adaptivity inherent to the self-organizing system, this is directly connected to Zadeh's definition: A good structure is one, under which the system maps Γ into W. The choice of W provides us with a binary decision as to whether a given structure is good or bad.

4.7   The Class of Self-Organizing Software Systems

From our discussion on the role of the system's description, it is clear that there is no absolute proof for a claim that a given system is self-organizing. Any given system can only be classified under a specific description. Thus, such a classification is always relative to that description. Our approach for classifying systems implies that there is a *class of self-organizing software systems* and that any system, when classified under a specific description, may either be in that class or in its complement.

Definition 4.7. *We define SO as the class of self-organizing software systems and $\overline{SO}$ as its complement. We say that a system $\mathfrak{S}$ is in SO under a description $\mathfrak{D}$ (denoted as $\mathfrak{S}_{\mathfrak{D}} \in SO$) if $\mathfrak{S}_{\mathfrak{D}}$*

1. *complies with the definition of adaptivity,*

2. *adapts by changing its structure,*

3. *does not employ central control.*

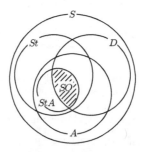

Figure 4.1: Graphical illustration of the classification of SOSS.

Figure 4.1 illustrates the relationship between the different classes (or sets) of systems we have discussed thus far. In this arrangement of intersecting sets, S is the set of all systems (defined in Definition 4.5), St is the set of all systems that create structure, D represents the set of decentralized systems, A is the set of adaptive systems, StA is the set of all adaptive systems that achieve their adaptation through structural changes, and SO (the hatched area) is the set of self-organizing software systems. Correspondingly, $\overline{SO}$ is everything that is outside the hatched area but inside S.

For any system $\mathfrak{S}_{\mathfrak{D}}$, the concrete containedness relationship within S (graphically spoken the position within the S circle) depends on $\mathfrak{D}$. More specifically, if we regard the same system under two different descriptions $\mathfrak{D}$ and $\mathfrak{D}'$, then $\mathfrak{S}_{\mathfrak{D}} \in SO$ might hold, while $\mathfrak{S}_{\mathfrak{D}'} \in \overline{SO}$.

4.8 The Classification Methodology

In the preceding sections, we have given a definition of what comprises a self-organizing system. This definition is based on the concept of adaptivity formally defined by Zadeh and contains the core ingredients found in a commonly accepted definition of self-organization by Camazine et al. from biology. Furthermore, we discussed the problem of defining the key elements of the system that is subject to classification. The complete classification methodology, which is based on the above definitions, is presented in this section. Apart from executing the necessary steps for classifying a system, a verification must be conducted. Any classification must be regarded as a proposal, rather than a proven fact. Ideally, the verification is done by a number of scientists in parallel and independently of each other. This resembles the review process that is common for scientific publications. A discussion should follow this individual review process, during which the reviewers should try to reach a consensus. In the following, we present the steps that are necessary for a classification and a proper verification.

4.8.1 Classification

The overall methodology for classifying any given system consists of four major steps:

1. **Define the key elements of the system as concisely as possible.** To enable other researchers to verify a classification, it is vitally important that this definition is not too detailed. In particular, the in-depth technical description of the system that is usually given before the classification does not serve this purpose. This definition is usually overloaded with details that are not relevant for the classification. Instead, the definition should be precisely targeted towards enabling the classification as well as the verification.

2. **Map the system $\mathfrak{S}$ to Zadeh's definition of adaptivity and show that it is adaptive.** This means that one has to identify the family of possible input functions $\{S_\gamma\}$, the performance function $P(\gamma)$, the class of acceptable performance functions W, and the subset Γ of the input space that $\mathfrak{S}$ shall adapt to. To proof $\mathfrak{S}$'s adaptivity, it has to be shown that it maps Γ into W.

3. **Show that the system adapts by changing its structure.** Assuming a proper definition of what *structure* actually means in the context of $\mathfrak{S}$, one has to show that the adaptivity of the system is indeed realized by changing (adapting) this very structure.

4. **Show that the system exhibits this kind of structural adaptivity without a central controlling entity.** This can be done by showing that a destructive decomposition according to Theorem 4.1 is not possible.

If one is able to complete these steps for a given system, then the classification is complete.

4.8.2 Verification

The fact that there is seldom a single canonical description of a given system may lead to descriptions being tailored solely for the purpose of proving the system self-organizing. Therefore, the normal process of validating scientific work becomes especially important in this context.

If a researcher presents a system $\mathfrak{S}_{\mathfrak{D}}$ and makes the case for its ability to self-organize, then the scientific community should research a number of questions in the attempt to confirm or dispute this hypothesis. The special focus here is on the validity of the system description chosen:

- Are all system elements defined properly in $\mathfrak{D}$?

- Are these definitions consistent with each other?

- Does $\mathfrak{D}$ present *a useful view* on $\mathfrak{S}$ that captures $\mathfrak{S}$'s essence, or is it rather artificial and unintuitive?

If these questions yield satisfactory answers, the latter three steps of the classification should be checked for validity. If, however, there is reasonable doubt concerning the validity of the system description $\mathfrak{D}$, then steps 2 to 4 may be formally correct, but the overall classification is not valid. In other words, $\mathfrak{S}_{\mathfrak{D}}$ may be formally recognized as belonging to SO, but this classification is based on an invalid description $\mathfrak{D}$ and is, thus, invalid itself. Furthermore, there may be a more useful definition $\mathfrak{D}'$ that is preferable and under which $\mathfrak{S}_{\mathfrak{D}'} \notin SO$. If such a $\mathfrak{D}'$ exists, then it should be specified as a part of any negative verification.

4.9　Discussion

At first glance, our classification methodology seems rigorous in creating the desired order among software systems. However, it seems foreseeable that there will essentially be three different outcomes of any classification attempt and the subsequent evaluation phase: The two obvious results are that, for a system $\mathfrak{S}_{\mathfrak{D}}$ the community either agrees that $\mathfrak{S}_{\mathfrak{D}} \in SO$ or that $\mathfrak{S}_{\mathfrak{D}} \in \overline{SO}$. We may be able to derive some common design principles that were not obvious in the first place from these cases. This could help in shaping a more general approach to engineering SOSSs. Generalizing the properties and principles found in existing systems into more abstract design methodologies, would clearly be a bottom-up process. Eventually, this bottom-up approach and the top-down approach, that was rather unsuccessful thus far, may meet in the middle. However, the third possible outcome of a classification attempt is simply that there is no consensus as to whether $\mathfrak{S}_\mathfrak{D} \in SO$ or $\mathfrak{S}_\mathfrak{D} \in \overline{SO}$. In our view, these cases may actually be the most interesting and the most important ones for furthering our understanding of SOSSs in general. A discussion about the proper classification of such a system might provide new insights into the general problem. Furthermore, it may indeed lead to an improvement of our classification methodology if it proves inadequate to classify certain systems.

Of course, a classification such as the one proposed here is no formal proof. Considering the nature of our definitions, it is hard to give a formal proof. Even though these definitions represent the current state of the art, they still involve some degree of fuzziness. In particular, the inability to offer a canonical description of a given system and the fact that any classification is relative to such a description contributes to this problem.

Chapter 5

Ad hoc Service Grid Model

Contents

In this chapter, we will introduce the Ad hoc Service Grid [73, 71] and all associated models. The ASG model represents the abstract infrastructure that is the foundation for all mechanisms, algorithms, and protocols that will be presented in Part III of this book.

5.1 Infrastructural Model

The basic infrastructure of an ASG network is quite simple and straight forward. An ASG consists of so-called Service Cubes. These Cubes offer the computational resources typical of modern standard personal computers from the low-end to medium price segment. We explicitly do not presume any high-performance computers. Cubes are equipped with a wireless networking interface that is capable of setting up a multi-hop ad hoc network. Furthermore, they do not possess any peripheral devices such as a keyboard, mouse, or display. However, they do have a power plug. Thus, we assume that Cubes have an unlimited energy supply and do not need any special precautions to save energy. Unlike other computers in public places (e.g. automated teller machines or information terminals), Service Cubes do not need to be visible to users. They can be hidden in any way that is unobstructive to the wireless transmissions.

5.1.1　Mobility

Service Cubes are assumed to be *semi-mobile*. We will quantify what this means below. Essentially, dynamic changes in the structure are explicitly handled, but they must not be as frequently as in a classical mobile ad hoc network where mobile users constantly move relative to each other.

5.1.2　Heterogeneity

The mechanisms we propose in this work do not deal with the aspects of heterogeneity. We assume that all nodes are in the same general performance range and that the differences in hardware architecture can be handled by using Java and similar technologies to abstract platform differences.

5.1.3　Modularity

A very important concept of the ASG is *modularity*. Each Service Cube is regarded as being a module of the overall system. Each module provides two kinds of resources that contribute to the possible performance provided by the ASG:

1. **Networking:** By providing its own network interface and the ability to relay network traffic, each Cube contributes to the overall networking resources. It should be noted that networking bandwidth cannot be scaled up arbitrarily by adding more nodes, though. The access to the shared wireless medium is limited depending on the specific technology used. However, within certain limits, adding new nodes can improve networking performance, for example, by providing alternative routes through the network. Additionally, extending the network at the edges and, thus, increasing the coverage area is possible.

2. **Computation:** Service provisioning relies on sufficient computational resources to satisfy the user demand. The basic concept of the ASG is to provide this computational power in a distributed fashion. Each Service Cube contributes a share of computing power that can be used to execute services. This is exploited by the ASG Serviceware through service replication: A single service may be replicated and run on more than one Cube in parallel. Moreover, several different services will be provided in a complex ASG. Thus, the distributed nature of the computational resources in the ASG does not present a general limitation for service provisioning.

The advantage of the ASG's modular structure is that new resources (both in terms of networking capacity and computational power) may be added at runtime. Conversely, Service Cubes may also be removed without having to shut down the complete ASG. This makes it easy to flexibly scale the capacity of a specific ASG to the user demand.

5.1.4　Basic Organization – Clustering

The ASG infrastructure of distributed Service Cubes explained thus far is an amorphous substrate for ambient services: A set of dispersed computers is connected via a wireless network. In order to ease the task of building a software infrastructure that is able to organize ambient services on top of this network, we use a *clustering algorithm* that divides the amorphous network into small clusters [17]. This enforces a rudimentary structure on the network that can be used to make message routing easier. It also assigns different roles to the nodes that will be used on a higher level: Some nodes become *cluster heads* and others become *ordinary nodes*. A simple example is depicted in Figure 5.1. In this network, nodes 4, 7, and 11 are cluster heads and the respective clusters are marked with dashed lines.

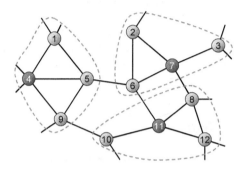

Figure 5.1: A network divided into 3 clusters.

At the network level, cluster heads function as gateways for routing messages. For example, if node 10 in Figure 5.1 needs to send a message to node 1, the routing protocol sends this message to the cluster head node 4 which is responsible for node 1. Node 4, in turn, delivers the message to the destination node 1. At the Serviceware level, cluster heads run the so-called *core services*. Core services provide basic functions needed to run, maintain, and organize value-added services. An example of such a core service is the Lookup Service that provides the current location of a specific service replica. Each core service runs in a distributed fashion being replicated on each cluster head. The clustering algorithm ensures that every node has a cluster head at most one hop away. Thus, each ordinary node may access the core services directly without any lookup.

Clustering Algorithm

The clustering algorithm used in the ASG is the *Distributed and Mobility-adaptive Clustering (DMAC) Algorithm* introduced by Basagni [17]. The DMAC algorithm establishes and maintains a clustered structure in a mobile ad hoc network, even if this network changes over time (that is, if links or nodes are added or removed). It requires only limited knowledge about the local neighborhood of a node (the neighbor's ID and its weight) to reach a decision about the role of that node in the cluster. IDs are assumed to be unique and the weight may be arbitrarily chosen to control the affinity of a node to becoming a cluster head. Each node takes on either the role of a cluster head or the role of an ordinary node. The basic idea of the algorithm is that each node decides which role to assume only when all its neighbors with bigger weights have decided their own role. This is achieved by using two types of messages: A CH message is sent by a node v to all neighbors in order to inform them that v

assumes a cluster head role. A $JOIN$ message is sent to the neighborhood to spread the information which cluster head an ordinary node joins. A node sends a $CH(v)$ message to all of its neighbors if it has the biggest weight among them. A node that has neighbors with bigger IDs than its own, waits until these nodes have either sent a CH message or a $JOIN$ message to indicate their role. Then it decides its own role: It either joins the cluster head neighbor with the biggest ID or (if there is no cluster head in the neighborhood) it becomes a cluster head itself. The mobility adaptivity is achieved by handling "link failure" and "new link" events. If these events corrupt the cluster structure, the nodes receiving such events take a new decision about their role to reconstruct the cluster.

This algorithm creates a cluster network in which two cluster heads are at most two hops apart. It introduces two levels of hierarchy: The cluster heads taking on coordinative roles in routing and service provisioning, and the ordinary nodes being reserved for value-added services.

5.2   Network Model

The idea of an Ad hoc Service Grid builds on the assumption that there will be a networking technology that is wide-spread and capable of building multi-hop ad hoc networks. At the moment, neither of the two most promising candidates for such a technology fulfills these requirements. The two contenders that are commercially most successful are IEEE 802.11 (WLAN) and Bluetooth. However, WLAN has a MAC (Medium Access Control) protocol that prevents any WLAN devices that are in transmission range from sending packets if another device is sending. This reduces the available bandwidth in ad hoc networks drastically since any communication that takes place inside the sender's transmission range is disrupted, even if it is unrelated. The reason for this is that WLAN was not designed for multi-hop ad hoc networking. It is mostly used between access points and user devices, and this access point mode has different requirements compared to ad hoc networking. Bluetooth, on the other hand, was explicitly designed for connecting a set of devices in an ad hoc manner. The standard also defines that so-called *scatternets* can be formed automatically. Scatternets are multi-hop networks composed of two or more *piconets* (small networks with one master and up to 8 slaves). However, most commercially available Bluetooth devices do not implement this feature since it is not necessary for the overwhelming majority of applications.

For a lack of applicable networking technologies, we present an abstract network model with some very basic properties. Any real-world networking technology that is to be used in ASGs has to possess these properties. In the simulations, we assume a standard *unit-disk graph* (see Figure 5.2). That is, each node has a fixed transmission range r and the area in which its transmissions can be heard has a perfect circular shape. Two nodes can communicate with each other if and only if they are within each others transmission range r. More formally, we adopt the standard definition of an undirected graph $G = (V, E)$ with a set of vertices V and a set of edges E. $d(u, v)$ is the distance between the nodes u and v. An edge (u, v) is in E if and only if $d(u, v) \leq r$. The transmission range r is the same for each node in V. Figure 5.2 depicts r as dashed circles and shows how a network (or graph) results from a specific topology of nodes.

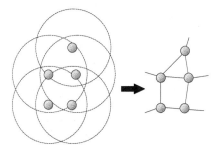

Figure 5.2: Unit-disk graph model for wireless networks.

5.2.1 Discussion

This represents a rather simplified network model. Due to different physical effects, most real-world wireless networks are far from being ideal unit-disk graphs. The transmission range varies with the physical conditions of the environment (e.g. temperature and obstacles). Real antennas do not produce a circular area in which the transmissions can be heard. Furthermore, due to reflection, interference, and distortion effects the areas reached by the transmission of a node can take arbitrary shapes. In particular, a signal may be detected by nodes that are far away while near-by nodes do not detect it. Moreover, the edges in a real wireless network may be unidirectional. That is, node u may be able to hear the transmission of node v but not vice versa.

However, as shown by Zhou et al. [189], the non-isotropic range found, for example, in wireless sensor networks does not affect common media access protocols to the extent that one might expect. Moreover, routing protocols can counter the negative effects by employing multi-round discovery techniques to explore alternative paths and to find symmetric connections. Based on these results, we argue that the unit-disk model used in our simulations is valid and does not void the results. There are no major limiting factors that may prevent us from implementing the measures advised by Zhou et al. in the routing protocol used in the ASG. The protocol overhead associated with multi-round protocols do not present a major problem in the ASG network as they are relatively small compared with the bandwidth of 802.11 networks, for example.

5.2.2 Preferred Network Technology

Due to the anticipated proliferation of the IEEE 802.11 technology in mobile devices, we think that WLAN is the best candidate for building ASG networks. However, in order to preserve the high bandwidth of WLAN even in a multi-hop ad hoc networking scenario, the 802.11 MAC protocol must be modified. We do not comment any further on these issues since they are out of scope in this work.

5.3   Usage Model

From the user's perspective, the interaction with an ASG is not directed towards a specific Service Cube, even though his mobile device is always connected to at least one of the Service Cubes. Instead, he interacts with the location as such. The user is unaware of the positions of individual Service Cubes and of the overall number of Cubes at his current location. As long as he has a connection to at least one Cube, he is not required to change his geographical location in order to access specific services. The distributed nature of the service provisioning shall be hidden from users. Thus, the ASG must offer distribution transparency to the user.

The goal set out by this research is to minimize and ultimately remove the necessity of manual intervention for the purpose of management and control. It is the very nature of a fully self-organizing software system that external organization is not necessary. Thus, ideally, there should not be any need to specify an administrative usage model. However, it is still unclear whether this ultimate goal can be reached. Certainly, we do not claim to remove the need for a human administrator in systems like the ASG. We only offer mechanisms to get closer to this goal. There is still the necessity to manage certain aspects of an ASG. For example, the "injection" of new services requires manual actions. However, since this book proposes algorithms and protocols for the self-organized distribution of services in the ASG, the human administrator is not required to control each Service Cube individually. Instead, the injection may take place at a designated control node or even at some arbitrary node. The service distribution algorithms do not presume any special start node for services.

In terms of general management actions and interfaces for executing them, we do not offer solutions here, as this is out of scope in this book. However, we imagine that an administrator may approach the ASG in much the same way as ordinary users do. Albeit, with a more in-depth knowledge about its structure and the positions at which Service Cubes are located. But issuing management requests is not much different from issuing service requests. Thus, an ASG administrator could have a mobile device that serves as a management station. He could connect to the ASG via the Service Cube closest to him and issues his control actions. There may be special security requirements involved with the transmission and execution of such commands.

5.4   Application Scenarios

ASGs may be applied in a wide range of scenarios due to the inherent flexibility of the model. Possible scenarios may be characterized as being of *medium size and medium dynamics*. The size of an ASG location is expected to range in the order of 1000 to 10000 m^2. The dynamics of the ASG infrastructure is given by the rate at which Service Cubes are added or removed. Even a large ASG will be able to handle such *structural changes* at a rate of a few hours. Tolerable levels of dynamics experienced due to use mobility include normal walking speeds.

These general assumptions apply to a range of different scenarios that are common in our daily life. We will briefly describe some of them to establish an intuition for the technical requirements and challenges. The following list is roughly given in ascending order according to the scenario's dynamics:

- **Hospitals:** Today, hospitals already possess advanced IT infrastructures to manage complex tasks, workflows, and schedules. However, in most cases, these infrastructures are centrally organized and the information is only accessible via non-mobile desktop computers or even through a single central terminal. By installing an ASG, information could be made omnipresent. The internal communication concerning tasks like scheduling working hours, planning operations, and presenting patients with up-to-date information about their health status, can be supported in this way.

- **Shopping malls:** Modern shopping malls offer many different services to customers. They consist of different shops with overlapping product lines. Moreover, they host restaurants, hair dressers, and cinemas. An ASG may be installed in such a mall in order to guide the customers through the complex set of offers. Product overview, navigation based on a shopping list, and infotainment services are only a few examples for ASG-based services that may enhance a shopping mall.

- **Construction sites:** Large construction sites pose big logistical challenges. Workers already use wireless communication means to span long horizontal and vertical distances in order to cooperate. An ASG may enhance the collaboration between foremen and co-workers. Today, the main means for communication on a construction site are walkie-talkies and mobile phones (for information exchange with external facilities). Therefore, communication is direct and synchronous. An infrastructure like the ASG can enrich this communication by adding an asynchronous communication medium. Information about available raw material, workflows, and time schedules can be supplied through information services. This can help to optimize efficiency.

- **Trade fairs:** Trade fairs are targeted towards information exchange. Potential customers and sellers come together and do business with each other. Navigation, information, and news services are required in this scenario. Exhibiting companies may contribute Service Cubes to the overall ASG in order to enhance this kind of services.

- **Concerts and other cultural events:** Today, some art exhibitions are already enhanced with electronic equipment in order to present visitors with additional information on the exhibits. Usually, the theme of a cultural event is rich of information that the interested visitor has to discover himself. More of this information could be presented to him via a supporting ASG providing knowledge and a new way of interacting with the event. In a concert, the people in the audience may obtain more knowledge about the artists and their background.

5.5 Business Models

The idea of a self-organizing service infrastructure also creates new business models. Classical infrastructures for covering locations like the ones presented above need to be set up and maintained by experts. Moreover, they are usually associated with high initial costs for server computers and high running costs for communication and support contracts. The vision of a self-managing, modular infrastructure of low-end computing devices changes this.

In the following, we give a list of business models that is enabled by an ASG infrastructure that is able to operate without manual administration:

- The operator of a location (the owner or the institution responsible for its maintenance) may decide to equip the location with a number of Service Cubes. Thus, the operator may finance and setup the ASG in order to attract more customers.

- Companies may specialize on offering Service Cubes for rent or sale. If an ASG is to be set up temporarily (e.g. for days or weeks), the best model may be to rent an appropriate number of Service Cubes for this period of time in order to minimize costs and still be able to provide Ambient Services. This may be the case, for example, at trade fairs.

- In a scenario in which multiple very small providers are present at the same general location, each of these providers may choose to contribute one or two Service Cubes for the sake of the whole community. This could be the case in the shopping mall scenario where multiple shop owners may join together to provide an overall infrastructure that may be used by each of them to make the whole location and consequently also the shops in the mall more attractive.

In general, there may be two motivations for setting up an ASG in the first place. First, operators and local providers may generate more profit directly by offering services that have to be paid by customers. The second benefit that is potentially presented by an ASG is the improvement of the attractiveness of an ASG-enhanced location. Customers may find it more enjoyable to do their shopping in a mall that supports them in the way that was sketched at the beginning of this book. Thus, without offering any commercial services, the operator of a location and the local providers may increase their profits, simply by attracting more customers.

All of this represents a vision that is really only possible with a modular, low-cost, zero-administration infrastructure like the ASG.

Part III

Algorithms and Protocols

Chapter 6

Introduction

In this part of the book, we investigate the principle of a *self-organizing replication and placement mechanism for ASG services*. Such a mechanism can dynamically change the overall configuration of the ASG in terms of the placement of service replicas in order to adapt to changes in usage patterns. This implies two other questions: *How can dynamically distributed service replicas be found by clients, and how can we achieve consistency among the replicas of stateful services in this environment?*

This defines the scope of this central part of our work. Three cooperating subsystems that are at the core of an ASG infrastructure will be discussed and studied in great detail to get a good understanding of their interactions. The general requirements for the respective mechanisms are that the consumption of wireless network bandwidth must be minimized and that the solutions must be decentralized and able to cope with dynamic changes in their environment.

1. The *service replication and placement system* provides a fully distributed algorithm that is able to adapt the service distribution within an ASG such that a stable and cost-efficient configuration is established. In this context, "cost-efficiency" means that the overall bandwidth consumption in the ASG network is minimized. The service distribution algorithms we present do not rely on any form of global knowledge. They are online heuristics that also do not require any communication between the replicas that are subject to placement decisions.

2. The *ASG Lookup System* consists of a group of distributed Lookup Service instances that collectively provide service discovery and lookup functionalities. Since services may dynamically replicate and migrate, it is a challenging task for clients to locate an appropriate replica. The Lookup System takes over this task and provides clients with the current addresses of such replicas. Since the Lookup System is distributed, the core problem is the dissemination of the changing location information. This has to be done with minimal network bandwidth overhead.

3. The *ASG consistency protocol* provides the means for keeping the data of replicated stateful services consistent. Without such a system, the dynamic repli-

cation and distribution of services would only be possible for stateless services which would severely limit the class of applications that may be run in an ASG. Our consistency protocol relies on an optimistic consistency model.

At the end of this part, we will derive an appropriate Serviceware architecture that fully supports the systems sketched above. The mechanisms used by this architecture are based on mobile agent technology and the tuple space paradigm. To enable the reader to fully understand our algorithms and protocols, we will first introduce these concepts without putting them into the architectural context of the final architecture.

Chapter 7

Middleware Mechanisms

Contents

The mechanisms, algorithms, and protocols introduced in the following chapters make use of some basic features of the underlying distribution platform. These features are specifically designed to meet the requirements laid out by the algorithms and protocols, and they were designed in parallel with them. We introduce them here, before explaining the higher-level mechanisms that make use of them. At the end of this Part, in Chapter 11, we will use these middleware mechanisms to design a Serviceware platform that is tailored to the requirements defined by the algorithms presented in the next chapters.

7.1 Mobile Agents

A mobile agent is a self-contained, autonomous software entity [130, 121]. It may travel across a network to migrate from one computer to another during runtime. Mobile agents are the most flexible form of mobile code [54] and they enable *logical mobility*: When mobile devices move and their connectivity changes over time, this is called *physical mobility*. *Logical mobility*, on the other hand, is present if software components may move between computers. The effects of physical mobility can be compensated by using logical mobility. For example, if two interacting devices are in danger of losing their connection, one of the interacting software components may be moved to the device of the other component. Thus, even if the connectivity is lost, the interaction may continue. Possible results of this interaction may be transported back to the original device of the migrated component later on, when both devices are connected again.

We assume that a middleware for the ASG is based on mobile agent technology. This means that a complex application is composed of several mobile agents that may use their mobility to restructure the application in order to adapt it to changing conditions. It should be noted that using mobile agents does not enforce mobility in any form. A mobile agent may also choose to stay where it was created for its entire lifetime. Furthermore, the possible internal complexity of a mobile agent is not restricted in any way. An agent may consist of many subcomponents and contain a considerable amount of code and data. Of course, there is always a trade-off between size and mobility, and the decision on how to structure a mobile agent is application-dependent.

The concept of agent mobility becomes of central importance when we introduce our service distribution algorithms in Chapter 8: Starting from some node in an ASG network, a service incrementally replicates and moves towards a position that minimizes network traffic and client response time. Thus, service replicas use their mobility to restructure their distribution and to adapt to changes in client request patterns.

7.2   Tuple Space Communication

This dynamics in an ASG represents a big challenge in terms of the communication between clients, services, and infrastructure facilities (e.g. middleware services). The ability to self-structure must not be hindered by communication. Conversely, the communication, e.g. between client and service, must not break down as a service moves. Thus, an ideal communication paradigm for the ASG supports the decoupling of communicating parties. Furthermore, the components inside the Serviceware layer, that are responsible for controlling the self-organization process, must be able to extract basic semantic information from the ongoing communication between clients and services. When a Serviceware daemon receives a message on behalf of a service, it needs to know which sort of message it is (e.g. a request) and, maybe it needs to get the size of the message to feed it into the self-organization algorithms that constantly monitor the local daemon. Finally, the Serviceware perceives communication as a stream of events that may trigger different actions below the actual communicating parties. A prime example for this paradigm is the message snooping mechanism (explained below) that enables arbitrary components at the Serviceware or application level to get copies of "interesting" messages without interfering with the actual communication.

In summary, the basic communication mechanism used in the ASG must support the following features:

- Decoupling of communication partners (clients, value-added services, middleware, and Servicware),

- Extraction of semantic information about messages to enable control algorithms to take decisions about self-organization actions, and

- Event-driven communication.

7.2.1 Tuple Spaces – Background

The best and most simple choice under these requirements are tuple spaces. Initially, tuple spaces where invented in the mid 80s as a means for the coordination of parallel processes [57, 2]. The first such system was called "Linda". A *tuple* contains typed data items and is written into or read from a *tuple space* by a process. Reading is done by partially specifying the content of the desired tuple. For some items in a so-called *template* the entire content is specified (*actuals*), and for others only the type is given (*formals*). Specifying a template in a read operation invokes a matching process during which the contents of the space is examined to find a tuple that matches the template. A match is found if the template and the tuple have the same number of data items, if all the actuals in the template and the tuple are equal, and if the tuple contains an actual for every formal in the template. If more than one tuple matches a template, then an arbitrary one is chosen. Typical tuple space implementations offer a set of blocking read and take operations and a set of non-blocking operations (e.g. JavaSpaces [160]). Processes that run in parallel can use blocking operations to coordinate their actions. One process may do a blocking read to wait for a result produced by another process. While the former operations block the caller until a matching tuple is put into the space (if none is found initially), the non-blocking variants examine the space and return immediately. They either return a matching tuple or some sort of notification that none was found. As an extension of the basic read and write operations some implementations offer a notification mechanism. Using this mechanism a caller can request to be notified by the space in case a tuple matching some template appears.

Tuple spaces enable applications to exchange data anonymously since tuples are addressed in an associative way by specifying their contents. It introduces a high degree of decoupling because two communicating entities do not have to exist in the same location or at the same time. In fact, they do not even need to have overlapping lifetimes. Tuples as the key element in this data-centric communication scheme can be conveniently transported to remote locations via some transport or dissemination mechanism.

7.2.2 Tuple-based Remote Communication

All communication in the ASG is based on tuples and tuple spaces. For example, when a client sends a request to a service, it creates a tuple containing the sender, the receiver, the data of the request, and other information that is necessary for sending the request. Subsequently, it uses a primitive provided by the Serviceware to send the tuple. The Serviceware in turn takes the tuple and routes it to the requested destination. It does so by using well-known routing protocols that establish multi-hop routes through the network. The choice of an appropriate routing algorithm is orthogonal to the idea of using tuple spaces. At the destination node, the message (the tuple) is put into the local tuple space and, thus, made available for local applications. It should be noted that the tuple is not directly delivered to any specific application. The destination may also be the local node, in which case the tuple is simply written into the local space.

7.3   Message Snooping

Any form of self-organization in artificial or biological systems relies on the ability of sensing changes in the environment. Changes are detected through sensors and the environment is manipulated as a result of these changes through some internal process. In an artificial communication system that shall optimize its own operation, one vital environmental factor is the flow of information between communicating parties. In order to sense important activities, and to adapt to them, the components responsible for structuring and organizing the system must be able to analyze the flow of messages.

In the platform proposed in this book, we introduce *message snooping* as a fundamental means for sensing the flow of information through the network, both in terms of its quantity and quality. Tuples, tuple spaces, and the associated routing infrastructure represent a middleware-level communication service. Based on the concept of tuples, the classical tasks of the network and transport layers are implemented in the middleware to gain full access to data about the flow of information. This access is realized through message snooping: An agent may register itself as a *snooper* at the middleware. It specifies a template that describes the tuples (messages) it is interested in. The middleware inspects any message that is destined for the local node or relayed on its way to some other node. If it detects a message that matches the template of a registered snooper, then that agent gets a copy of the message. This does not interfere with the normal transport of messages in any way. Sender and receiver are not aware of snoopers.

Note, that this approach is fundamentally different to that taken by the layered system model that has been adopted for Internet-based distributed systems many years ago. The OSI reference model propagates the usage of layered services that offer a high degree of transparency: One layer does not need to care about the way in which the service at the layer below functions. This is a very effective way to simplify the construction of complicated communication systems by deliberately hiding information. However, the emerging field of mobile and embedded systems and the trend towards self-organizing computing systems necessitate a different view on transparency. Operating systems and middleware platforms are much more tightly integrated with the functions at lower layers. For example, the all-important issue of energy conservation in small mobile devices raises the need for making much more data from the physical layer visible to applications.

Obviously, the snooping mechanism has implications in terms of the privacy and security of communication. The corresponding middleware implementation should provide means for restricting the information handed out to snoopers. For example, they may only be allowed to see source and destination, or they may only access a message's meta data etc. The nature of these restrictions is depending of the desired level of privacy and the requirements of the self-organization mechanisms implemented by the snoopers.

7.4   Message Meta Data

The communication model introduced for the ASG, allows arbitrary data to be put into messages independently of their payload. Any participant along the path of a message, including the sender and any snoopers, may read and manipulate this meta data. The meta data can be used, for example, to describe the nature of the message or any important properties of the message path or the participants. For example, the update mechanism of the ASG Lookup Service uses meta data to indicate whether a message has been redirected. Somewhere along the path of a message, a redirection is caused if a destination service has moved. New meta data is added to the message to indicate this fact before sending it to its new destination. The receiver in turn may inspect the meta data to find out whether it has been redirected. The receiver may also generate a new message and copy the meta data from the received one into the new one. Thus, meta data may be transparently transferred between messages in order to create a logical connection between the two. For instance, a reply message may contain information about the corresponding request to enable the receiver to draw a connection between the two. Combined with message snooping, meta data is an effective means for accumulating data in messages that is needed to observe and control their flow through the network.

7.5   Proxy Agents

An important feature of an ASG is the mobility or, more generally, the flexibility of service replica. However, this flexibility does not only have advantages. It also introduces a large degree of uncertainty: Does a replica really exists at a specific point in time? Is it still running at its last known location? Is a message really delivered if the target replica has moved to a different node? The fact that replicas may migrate, replicate, and remove themselves autonomously necessitates that we introduce some additional component that runs on all Service Cubes and handles all aspects of a replica's dynamics in order to restore the reliability and dependability of replicas. In the ASG, this component is called the *Proxy Agent*. A Proxy is running on each node in the network. It manages and maintains all replicas that are running (or that have been running) on its node. For example, it receives all messages destined for any of these replicas and decides how to handle them. If the target replica is still at the node, it simply forwards the message locally to that replica. If the replica has moved, the Proxy forwards the message to its new location. Furthermore, the Proxy plays a vital role in the adaptation process since it may monitor request traffic and initiate adaptations on behalf of replicas.

Chapter 8

Service Distribution

Contents

In Part I, we stated that manual control actions in an ASG infrastructure are undesirable and infeasible. Due to the decentralized and dynamic nature of an ASG, it is necessary, that the Serviceware platform has the ability to self-organize. One aspect that requires particular attention in this context is the distribution of services within an ASG network. If we want to deploy a particular service in an ASG, the following questions arise:

- Where (at which node(s)) shall a service be running?

- Should a service be replicated to run at more than one node in parallel?

- How many replicas are adequate in a particular situation?

- How can a set of replicas adapt to changes in the request patterns or the network topology?

A human operator may not be present, or he may not be able to answer these questions. He may not have sufficient knowledge about the changing network and about the dynamics in request patterns exhibited by clients. Classical network and system management assumes that the time period between relevant changes in the system are long enough such that an administrator can detect them and execute appropriate control actions to adapt the system accordingly. Moreover, the system that is subject to management decisions is controlled centrally: Relevant decisions about its configuration are usually made by the same personnel that manages the system. A global view is available to the administrative personnel such that the system can be monitored effectively, and adequate reactions can be issued if it is operating outside normal parameters[1].

All of these assumptions do not fit the concept on an Ad hoc Service Grid as we presented it in the preceding sections. An ASG may grow or shrink as it is running. Such topological changes may not be under the central control of any administrative personnel. They may occur as participants contribute their own Service Cubes. Request patterns may change more or less abruptly due to changes in client behavior. Such changes may happen frequently, and they may render an existing service distribution suboptimal or even counterproductive (e.g. if requests have to traverse the entire network). In the face of these dynamic changes, the manual control of the distribution of services is not feasible.

---

[1]This is at least how it should be in theory.

In this chapter, we introduce algorithms for the automatic distribution of service replicas in an ASG [73, 71] (called *service distribution* or *replica placement* in the following). Starting from a single, initial service replica that may be injected at an arbitrary Service Cube, our algorithms can migrate, replicate, and dissolve replicas to produce an appropriate replica placement incrementally. They achieve this without a global view on the network using client requests as a stimulus. The placement algorithms are run in a distributed fashion by each replica. They do *not* directly communicate with each other in order to coordinate, but nonetheless, they achieve a coherent, stable, and adaptive global placement pattern that minimizes the overall network load.

The rest of this chapter is structured as follows: We start by analyzing solutions in related research areas to assess their applicability to our problem domain (Section 8.1). We go on by formalizing our model and the replica placement problem as a basis for the presentation of our algorithms and the subsequent evaluation. Then, we explain the simulation models used to produce our results in Section 8.3. In Section 8.4 we describe our replica placement algorithms, before we give a detailed quantitative and qualitative evaluation of our results and concepts in Sections 8.7 and 8.8. In our qualitative evaluation, we show that our replica placement system is indeed self-organizing according to the model given in Section 3.4, and we present a detailed discussion on their specific self-organization and adaptivity features. We conclude this chapter with a discussion of our results.

8.1 Foundations and Related Work

The problem of placing software components in a computer network in order to optimize certain aspects of the overall system is not new. Before we formalize the model of our system and define the concrete optimization problem that shall be solved by our replica placement algorithms, we analyze the current state of the art in related problem domains. Specifically, we review agent-based approaches to service provisioning, techniques for placing services and resources in a networked infrastructure, and finally, we take a look at similar problems in the area of multiprocessor systems. While these domains have different underlying assumptions and goals, each of them deals with the same basic problem: *How can we adapt the structure of a specific distributed system by placing components (programs or resources) in order to improve its performance?*

8.1.1 Mobile Agents and Services

As we explained in Section 7, the fundamental mechanism for achieving a dynamic replica placement that may adapt during runtime, are mobile agents [121, 54, 130]. Most systems that employ mobile agents, either equip them with some task and send them to a remote host [187, 72] or they specify some sort of itinerary for an agent and let it migrate in a coordinated fashion over a set of computers in order to execute some task or to collect or disseminate data [183, 132].

The association between mobile agents and services has been made more explicit in the context of the World Wide Web. Bryce et al. employ them to deploy new services to information portals [24]. In this approach, a service is encapsulated in a set of mobile agents. In our approach, a self-contained service is realized as a single agent. However, we do not explicitly restrict a service to one agent. Since one service may employ another service to execute a client's request, one may view the overall service as being composed and, thus, consisting of multiple mobile agents. Another approach in the Web context is proposed by Nitto et al. who provide a platform that uses mobile agents to coordinate and execute a user's search requests on multiple websites [120].

Besides the research strand that concentrates on enhancing the classical Web, there is also a considerable interest to merge mobile agents and Web Services with each other. In these projects, mobile agents are essentially used to implement Web Services [35, 85, 19] and also Web Service clients [127] in order to render Web Services more dynamic and flexible.

Another important area where services based on mobile agents are studied is mobile computing. Their ability to decouple interacting software components (e.g. a client and a service) is a very desirable property in an environment where mobile devices may only have intermittent connectivity and must roam between different access networks while keeping the same communication session alive. Bellavista et al. employ this well-known concept and propose to use mobile agents as proxies for portable devices [20]. These proxies follow the clients' mobile devices during service provisioning to maintain and migrate session information. Samaras et al. propose services for providing views on Web-accessible databases. These services are based on mobile agents and are tailored to mobile client devices [149].

An idea that resembles the replica placement mechanisms we propose, is presented by Nakano et al. [118]. The authors claim that their "Bio-Networking Architecture" is able to offer adaptive and scalable network services that are implemented using mobile agents. It is applied to implement a distributed HTTP service that adapts to the current user demand by replicating and migrating *cyber entities* (mobile agents). The authors assume that every node in the Internet runs their platform in order to achieve this. A cyber entity's behavior is based on a set of linear threshold functions applied to some internal variables. The whole idea of this architecture is that agents spend energy and receive energy. The internal variable used in the threshold functions are somehow depending on this energy. Unfortunately, the results presented by the authors are not verifiable and not reproducible since vital information is missing. The numeric values used in the threshold functions are not motivated and seem to be rather arbitrary. The amount of energy that is spent and received by agents for the execution of certain actions are based on rather awkward assumptions about hardware platforms, the size of web pages, the support cost for a Bio-net platform, the cost and bandwidth of specific network links, and some further hard-to-verify statements [177]. Furthermore, the experimental results show that the system exhibits only a marginal increase in performance over a random algorithm. The optimal algorithm that is used for comparison seems rather arbitrary as well, since it uses a fixed number of three replicas.

8.1.2   Service Placement

Existing algorithms for the placement of servers are mostly targeted towards the Internet. The preferred application domain in this area is the Web. There are numerous approaches to placing web servers or web proxies such that some performance measure is optimized [90, 89, 99, 100, 164, 136]. The placement algorithms applied in all of these cases use global knowledge about the topology of the network and about client requests.

Lee et al. propose a replication architecture for a so-called *service grid* [98]. A service grid shall deliver generic services to Internet users. In order to be adaptive to the current user demand, these services may replicate. This idea is similar to our Ad hoc Service Grid concept. However, the application domain of the Internet is a different one, considering the scale and the nature of the network (fixed-wired vs. wireless). The replication architecture of the service grid is centralized and builds on a so-called replication manager that has complete information about all existing replicas of a service. This manager makes all decisions about replications in the network. Replicas in the service grid may not migrate during runtime and remain static after their creation. In contrast to this, we propose a completely decentralized approach in which the global, collective replication strategy emerges from the local decisions taken by the replicas themselves. Furthermore, replicas may autonomously migrate in the ASG to optimize the replica placement.

Andrzejak et al. present several service placement algorithms for grid environments [8]. These algorithms range from centralized ones that employ integer programming to decentralized ones that use ant-based optimization techniques and mobile agents. The specific focus of the authors is on the placement of a group of different interacting services such that the assignment of services to nodes obeys the nodes' constraints on processing and storage load. In addition, highly interactive services in the group shall be placed such that they have sufficient network bandwidth between them. Dynamic replication is not considered, and services do not migrate. Instead, they are stopped and restarted. The authors do not explain how stateful services are handled. Thus, the requirements for these algorithms are quite different from those in the ASG. Moreover, the placement of a group of services is a heavy-weight process, whereas placement in the ASG needs to be light-weight and continuous. The algorithms presented by Andrzejak et al. are not evaluated properly. They may not even be implemented. This makes them irreproducible and non-verifiable. It remains unclear how they behave in practice.

Lui et al. propose an algorithm for dynamic service replication in an Internet-based Service Overlay Network (SON) [103, 104]. The algorithm searches for the best node in the tree that has a service at its root and clients at its leafs. It applies a cost function that expresses the net income that is possible for the whole SON assuming that links need to be paid proportionally to their bandwidth. The algorithm takes a greedy approach and replicates services iteratively until no further gain is produced. The aim is not to reduce bandwidth consumption or to improve client-perceived latency, but to maximize the income of the SON's operator. The biggest drawback, however, from the ASG perspective, is that the greedy algorithm proposed by the authors is centralized and needs global knowledge on all source-destination pairs in the SON.

Choi et al. propose a system that is very similar to that targeted by Liu et al. [33]. They tackle the problem of minimizing the configuration costs for communication sessions between clients and servers in a SON. They propose five algorithms (including a random algorithm used for comparison) to solve this problem. However, like Lui et al. they only consider centralized solutions that require global knowledge.

More specifically, the algorithms proposed by Lui et al. and by Choi et al. are not distributed. One algorithm runs on some node, and as its input, it gets information about the network topology and about the associations between clients and services (paths, request volumes etc.). Based on this information, the algorithm heuristically finds a good service placement. In general, the aim of the approaches discussed here is to solve the NP-hard placement problem [33] heuristically. They are not targeted towards providing decentralization and autonomy in order to create a flexible system.

8.1.3   Resource Placement

The problem of *resource placement* is closely related to the server placement problem. Both try to place resources inside a network such that some performance measure is optimized. This may be a client-related measure like response time or a server-related measure of resource consumption (CPU cycles, storage space, bandwidth etc.). Sometimes, a combination of both is used [137, 138]. A service placement algorithm assumes a rather coarse-grained view by placing a whole set of resources (data, documents) provided by a single server. In contrast to that, we use the term *resource placement* to denote the placement of individual resources like, for example, web pages. These resources may be dynamically placed on a subset of a set of so-called *surrogate servers* that are running in fixed locations inside the network. Thus, servers remain fixed and resources are moved and replicated dynamically. This represents a more fine-grained approach compared to server placement. However, the basic optimization problem is very similar. A survey concerning both server and replica placement in the context of the World Wide Web is presented by Manzano and Yilmaz [109].

The WWW is the most prominent application domain for placement algorithms. This includes the placement of web proxies (see 8.1.2) as well as the placement of web pages among fixed servers. More generally, the corresponding networks are called *Content Distribution Networks* (CDNs). Akamai is a prominent example of a commercially successful company that runs such a CDN.

Most existing replica placement algorithms (RPAs) for CDNs try to minimize the distance between requesting clients and the resources they request. This distance is essentially measured in network hops. However, other metrics like bandwidth or latency may be included into that distance measure. Kangasharju et al. present RPAs that minimizes the average number of hops a request must traverse [91]. Objects are initially placed on an origin server and then replicated to other servers. The algorithms require global knowledge of the network topology and the popularity of documents to make a placement decision.

Crorin et al. address the problem of placing download mirrors in the Internet such that the client download time is reduced [37]. The authors explicitly mention the fact that keeping mirrors (replicas) consistent causes an increase in network traffic that is linear in the number of mirrors. However, they ignore this cost component since it does not take effect in their case.

Crorin et al. [37] and Radoslavov et al. [139] are both considering the outdegree of a potential replication site as a good indicator for its appropriateness to host a replica. A node that is highly connected to other nodes is assumed to be a good location for replicas. The validity of this assumption is, of course, highly dependent on the network's topology. In a network that has a scale-free topology, like the Internet or the WWW, this could lead to overload situations and congestion at the hub nodes. In such a network, very few nodes are highly connected (so-called *hub nodes*) while the majority of nodes has only few connection [6].

While all of the above algorithms are purely centralized, Coppens et al. present an architecture and algorithms for a semi-centralized content delivery service [36]. In their system, each request is sent to a central *Content Retrieval* module (CR) that finds the appropriate server (providing the requested replica at minimal cost) and a path from the client to that server. The actual placement is executed decentralized using the information provided by the CR. While this is more scalable in terms of processing load, it produces considerable network overhead. Moreover, the CR is still a bottleneck and central point of failure.

Ko and Rubenstein introduce a replica placement system in which the servers decide which resources to host based on the distance of nearby clients requesting resources [96]. This is realized by a distributed algorithm. Each server has a color (representing a specific resource required by clients). In a distributed fashion, servers cooperate with the other servers in their neighborhood to find a global color distribution that minimizes the overall distance of clients to the closest server that hosts their required color. When a server applies the color change rule (run by all servers locally), it first has to measure the distance to all clients by sending a request to those clients, asking each of them to confirm the server's current information on the distance. This assumes that clients are static and that the distance between a client x and a server y does not change frequently due to client and/or server mobility. Another reason why this system is not applicable in our scenario is that it produces considerable network overhead for the distance probing. Finally, the fact that a server can only resume properly if all clients have answered reduces the robustness of this approach drastically.

Interesting work with respect to the adaptivity of replica placement is described by Pierre et al. [131], who propose an architecture for the replication of web documents among servers. They describe a per-document selection of a specific replication strategy and show that this algorithm outperforms a system with a global strategy. The authors use adaptivity in the sense that the strategies for each document may be changed during runtime. To achieve this, the documents' servers periodically run a simulation and, based on the result, they choose the best strategy. Thus, not the placement is adapted, but the placement strategy. This introduces a meta level.

Rabinovich et al. propose the RaDaR architecture [137] for monitoring a large pool of servers and migrating and replicating resources among them. The objective is to move replicas of objects (resources) closer to requesting clients and to relieve overloaded hosts. The RaDaR approach resembles that taken in one of our placement algorithms in that it uses the paths taken by requests to find better locations that are closer to requesting clients. RaDaR employs routing information extracted from the OSPF (Open Shortest Path First) routing system. However, the algorithms used in RaDaR are not applicable to the ASG since they make different assumptions concerning the placement granularity. RaDaR places resource objects (single web pages). The restrictions on the number of objects replicated throughout the network are much weaker than the restrictions that apply to complete service replicas in the ASG. Additionally, RaDaR may ignore any consistency considerations based on the arguments that web pages are static and that update traffic is negligible. In the ASG, service replica consistency is a key factor in placement decisions. Finally, RaDaR assumes a hierarchical structure of so-called replicators. Such a structure is problematic in an ASG as its maintenance imposes additional overhead and network dynamics may cause inconsistencies that may prevent proper placement decisions.

8.1.4 Task Assignment in Parallel Computing

Another area of research that deals with placement problems is high-performance parallel computing [105]. The research in this area is concerned with the solution of computationally intensive problems. These problems are usually divided into smaller subtasks, distributed over multiple processors, and computed in parallel to reduce the overall computation time as much as possible. The hardware and software platforms employed here range from highly integrated multiprocessor systems to cluster computers [14] and grid solutions [15, 52]. In multiprocessor systems, a large number of processors are essentially running inside one computer. They communicate over a classical bus system. A cluster computer is a set of interconnected workstations that are dedicated to the cooperative solution of computational tasks. Such a workstation cluster is usually under a single administrative domain and often concentrated at a single geographical location. A computing grid is a collection of loosely coupled multi-purpose computers that may join and leave autonomously. Thus, a grid computes its tasks based on a dynamically changing set of computers that are connected over the Internet and are possibly dispersed over the whole world.

A common problem in all of these parallel computing infrastructures is the assignment of subtasks to individual computers (or processors). This assignment must obey two fundamental constraints:

1. Tasks must be allocated such that the communication cost is minimized. Two tasks may have to communicate, and this communication may have different intensities depending on the pair of tasks. Two tasks that must communicate heavily should be placed close together to minimize the latency of communication and, therefore, increase the speed of computation.

2. The load must be balanced as evenly over the processors as possible in order not the create hotspots that slow down the overall computation. In particular, the tasks of the same parallel program should not be concentrated on a few processors since this would hamper its parallel execution.

Some interesting, self-organizing approaches to the task assignment problem have been presented by Heiß et al. The authors applied Kohonen self-organizing maps to map a task graph onto a multiprocessor system in such a way that the graph's topology is preserved [65]. That is, highly interactive tasks are mapped to neighboring processors. This approach yields excellent results with respect to the load balancing among the processors. However, the underlying concepts and assumptions differ from the ones found in the ASG as it is assumed that the task graph as well as the dependencies between the tasks are known in advance.

In a different approach, Heiß et al. propose a model that is based on the interactive behavior of viscous fluids [66]. Communication, load balancing, and migrations are modeled as physical forces (viscosity, gravitation, and friction) that act upon tasks.

Tasks are modeled as fluids and the multiprocessor system is viewed as a tank containing the different fluids. The resulting overall force is computed in a decentralized way and may lead to task migrations if such a migration reduces the force on the task. This process eventually leads to a balance of forces which represents a good solution to the task assignment problem. This approach has some appealing properties, especially for the application to the ASG replica placement problem. However, there are some fundamental differences that prohibit a direct usage:

- There is no concept for replication in the physical model. Tasks may not decide to replicate in order to react to the forces they experience.

- Load balancing is not considered an issue in the ASG. While an unbalance in load may degrade the overall execution time of a task in a parallel program, the ASG has no notion of an overall execution time. Services run indefinitely long and do not terminate automatically. Moreover, "tasks" in the ASG do not execute intensive computations. Therefore, we do not consider processing load as an issue. On the other hand, the network load in the wireless medium has a much higher significance to us.

- Heiß et al. model migration cost as friction. Thus, they assume that two tasks must exchange a specific amount of data that exceeds the data that needs to be transferred in a migration before a migration may happen. This is only possible, if precise a priori information about the communication habits among tasks is known. In the domain of parallel programming, there are certain mechanisms to get this information (e.g. by monitoring prior program runs or by inferring it from the software). This is not possible in the ASG. In Section 8.4.2, we will discuss the role of migration cost in great detail. We will show that it may not be used in the decision for or against a migration in our case.

These differences imply that the physical model would be reduced to modeling the communication cost in the ASG. In fact, our model for communication cost resembles that of the physical model closely. This is not surprising due to the nature of this cost component.

8.1.5 Discussion

From the preceding review of related projects, we conclude that none of the solutions proposed in literature thus far complies with the requirements of an ASG. The approaches with respect to mobile agent based services do not offer solutions to the replica placement problem. The core domain of service placement concentrates mainly on centralized solutions that are concerned with designing heuristics for solving the NP-Hard placement problem more efficiently. None of these algorithms operates decentralized using local knowledge only. This is also true for the closely related domain of resource placement. Finally, the assignment of tasks to multiprocessor systems provides some interesting approaches. However, the assumptions about the nature of a task and the optimization goals are quite different, such that a direct application of the proposed models to our problem is not feasible.

8.2   Formal Problem Statement

In order to capture the nature of the service distribution problem, and to be able to define the respective optimization problem and reason about it as precisely as possible, we give a mathematical definition of the relevant aspects of the ASG in this section. We will define the relations between the key elements clients, replicas, and network nodes. We go on by defining a cost model before we present functions that model the dynamics in the system. These functions generate the mobility and request patterns of clients and the allocation of replicas to clients. We also describe the functions that must be implemented by any algorithm that could be used to solve the problem of distributing replicas optimally over the nodes.

The ASG network is given as a graph $G = (N, L)$ where N is the set of nodes (the Service Cubes) and L is the set of communication links between them. K is a set of clients with each client being connected to a Service Cube. To keep our model simple, we assume that the client software that generates service requests runs on the nodes in N. Thus, we do not model mobile devices and their connections to the network explicitly. A mobile client device that connects to different Service Cubes $\{x_1, \ldots, x_k\}$ at time indices $\{t_1, \ldots, t_k\}$ on its way and send its requests via these nodes is equivalent to this simpler model that assumes that the client is running on node x_i at time t_i.

There may be an arbitrary number of different *service types* that coexist in parallel in the same ASG. We denote the set of service types as S, and a single service type as $s \in S$. In a shopping mall scenario, for example, there may be a navigation service, a product information service, and an entertainment service. These are three different service types. For each of these service types, an arbitrary number of replicas may exist. In principle, each replica of a specific service type provides the same service to its clients. The only difference between two replicas is that they may store different data as it may temporarily diverge between replicas. Section 10 will introduce an appropriate consistency protocol to deal with this issue. In this section, we abstract from the details of this protocol and simply assign a cost for keeping data consistent.

In order to keep the following formal definition as simple as possible and without loss of generality, we assume that there is only a single service type in the system. R is the set of replicas of that service type. The number of replicas in R may grow (replication) and shrink (replica removal) as needed, but $|R| \geq 1$ must always be guaranteed. Since R changes over time, we also write $R(t)$ to refer to the set of replicas a time t. Hereafter, we will use R to denote $R(t)$ unless stated otherwise. The optimization problem we are defining here can easily be extended to multiple service types since the optimizations for individual types are independent of each other. There may be dependencies between service types, for example, if a service type A requires a service type B and A's replicas send requests to replicas of B. However, for B, these replicas are merely clients and the interaction is not different from the normal interaction between service replicas and clients.

A client in K always chooses the replica closest to its current location. This is a very fundamental assumption that is essential for the algorithms that we will introduce. These algorithms build on this assumption by trying to push replicas closer towards clients to shorten the distance and to avoid costly wireless transmissions. The distance metric used here is the number of network hops between the client and the available replicas. In Section 9, we present the ASG Lookup Service that provides clients with a good approximation of the distance to a specific replica.

Finally, we assume that messages that are exchanged between two nodes u and v in N are always routed over the shortest path between u and v.

8.2.1 Cost Function

Before we can formalize our optimization problem, we need to define a cost function that is to be minimized by the optimization. Our central assumption is that the wireless medium is the most critical resource in an ASG. Other resources like memory, CPU cycles, or energy are much less relevant in our context. Therefore, we employ a cost function that measures the overall number of transmitted messages per time unit, and we ignore costs associated with other resources. However, as we will show in the following sections, placing replicas in a way that minimizes network load also balances the load with respect to CPU cycles and memory.

The cost function that we develop consists of three components:

- the *request costs*, caused by clients sending requests to replicas,

- the *migration costs*, associated with transporting replicas to better locations in the network, and

- the *replication costs*, caused by multiple replicas of the same service type having to keep their data consistent.

All of these costs are generated by sending message through the network for the respective purpose. The measurement unit for these cost components is *message transmissions per time unit*. A message transmission is caused whenever one node sends a message through the wireless medium to a neighbor node. If the distance between the two nodes is n hops, a message sent between the two causes n message transmissions. We count each transmission individually since on every hop, the sender needs to acquire access to the shared wireless medium, affecting all other nodes in its transmission range[2]. Thus, the goal of our optimization is to save as many of these transmissions as possible to take load off the network and free up networking resources. We will now define the three component cost functions before we combine them to get the overall cost function.

Let $A_{RN} = \mathcal{P}(R \times N)$ be the power set of all possible replica allocations a_{rn}. Each element in A_{RN} is a set of pairs allocating each replica in R to some node in N. For example, $a_{rn} = \{(r_1, 17), (r_2, 23), (r_3, 47)\}$ would be a valid element of A_{RN} if $|R| = 3$ and $|N| = 50$. In this specific allocation, the first replica r_1 runs on node 17, the second replica runs on node 23, and the third one on node 47.

Let $A_{CN} = \mathcal{P}(K \times N)$ be the set of all possible client allocations a_{cn}. Each element in A_{CN} is a set of pairs allocating each client in K to some node in N.

The replication cost function

$$C_R : A_{CN} \times A_{RN} \to \mathbb{R} \tag{8.1}$$

---

[2]The degree of this interference is dependent on the specific networking technology. However, the general concept of a shared medium is common to all existing wireless technologies.

maps each pair consisting of a client allocation and a replica allocation to a real-valued cost associated with keeping the replicas in R consistent. The number of transmissions necessary for keeping the replicas in R consistent is depending on the distance between the replicas which can be calculated using G (more precisely, the shortest paths between any pair of nodes in G) and a_{rn}. Together with the number of messages that the replicas exchange for achieving consistency, C_R can be calculated. This number of consistency protocol messages, in turn, depends on the volume of client requests received by the replicas and, thus, on A_{CN}. Remember that each client is mapped to its nearest replica.

The request cost function

$$C_Q : A_{CN} \times A_{RN} \to \mathbb{R} \tag{8.2}$$

maps each pair consisting of a client allocation and a replica allocation to a real-valued cost associated with the exchange of requests and responses between clients and replicas.

The migration cost function

$$C_M : A_{RN} \times A_{RN} \to \mathbb{R} \tag{8.3}$$

maps each transition between two replica allocations to a real-valued cost. For example, let $a_{rn}^1 = \{(r_1, 17), (r_2, 23), (r_3, 47)\}$ and $a_{rn}^2 = \{(r_1, 32), (r_2, 5), (r_3, 21)\}$ be two replica allocations. The transition from a_{rn}^1 to a_{rn}^2 is done by migrating $\{r_1, r_2, r_3\}$ from nodes $\{17, 23, 47\}$ to nodes $\{32, 5, 21\}$ which is associated with costs expressed by $C_M\left(a_{rn}^1, a_{rn}^2\right)$.

At this point, a problem occurs. The migration costs are fundamentally different in nature when compared with the request and replication costs. C_R and C_Q are associated with a specific replica allocation $a_{rn} \in A_{RN}$ (and client allocation A_{CN}). C_M, however, cannot be directly attributed to an element of $a_{rn} \in A_{RN}$. Instead, it is associated with the *transition* between two replica allocations $a_{rn}^1, a_{rn}^2 \in A_{RN}$. As a result, C_Q, C_R, and C_M cannot be linearly combined in an overall cost function in a straight-forward way. This would be the same as if we simply added a distance to a velocity. Doing so would yield a result that is not useful. Instead, one would have to convert one into the other using time: If a person has traveled 180 *kilometers*, and if he would like to know if a train traveling at 90 *kilometers per hour* can take him back to his starting point, he has to make a statement about how long he would be willing to travel by train.

We will do the same with respect to the overall cost function by considering the time period between two successive replica allocations and by distributing migration costs evenly over this time period. We will regard time as being discrete.

Let us assume that the replica allocations change at times $\{t_1, t_2, t_3, \ldots\}$ with $t_i < t_{i+1}$ and that $a_{rn}(t_i)$ is the replica allocation that is active in the time interval $[t_i, t_{i+1} - 1]$. We define the time-dependent migration cost function as follows:

$$\forall t \in [t_i, t_{i+1} - 1] : C_m(t) = \frac{C_M\left(a_{rn}(t_i - 1), a_{rn}(t_i)\right)}{t_{i+1} - t_i} \tag{8.4}$$

In other words, if t is in the interval $[t_i, t_{i+1}]$, then the migration costs associated with t are the costs caused by the migration from the previous replica allocation $a_{rn}(t_i - 1)$ to the current allocation $a_{rn}(t_i)$ divided by the length of the time interval during which $a_{rn}(t_i)$ will be active. If either $a_{rn}(t_i - 1) = \emptyset$ or $a_{rn}(t_i) = \emptyset$, or if $a_{rn}(t_i - 1) = a_{rn}(t_i)$ then $C_m(t) = 0$.

In a straight-forward way, we define $a_{rn}(t)$ as the replica allocation and $a_{cn}(t)$ as the client allocation that is active at time index t. Furthermore, we define $C_q(t)$ and $C_r(t)$ as the request costs and replication cost at time t. We can convert C_Q and C_R into the time-dependent functions $C_q : [0, \infty) \to \mathbb{R}$ and $C_r : [0, \infty) \to \mathbb{R}$ by defining

$$C_q(t) = C_Q(a_{cn}(t), a_{rn}(t)) \quad \text{and} \quad C_r(t) = C_R(a_{cn}(t), a_{rn}(t)). \tag{8.5}$$

Based on these definitions, the overall cost function becomes:

$$C(t) = C_q(t) + C_r(t) + C_m(t) \tag{8.6}$$

Using an analogon from physics, we may interpret these three components as forces that pull replicas into different directions: C_Q pulls a replica towards clients. The request costs get smaller if a replica is closer to its clients since the number of message transmissions needed to transport the same number of requests (and responses) between the replica and its clients is reduced. C_R forces a group of replicas to stay close together. The closer the replicas stay together, the less message transmissions are necessary for the exchange of consistency protocol messages. Finally, C_M may be interpreted as the *inertia* or the *friction* of a replica: The higher the costs for moving a replica from one node to another, the greater the force C_Q must be to make it move.

8.2.2 Definition of System Dynamics

Before we go on to define the optimization problem, we first give some functions that describe the system that is subject to optimization:

Let

$$f_C : K \times [0, \infty) \to N \tag{8.7}$$

be the time-dependent client allocation function that defines which client in K is running at which node in N at time t. f_C generates a client allocation $a_{cn} \in A_{CN}$ such that

$$a_{cn}(t) = \{(c_1, f_C(c_1, t)), \ldots, (c_m, f_C(c_m, t)\} \tag{8.8}$$

for $K = \{c_1, \ldots, c_m\}$.

The client request function

$$f_Q : K \times [0, \infty) \times N \to \mathbb{N} \tag{8.9}$$

specifies the number of requests that a client at a specific node sends at time t. $f_Q \circ f_C$ is a model for the request patterns that our algorithms shall adapt to. f_Q generates a request distribution $q(t) \in \mathcal{P}(N \times \mathbb{N})$ at time t as follows:

$$q(t) = \left\{ (v_i, m_i) | \forall i \in \{1, \ldots, |N|\} : v_i \in N \wedge m_i = \sum_{j=1}^{|K|} f_Q(c_j, t, v_i) \right\} \tag{8.10}$$

$q(t)$ simply defines how many request messages m_i are sent from node v_i at time t for each node in N.

Let $U_R = \{r_1, r_2, r_3, \ldots\}$ be the set of all possible replicas. The replication function

$$f_R : \mathcal{P}(U_R) \to \mathcal{P}(U_R) \setminus \emptyset \tag{8.11}$$

maps one set of replicas to another set by creating new replicas (from existing ones) and by removing replicas. The set of replicas that is active at time t may be written as $R(t)$ and $f_R(R(t)) = R(t+1)$.

The migration function

$$f_M : R \times [0, \infty) \to N \tag{8.12}$$

defines a mapping of each replica in R to a node in N at time t. This is the function that establishes the time-dependent distribution of the existing replicas over the nodes. f_M generates a replica allocation $a_{rn} \in A_{RN}$ such that

$$a_{rn}(t) = \{(r_i, f_M(r_i, t)), \ldots, (r_j, f_M(r_j, t)\} \quad \text{for} \quad R = \{r_i, \ldots, r_j\}. \tag{8.13}$$

Next, we define the time-dependent allocation of clients to replicas more precisely. Above, we only stated that a client always chooses the nearest replica. However, this replica also has to be *appropriate*. In some cases, a specific client $c \in K$ may be restricted to using only a subset of the replicas available in $R(t)$. For example, c may have started a communication session with a replica r_j. For the duration of this session, c may choose to continue its interaction with r_j instead of switching to a replica r_k that moves closer. Therefore, we define a function f_A that chooses a set of possible candidate replicas for a given client at a specific time:

$$f_A : K \times [0, \infty) \to \mathcal{P}(R) \tag{8.14}$$

In our example, where client c has an ongoing session with replica r_j at time t, the candidate set would be $f_A(c, t) = \{r_j\}$.

Let

$$d : N \times N \to \mathbb{N} \tag{8.15}$$

be the distance function for the network G. d maps each pair of nodes in G to the length of the shortest path between them:

$$d(n_i, n_j) = \begin{cases} \text{length of shortest path bt. } n_i \text{ and } n_j & : & (n_i, n_j) \in L \\ \infty & : & (n_i, n_j) \notin L \end{cases} \tag{8.16}$$

We define

$$d_{CR} : K \times R \times [0, \infty) \to \mathbb{N} \tag{8.17}$$

as the distance function that maps each pair consisting of a client and a replica to the length of the shortest path between them in G at time t:

$$d_{CR}(c_i, r_j, t) = d(n_k, n_l) \text{ with } (c_i, n_k) \in a_{cn}(t), (r_j, n_l) \in a_{rn}(t) \tag{8.18}$$

Let $A_{CR} = \mathcal{P}(K \times R)$ be the set of all possible allocations of clients in K to replicas in R. The allocation function that maps each client to a replica is given by:

$$f_{CR} : [0, \infty) \to A_{CR} \tag{8.19}$$

with

$$f_{CR}(t) = \{(c_i, r_j) | c_i \in K \wedge r_j \in R(t) \wedge$$
$$d(c_i, r_j) \le d(c_i, r_k) \forall k : (r_k \in R(t) \wedge r_k \in f_A(c_i, t))\}. \quad (8.20)$$

In other words, each client c_i chooses the replica r_j among all appropriate replicas ($f_A(c_i, t)$) that is closest to c_i. We will also denote the allocation of clients to replicas at time t by $a_{cr}(t)$, analogous to the other allocations $a_{cn}(t)$ and $a_{rn}(t)$.

In a real system with real users, f_C and f_Q are given by the behavior of human clients that move through the network and post requests according to some pattern. In the simulation, f_C and f_Q are modeled by stochastic processes with specific properties that will be discussed in Section 8.3. The set of possible candidate replicas f_A and the mapping between clients and replicas f_{CR} are partially influenced by client behavior and by technical issues like sessions. f_R and f_M, on the other hand, are the functions that are implemented by the service distribution algorithms and the reference algorithms introduced in Section 8.4.

A *configuration* $\mathcal{C}$ of the system is defined as a triplet consisting of a network graph, a client allocation, and a replica allocation: $\mathcal{C} = (G, a_{cn}, a_{rn})$. $\mathcal{C}(t) = (G, a_{cn}(t), a_{rn}(t))$ is the system's configuration at time t.

8.2.3 Definition of the Optimization Problem

The following definition formalizes the basic problem of finding a replica allocation or a series of replica allocations that minimizes the cost function C over a given time interval. Any service distribution algorithm that is applied to the ASG has to solve this basic problem.

Definition 8.1 (Replica Placement Optimization Problem). *Find a replication function f_R and a migration function f_M such that the average cost $\overline{C} = \frac{\sum_{t=0}^{T} C(t)}{T+1}$ in a given time interval $[0, T]$ is minimal for a given network $G = (N, L)$, under a given client allocation function f_C, client-to-replica allocation function f_{CR}, and client request function f_Q.*

In the following, we will denote the duration of a complete simulation run as T. Thus, any point in time t is in the range $[0, T]$, and T is measured in simulation ticks. This definition leaves the question open, as to whether $f_R \circ f_M$ generates a single static replica allocation $a_{rn}(t)$ with $a_{rn}(t_i) = a_{rn}(t_j) \quad \forall t_i, t_j \in [0, T]$ or whether $a_r n$ may change over time. Both choices are possible. A dynamic series of allocations may be beneficial if f_C, f_Q, and f_{CR} are dynamic. Furthermore, the definition does not state whether the mechanisms that are used for implementing $f_R \circ f_M$ use global knowledge over the complete time interval or if they are distributed and use local knowledge extracted from past events at any point in time t.

8.2.4 Optimal Solutions

The optimization problem that we have defined above is closely related to the well-known *facility location problem* which is defined as follows: Given a set of locations

N, a set of facilities has to be built on these locations such that a given set of clients (also residing on locations in N and using the closest available facility) produces the lowest possible cost when connecting to these facilities. The cost produced by a client j connecting to a facility i is defined as $d_j c_{ij}$, where d_j is the client's demand, and c_{ij} denotes the distance between i and j. In addition to these costs, building a new location i incurs a cost of f_i. $G = (N, E)$ is a graph that has the potential locations as its nodes, and c_{ij} is given by the topology of G. The objective is to find a number of facilities and their locations such that the overall cost is minimal.

The facility location problem is NP-hard. This can be shown by reducing it to the set cover problem. Efficient algorithms producing approximations whose cost is within a constant factor of the optimal solution have been proposed in a number of publications (cf. [31, 88]).

Our online placement algorithms solve the same basic problem of finding a placement (number of replica and their locations) that minimizes the cost of client requests. This request cost is depending on the distance between replicas (facilities) and clients and on the client demand (number of requests), too. The migration cost component in our model can be mapped to the cost component f_i in the facility location problem. Thus, the cost for migrating a replica to a new location may be interpreted as the cost for building this facility. The replication cost component, however, introduces a new element not present in the original facility location problem: In our model, facilities also produce costs that depend on their mutual distance. Thus, if our algorithm was able to do the optimization with a global view, as it is the case in the facility location problem, it would still be faced with a problem that is at least as hard. However, our algorithm only has a local view. We conclude that an optimal online solution is not efficiently computable in our case. Therefore, our algorithms use a heuristic approach.

8.2.5   The Use of Simulations – Motivation

We evaluate our algorithm by simulating them. An obvious alternative would have been an analytical approach by employing tools like Makrov chains or Petri nets. However, these techniques have several limitations that make them infeasible for the analysis of a system like the ASG: First of all, they may give us insight into the behavior of systems that are in a stationary state where the underlying probability distributions are invariant. However, the processes we are interested in are non-stationary by their very nature. In the next section, we introduce dynamics models that are used to simulate changing client behavior. One of the interesting questions studied in this book is related to the ability of our placement algorithms to adapt to such changes. Essentially, the system undergoes repetitive dynamics changes, and we study the behavior of our placement system on the way to the next stationary state.

Another reason why the use of established analytic methods is prohibitive in our case is the fact that they rely on a concise definition of the system's state space. With the complexity involved with modeling the actors in an ASG system, this state space can get extremely large. Moreover, to produce the wealth of quantitative results presented in the three core chapters of this book, different analytical models would have to be built and analyzed.

Finally, the work and the results presented exhibit a strong experimental character. The difficulties involved with designing and evaluating a self-organizing system have been discussed in depth in Section 3.4 and in Chapter 4. In most cases, this is not a straight-forward process. Biologists, for example, are starting from a basic hypothesis about a certain behavior (e.g. the foraging of ants) and build models to test this hypothesis. Often, these initial models do not really reflect the behavior observable in the real world. However, they provide vital insights and point to new directions. Subsequent improved versions of the model eventually lead to the desired behavior which results in new findings about the original subject of investigation. We took the same basic approach to develop our algorithms: An initial hypothesis had to be tested and improved until a working algorithm was found that could be analyzed in depth. Many of the results were only discovered in this analysis. This methodology requires a simulation that can be changed very flexibly to test and refine the solutions. With an analytical approach, however, fundamental assumptions (e.g. probability distributions) would have determined the choice of an appropriate analysis tool and they could not have been easily changed without having to build a new model. Thus, a sophisticated simulation had to be created anyway. Therefore, beyond the fact that known analytical means do not really match our system, we chose to use this simulation for our evaluation for practical reasons.

8.3 Simulation Models

This section describes the different models that work within our simulation of the ASG environment. In particular, we explain the implementation of the client allocation function f_C and the client request function f_Q in the simulation. That is, we present the model for client mobility and the model according to which clients generate requests. Before that, we start by presenting the mechanism used to generate a random network graph $G = (N, L)$.

8.3.1 Topology Model

We assume that the building process of an ASG network is motivated by the objective to distribute nodes evenly across the available space to fill gaps that may occur and to improve connectivity. Thus, if a new node was to be added to the ASG, it would rather be put in a place where there are few other nodes than in a spot that is already crowded with nodes. Furthermore, if a node is put up purposefully, the person choosing a place for it would try to put it somewhere where it has at least a certain number of neighbors (other nodes in transmission range). This helps to minimize the risk that the removal of one node partitions the remaining network and to maximize the number of alternative routes through the network without crowding an area.

Motivated by this intuitive description of the expected building process, we implemented the random creation of an ASG network as follows: The first node is put in the center of the available plane and serves as a nucleus. For every new node, a random node is chosen that has already been placed. Starting from this node, the algorithm chooses a random angle between 0 and 359 degrees and a random distance between the transmission range (equal for all nodes) and twice the transmission

range. This defines a new point on the plane. If this point is within transmission
range of at least one and at most three other nodes, the new node is placed at this
position. We repeat this procedure until the node can be placed in a valid position
and go on with the next node that has not yet been placed.

Applying this algorithm for $|N| = 50$, we get networks with the measures listed in
Table 8.1. These are average numbers that have been measured for 1000 random
networks. All experiments have been conducted with this class of networks unless
explicitly stated otherwise. The node degree is the number of nodes that a given

	average value	95% confidence interval
node degree	3.85	0.0125
shortest path length	4.57	0.0174
diameter D	10.35	0.0646

Table 8.1: Properties of randomly generated ASG networks with 50 nodes.

node may connect to directly. In the unit disk model this is the number of nodes
within transmission range of a given node. The network diameter D is the longest
shortest path between any two nodes.

8.3.2   Client Model

The formal model presented in Section 8.2.2 defines two core functions that describe
the client behavior: $f_C(t)$ generates a time-dependent allocation of clients to nodes
and $f_Q(t)$ generates the number of requests sent by a client at a specific node at time
t. Both are modeled in the simulation to create the client behavior. In the following
sections, we describe these models.

Mobility Model

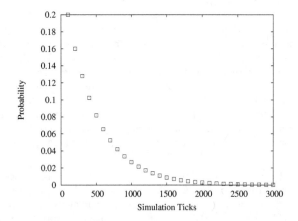

Figure 8.1: Probability distribution for the time interval between client moves.

Clients move within the ASG network according to a *random waypoint model*. Each client is modeled by an agent running directly on a Service Cube (cf. page 76). It chooses a random node as its new waypoint and calculates the route from its current node to this waypoint node. After that, it moves hop by hop from its current location to the new way point. In regular intervals (every 100 simulation ticks), the client takes the next hop with a probability of p. Thus, a client stays at its current node with probability probability $1 - p$. If a client has reached its destination waypoint, it chooses a new one and the whole process starts anew. The probability used for all experiments (unless specified otherwise) is $p = 0.2$. The discrete probability distribution for the time interval between two consecutive moves of a client is the geometric distribution. Thus, the probability p_k that a client moves after k steps ($k \cdot 100$ ticks) is

$$p_k = p \cdot (1 - p)^{k-1}. \tag{8.21}$$

Figure 8.1 depicts the distribution of the migration interval for $p = 0.2$. The expected value for interval with $p = 0.2$ is 500 ticks.

Request Model

The purpose of the service distribution algorithms that we will introduce in the following sections is to adapt the system to request patterns in order to minimize the costs according to Definition 8.1. The underlying assumption here is that such patterns exist. That is, requests are not created in a uniform fashion throughout the entire network. Instead, in some locations, clients generate more requests than in others. Intuitively, this seems to be a realistic assumption since real users in a real network tend not to be uniformly distributed geographically at any point in time. Furthermore, interests and requirements that drive users to request a certain service are not uniformly distributed either. For example, the necessity to employ a navigation service at the entrance of a shopping mall would be higher than at the center since people entering the mall have to accustom themselves to the topology of the mall and to the locations of interesting shops.

We model these non-uniform request patterns using *request hotspots*. When a client moves through the network in the simulation, it sends a requests at time t with a probability p_r that depends on the node the client is on at time t. A specific request pattern is enforced by these probabilities that are stored at the nodes in the network. Such a pattern may be static throughout the simulation run, or it may be changed dynamically using an arbitrary model. Thus, the overall request pattern may change in space (since at time t different nodes have different probabilities) and in time (by changing request probabilities on the nodes relative to one another over time). This is a simple model of our intuitive view on request patterns presented in the preceding paragraph.

The non-uniform spatial distribution of request probabilities is generated by using request hotspots. Each service type $s \in S$ has a set of request hotspots $H_s \subset N$ with $|H_s| \ll |N|$. These hotspots govern the request probabilities for service type s in the entire network. The steps of the algorithm for creating these probabilities are the following:

1. The number and the locations of the hotspots are chosen randomly. At each hotspot $h \in H_s$ the probability $p_r(h, s)$ that a request is created for service

type s is initially set to 1. This is done for each service type $s_i \in S$ and it is guaranteed that $\forall\, i \neq j : H_{s_i} \cap H_{s_j} = \emptyset$ and $\forall h_i, h_j \in H_s | i \neq j : h_i \neq h_j$ (no node hosts more than one hotspot) holds.

2. After the initialization of all hotspots, the probabilities are *diffused* over all nodes: Each node n receives a fraction of the probability of each hotspot h inversely proportional to the distance $d_g(n, h)$ between n and h. This distance is not measured in network hops but represents the real distance between n and h on the plane.

3. Each node $n \in N$ is given a distance factor $d(n)$ with $0.5 \leq d(n) \leq 1$ depending on its distance from the nearest hotspot h_k (irrespective of the service type that hotspot is for): $d(n) = \frac{1}{2} + \frac{1}{2} \cdot (1 - \frac{d_g(n, h_k)}{d_g^{max}})$ where d_g^{max} is the maximum over all distances between any node and its nearest hotspot. Thus, for each hotspot, $d(n) = 1$ and for all other nodes $\frac{1}{2} \leq d(n) < 1$.

4. The probabilities $p_r(n, s_i)$ at each node n in the network are normalized such that $\sum_{i=1}^{|S|} p_r(n, s_i) = d(n)$. Thus, when a client is at node n, the probability that it sends any request at all is $d(n)$. The probability that the client sends a request for service type s, is $\frac{p_r(n, s)}{d(n)}$.

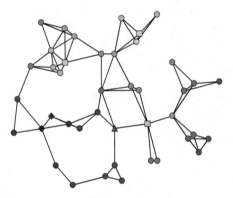

Figure 8.2: Request probabilities for one service type in an ASG network.

Figure 8.2 depicts an example network with hotspots for three service types (diamonds, triangles, and squares). The request probabilities for the service type with the squared hotspots are represented by different shades of gray, with light gray indicating a high probability and dark gray indicating a low probability. The probabilities for the other service types are not shown.

In addition to the request probabilities $p_r(n, s)$, each client has a general probability p_c for sending a request at each time index. Unless stated otherwise, $p_c = 0.5$ for all clients. Thus, the overall probability for a client running at node n to issue a request for service type s is $p(n, s) = p_r(n, s) \cdot p_c$ at each time tick. The probability for sending any request is $p(n, s) = d(n) \cdot p_c$ at each time tick.

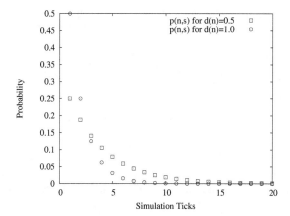

Figure 8.3: Probability distribution of the time interval between client requests.

Figure 8.3 shows the geometric distribution of the time intervals between two consecutive client requests for hotspots $(d(n) = 1)$ and the nodes that are at the maximum distance d_g^{max} from any hotspot $(d(n) = 0.5)$.

Discussion

The behavior of clients and, thus, the request pattern in the simulation is generated by the two separate models for mobility and requests. Intuitively, one may expect that request patterns are attributed to clients, and that each client would have a time-dependent function deciding for which service types it sends requests. We argue that such a client-specific model can be mapped to our model. Client-specific request patterns that move with the client can also be attributed to the locations the client visits. Thus, the two are equivalent for describing client behavior.

Note that the client mobility, and, thus, the client allocation, is independent of the replica allocation. That is, clients do not purposefully move in any direction because of the current distribution of replicas. This is realistic since in reality, users are not aware of the replicas' current locations. The fact that client movement is independent of replica locations is important as it enables us to use recorded client traces and replay them to test different offline algorithms as benchmarks for the performance of our algorithms.

8.3.3 Dynamics Model

In order to evaluate our algorithms under dynamic conditions, we have to model this dynamics within the ASG simulation. The real pattern that the algorithms should adapt to is the distribution of request probabilities over the nodes. Since clients move randomly, they do not enforce any specific non-uniform pattern (at least when they are observed over a sufficiently long period of time) in addition to the pattern generated by node request probabilities. Moving clients manifest this pattern with their requests, they do not generate it. Thus, in a sense, they represent the noise rather than the relevant signal in our simulation[3]. With a large number of clients who cover the whole network with their mobility, the request pattern perceived by replicas approximates the real pattern encoded into the nodes' request probabilities very accurately since at any point in time enough requests are generated by clients to "report" this pattern. If the number of clients and/or their mobility is reduced, then replicas may perceive only an incomplete view of the real pattern.

As a consequence, in order to simulate dynamics (i.e. to change request patterns over time), we have to change the request probability distribution in some way. Two central questions occur when we try to do this:

1. How can we model the complex dynamics in usage patterns that emerge in a network with many nodes and many clients? Real human behavior is dictated largely by the rhythm of the day. It usually undergoes periodic changes with frequencies that are normally in the order of weeks, days, hours etc. The collective behavior of a group of users is the superposition of each individual behavior. In addition, some effects resulting from the users' interactions (communication, coordination) and from the interaction of users with the hardware and software infrastructure (overload, congestion) influence these overall patterns. It is the very nature of such a complex collective behavior that it can only be modeled approximately and in a very crude way. Since the interaction of the behavioral model and the algorithms acting on that model is non-linear by nature, small deviations of the approximated simulation model from the real model can have large effects. Therefore, introducing sophisticated models that shall reproduce real behavior as accurately as possible may result in the opposite. Such a model may introduce its own intricacies and idiosyncrasies that may be amplified non-linearly by the feedback mechanisms inherent to complex systems. Of course, this reduces the usefulness of such models considerably.

2. How can simulation ticks be mapped to real time in a useful way? This question is important if we ask how much dynamics is realistic. The periodic changes in usage patterns have to be mapped to simulation ticks in some way in order to create periodic behavior with certain frequencies. However, the concept of a simulation tick in an event-based simulation is completely different from the concept of real time. The different events that are triggered by advancing simulation time by one tick may happen in different time scales in reality. For example, sending an arbitrary number of messages takes one tick. The fact that it takes proportionally longer to send a larger number of messages is not modeled in the simulation to keep things simple. Thus, every measured simulation tick potentially runs at a different speed when mapped to real time. In consequence, there is no satisfactory mapping of simulation time to real time or vice versa.

In order not to fall victim to either of these problems, we take a rather simple approach to model dynamics. We employ three artificial models. Each of these models has a single parameter that controls the degree of dynamics applied in the simulation. Thus, in each model we may create a very wide range of dynamic changes

---

[3]Regarding human users as "noise" may not be a very pleasant idea, but this is only a property of our simulation model rather than a philosophical view.

from *no dynamics* to *unrealistically high dynamics*. We will show that throughout this entire range of dynamics, our algorithms perform acceptably well. Even though the models are artificial and may not be directly mapped to any form or degree of dynamics found in real life, the result that our algorithms exhibit good performance throughout the entire range of dynamics is an important one and the best we can achieve in a simulation.

The dynamics models that represent different qualities of dynamic behavior in our simulation are the following:

- **Moving hotspot dynamics** employs a concept that is similar to client mobility: Each hotspot moves after a fixed time interval (100 ticks) to a neighboring node with probability p_m. The system is static if $p_m = 0$. With this form of dynamics the request patterns change more or less slowly over time. In this model, p_m is the parameter controlling the degree of dynamics. Note that if p_m is close to 1, request hotspots move more frequently than clients. This represents an unrealistically high degree of dynamics which serves as a yardstick for measuring the algorithms' ability to tolerate even extreme conditions.

- **Sudden change dynamics** periodically reconfigures the distribution of request probabilities after a given time interval. There is no smooth transition from one pattern to a slightly different one, like in the moving change model. Instead, a new pattern is formed randomly from scratch after each interval. This is used to show how our algorithms perform when they are thrown off target completely and suddenly. The degree of dynamics in this model is controlled by the interval between sudden changes.

- **Oscillating dynamics** uses fixed hotspot positions throughout an entire simulation run. The degree of dynamics is adjusted via the parameter δ. In this model, the request probabilities of the hotspots oscillate with a period given by

$$T_o = T_{min} + (T - T_{min}) \cdot (1 - \delta). \tag{8.22}$$

  T (the length of the simulation) is in the order of 10^5 ticks, and T_{min} is set to 400 ticks. Thus, for $\delta = 0$, one oscillation covers the entire duration of the simulation, and for $\delta = 1$, one oscillation takes only 400 ticks which results in about 10^3 oscillations throughout the simulation. Moreover, δ controls the amplitude of the oscillation since we use it as a factor in the request probability of each node such that at $\delta = 0$ the probabilities remain constant and at $\delta = 1$ they oscillate between 0 and their maximum value.

8.4 Distribution Algorithms

In this section, we present two algorithms that implement f_R and f_M in a distributed fashion using local knowledge only. We will refer to these algorithms as *online algorithms* to point out that at time t_k they may only use information gathered in the past, over some interval $[t_l, t_{k-1}]$ with $l < k$. Moreover, this information only refers to some local environment. We will specify what "local" means later. For now, it suffices to say that an online algorithm has no complete knowledge of the system, neither in space nor in time. In contrast to this, an *offline algorithm* has a global view of the system. Specifically, it may use any information available in the complete time interval $[0, T]$ when faced with the task of finding a good configuration for the system at time t_k with $0 \leq t_k \leq T$.

Despite the fact that our algorithms (like any other algorithm that can be employed to solve the optimization problem of Definition 8.1 in practice) may only use *local knowledge*, they find a *global function* $f_R \circ f_M$ to minimize the cost function C and, thus, the network traffic in any given ASG network and under the client allocation function f_C, the client-to-replica allocation function f_{CR}, and the client request function f_Q defined in the preceding sections.

8.4.1 Basic Feedback Mechanism

Both algorithms that will be presented make use of the same fundamental principle. They use a simple feedback mechanism based on the following two rules:

1. **Clients always choose the closest replica.** We have defined this fundamental property of ASG systems in Section 8.2.2 (cf. Equation (8.20) on page 81). This is a property of the environment.

2. **Replicas try to get closer to clients.** This rule is enforced by the online algorithms we propose.

Intuition tells us that the shorter the distance between clients and replicas on average, the lower the number of message transmissions. Of course, this is not true per se since a reduction of the average distance beyond a certain point requires replication and replication adds to the costs through the consistency protocol that is run between replicas. Thus, there are two opposing forces. One is pushing the system to create replicas and to migrate them closer towards clients, and the other is limiting the number of replicas keeping them as close together as possible. The basic task of our online algorithms is to find and maintain the balance between these two forces in the most efficient way. "Most efficient", of course, means with as few migrations as possible.

As we have seen in Section 3.4, the combination of positive and negative feedback is one of the fundamental concepts of self-organization. In general, positive feedback stimulates the spontaneous buildup of structures and negative feedback limits their growth beyond a certain point to stabilize them. In Figure 8.4, an example is shown that illustrates how our two feedback rules interact.

Five clients and two replicas are running in a network with 13 nodes. The replicas r_1 and r_2 are of the same service type and the clients all send requests for this service type. Let us assume that each client sends an equal amount of requests per time unit and that they do not move. Furthermore, the service implemented by the replicas is stateless. Thus, they do not need to exchange messages to keep their data consistent. Finally, we ignore migration costs. This leaves us with the request costs as the only cost considered in this example. Initially, clients c_1, c_2, c_4, and c_5 send their requests to replica r_2 (right side of Figure 8.4a). This group of replica r_2 and its four clients is stable. An equal force is imposed upon r_2 from both sides such that they cancel out each other and r_2 does not need to move. However, r_1 and c_3 are in an unstable state. Since c_3 is r_1's only client, r_1 complies with the second rule and moves from

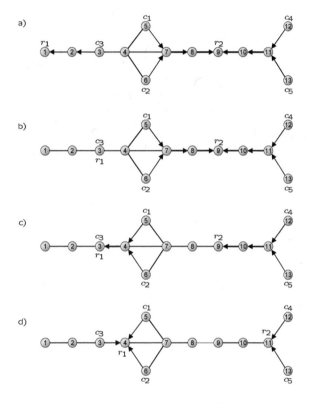

Figure 8.4: Feedback effects in an ASG network.

node 1 to node 3 as this is the location where all forces on r_1 are balanced out and where it is as close as possible to all of its clients (Figure 8.4b). By making this move, r_1 suddenly becomes the closest replica to c_1 and c_2. Obeying the first feedback rule, both clients switch to replica r_1. This, in turn, introduces a new force pulling r_1 even further into the same direction to node 4 (Figure 8.4c). r_1 reacts to the imbalance of forces that occurs due to loosing c_1 and c_2 by moving to node 4.

This is a classical case of positive feedback: Moving to node 3 caused the force to move into this direction to grow even stronger which caused the replica to move even further into this direction. In a more complex scenario, such a feedback loop may sustain for several steps. As r_1 arrives at node 4, all forces are in balance again. Thus, the move from node 3 to node 4 has terminated the positive feedback loop. The force to migrate into that direction, which has been amplified by the previous move, has now been depleted. This is a case of negative feedback that establishes a stable structure. Positive and negative feedback work together to create a *good configuration* fast and then stabilize it.

In the meantime, r_2 has migrated from node 9 to node 11 and, thus, has also reestablished its local balance again that has been disturbed by r_1's initial move. Figure 8.4d shows a system that is stable again. Extending our analogon from physics, we could say that the system has found its state of lowest energy. Or, put in complex system parlance, the system has "converged to an attractor" [112]. This attractor could be defined as the set of all configurations whose cost is within a certain distance from the optimal cost. It should be noted that a system in which clients behave dynamically does not necessarily have a stable state. And even if it has such a state in theory, it may never be reached. Such a system tends to oscillate. We will investigate this problem in detail when we introduce our algorithms.

8.4.2   Common Aspects

Before we present and evaluate our algorithms, we explain some fundamental properties that they have in common.

Usage-driven Adaptation

Both algorithms are *usage-driven*: They try to find a better distribution for the replicas of a service type by exploiting data about the flow of request messages that were issued by clients. More precisely, they collect historic data about the flow of requests in a certain time window that ranges from the current time index to some time index in the past. Based on this data, the algorithms try to decide which action has to be taken next. Self-organization is often associated with so-called *dissipative structures* that consume energy from external sources to build up an internal structure. In a sense, the flow of messages into the system of distributed service replicas can be regarded as a kind of energy flowing into the system to help it self-organize. In particular, if this flow stops, the structure of our system (the distribution of replicas) remains static. As long as there are no client requests, there is no stimulus to evolve towards a better configuration.

Trivial Predictive Mechanism

We do not employ any form of explicit prediction mechanism to extrapolate the behavior of the message flows into the future. The validity of such a prediction depends on how good the prediction model matches the real model underlying the overall process for creating requests. To employ some specific prediction mechanism, one first has to decide how the data that is to be predicted behaves in general. This model is then applied to extrapolate past data into the future. However, if the assumed model is wrong, the extrapolation will be incorrect, too. For example, if we assume that the overall number of messages arriving at a replica behaves according to some polynomial of degree n and the real behavior is closer to a polynomial of degree m with $m \gg n$ than the extrapolation of the predictor will not match the behavior of the system. The decisions resulting from such an inaccurate prediction may drive the system into future configurations that are worse than the current configuration. On top of that, they may impose high migration costs for reaching that suboptimal configuration. Finding an accurate model for the flow of messages in a system like the ASG is non-trivial. Moreover, it is not clear if a unique, well-defined model exists for this process. It is possible that the process underlying the arrival of requests at a replica changes with time and also with the current location of the replica. Furthermore, as we stated in Section 8.3.3, our simulation only provides a rather artificial model for the dynamic behavior of clients for this very reason. Thus, we decided not to delve into the task of *explicitly* predicting the behavior of request flows. This could be possible future work.

However, it should be noted that any process $\mathcal{P}$ that analyzes past data and derives appropriate actions to influence future data, inherently assumes some behavioral model $\mathcal{M}$ of this data. In the most simple case, $\mathcal{P}$ assumes that the data produced by $\mathcal{M}$ is constant over time. We call this a *trivial predictive mechanism* as prediction is inherent to it but it uses the simplest model conceivable.

This is also the approach taken by our algorithms. They implicitly extrapolate the system's behavior into the future by assuming that it will be invariant. This makes them prone to counterproductive behavior if the length of their time window of past data T_h is short. They may overreact to short-term fluctuations which could force them to execute repeated replications and/or migrations and, thus, lead to oscillations or even catastrophic build-up. Such an unstable behavior is well-known in dynamic systems from areas such as control theory. The strategy we employ to avoid this is very simple, too: We choose T_h large enough and assume that the data in $[t_0 - T_h, t_0]$ is constant (*trivial predictive mechanism*). Thus, we apply a simple low-pass filter to the data. The ratio behind this is that we would like the algorithms to react to long-term changes only, whereas we consider short-term changes as irrelevant. Since adaptation always requires an investment (migration costs), we choose a low frequency of adaptation $\frac{1}{T_a}$ with a fixed adaptation interval T_a. Thus, every T_a time units, each replica is allowed to adapt. T_h is chosen such that T_a and T_h are in the same order of magnitude. By doing so, we enable the algorithm to adapt to changes that take place in a time frame in the order of T_h and to ignore changes that take place in time frames much smaller than T_h. In a real system, T_h and T_a could be set to some time in the order of days. Of course, this depends on the cost associated with the migration of a replica.

The charm of this mechanism is its simplicity. It can be easily implemented and, what is much more important, analyzing and tuning the behavior of the overall system is greatly simplified. Keep in mind that, in the end, we will not be faced with one instance of this algorithm acting in isolation, but with multiple instances (replicas) interacting with each other via their environment (network and clients). This adds considerable complexity to the overall system. Having complex mechanisms with a multitude of tunable parameters working inside each component would render the tasks of analyzing the behavior of the system and tuning it to work properly much more difficult[4].

The Role of Migration Costs

As we have explained in Section 8.2.1, migration costs are one component in the cost function we use to evaluate our algorithms and to compare them with other approaches. However, it turns out that without sufficient predictive ability an online algorithm cannot make use of this cost component to guide its decisions. In order to compare the costs caused by a migration with the costs caused by client requests and a consistency protocol, the migration costs have to be regarded over some time interval. This means that if a replica was to consider the costs of a migration in its decision to migrate, it would have to know how long it was going to stay at the destination node, and it would need a good approximation of the value of each cost component over this time interval. This would be necessary to judge if the migration would be beneficial. However, making a good estimation of this data is very hard or even impossible. Consider the example presented in Figure 8.4 again. As replica r_1 migrates to node 3, it is not able to recognize that clients c_1 and c_2 will stop using r_2 and start using r_1 as a consequence of this move. As a matter of fact, without global knowledge, it may not even know that c_1 and c_2 exist. Thus, vital information is missing in order to evaluate explicitly if the migration would be beneficial. Moreover, the fact that c_1 and c_2 switch to r_1 causes this replica to migrate to node 4 after the next adaptation interval. This, too, cannot be predicted by r_1 prior to its move to node 3. As a consequence, it does not possess sufficient capabilities to asses precisely whether investing the migration costs will really pay off.

Nevertheless, let us assume that r_1 has a good approximation of the time interval $[t_1, t_2]$ it will spend at node 3 and of the value of C_Q and C_R during that period. Let us further assume that the costs that could be saved during that time are smaller than the costs caused by migrating there:

$$
C_M(a_{rn}^1, a_{rn}^2) \; > \; \sum_{t=t_1}^{t_2} (C_Q(a_{cn}(t), a_{rn}^1(t)) + C_R(a_{cn}(t), a_{rn}^1(t))) -
$$

$$
\sum_{t=t_1}^{t_2} (C_Q(a_{cn}(t), a_{rn}^2(t)) + C_R(a_{cn}(t), a_{rn}^2(t))) \qquad (8.23)
$$

Should the replica decide against the migration? Knowing the developments presented in Figure 8.4, we can certainly say that the initial migration will lead to a series of events that eventually result in a stable configuration that produces the

---

[4]As a side note, keeping things simple is a basic rule in the process of engineering a system that employs feedback mechanisms to achieve adaptivity. The non-linearity inherent in such systems lets things get out of hand very quickly, and the ability to be able to reason about the system and analyze its behavior is vital.

smallest possible costs for this system. The configuration shown in Figure 8.4d is optimal. Therefore, the initial move of r_1 was beneficial in the end despite the fact that it cost more than the sum of the immediate savings. This example shows that migration costs may be used for an a posteriori evaluation of a series of adaptations, but it is useless in an online decision. An online algorithm simply does not have enough information to use this cost.

The strategy used in our algorithms just ignores the cost of a migration and tries to estimate the potential reduction in request and replication costs to decide about a possible migration. Based on the trivial predictive mechanism, which assumes that the status quo will sustain, this is sensible because even for a small reduction in the sum of C_Q and C_R, there will be a time interval Δt after which the migration costs C_M amortize:

$$\exists \Delta t : C_M(a_{rn}^1, a_{rn}^2) \ < \ \sum_{t=t_0}^{t_0+\Delta t} (C_Q(a_{cn}(t), a_{rn}^1(t)) + C_R(a_{cn}(t), a_{rn}^1(t))) -$$
$$\sum_{t=t_0}^{t_0+\Delta t} (C_Q(a_{cn}(t), a_{rn}^2(t)) + C_R(a_{cn}(t), a_{rn}^2(t)))$$

$$(8.24)$$

Based on this fact, it may be argued that the replica should make the move but then stay at its destination node at least until Δt has passed such that the migration costs have amortized. However, this implies that even if a better configuration could be reached from a_{rn}^2 by a migration of the replica r_i to node n_k, it would stay at its current location $n_j | (r_i, n_j) \in a_{rn}^2$. This may be beneficial if the designated migration target n_k turns out not to be a good location after a while, but it may also be a suboptimal choice if n_k continues to be a better location than n_j. Without the ability to predict the future, there is no way to decide this. Thus, in summary, we can say that it is neither feasible to avoid migrations due to their costs, nor is it feasible to delay the next migration until migration costs have amortized. Therefore, our algorithms follow a greedy strategy by investing what it takes to get to the best location, and they *hope* that their investment will *pay off* in the long run. We avoid the inherent instability that such a strategy has in a dynamic system by introducing mechanisms for damping oscillations.

It is important to note, at this point, that the strategy laid out thus far will fail in a *competitive analysis*. Such an analysis is usually conducted for online algorithms [5] by designing an *evil adversary* A for the algorithm. A generates the worst case input for the online algorithm, and the analysis shows how good (or bad) the algorithm performs under this input compared to the optimal offline algorithm (with complete, global knowledge). If A knows our algorithms' strategy, it can exploit their inability to predict the future and their greediness by choosing f_C and f_Q such that investments never pay off. Thus, our algorithms end up paying migration costs without ever reaping the reward for it. In the jargon used in competitive analysis, our algorithms are likely to have an *unbounded competitive ratio*. A formal proof of this hypothesis is out of scope of this book. Note that this would represent a theoretical worst case result. In our case, we are more interested in the ability of our algorithms to perform well in the average case.

Basic Replica Adaptations

Our algorithms assume that a replica may execute one of the following basic adaptation actions every time it is allowed to adapt:

- $migrate(v)$ causes the replica to migrate from its current node to node v.

- $replicate(v, w)$ causes the replica r (running on some node u) to be cloned (clone r' is created from r, denoted as $r \succ r'$), and the replicas are migrated to node v and w, respectively.

- $dissolve()$ causes the replica to remove itself from the system.

We also use the following short notation for adaptations:

- $(u \xrightarrow{r_1} v)$ represents a migration: r_1 migrates from node u to node v.

- $(u \to \overset{r_1}{\cdots} \to v)$ represents a series of one or more migrations of r_1, starting at node u and ending at node v.

- $(u \xrightarrow{r_1 \succ r_2} v, w)$ is a replication: r_1 at node u spawns a new replica r_2. r_1 migrates to node v, and r_2 migrates to node w.

- $\overline{r_1}$ signifies that r_1 dissolves.

- A sequence on adaptations a and b is written as $a; b$.

- If adaptations a and b are executed concurrently, then we write $a|b$.

Architectural Assumptions

The algorithms we are about to introduce, have to be executed by some entity in our system. Intuitively, we may associate them with replicas, such that each replica runs its own algorithm and decides about its own adaptations independently. However, it proves to be more beneficial to let the local Proxy Agent, running at the replica's current node, take over the decisions about adaptations. First of all, the proxy manages the message exchange between the replica and the outside world (clients). Thus, it may easily accumulate historic data characterizing message flows. Data about message flows collected on one node is generally useless on another node. Thus, there is no need for the replica itself to store and transport this data. Therefore, it is better to maintain the data on the node on which the adaptations were executed. For these reasons, we let the proxy make adaptation decisions, and the respective replica is simply instructed to execute a specific adaptation. Thus, all algorithms pertaining to the process of adapting are executed by the proxy. This is reflected in the structure of the algorithms where replicas appear as parameters in operations.

Core Adaptation Algorithm

Our distributed adaptation algorithms are based on the same core algorithm presented in Figure 8.5. To facilitate the notation, we introduce the special node $\bar{v} \notin N$

representing the *invalid node*. Whenever a function shall return a node from N fulfilling a specific condition but no such node can be found, the function returns the value $\overline{v}$. If, for example, $w = \text{GETMIGRATIONTARGET}()$ in the following algorithms, then $w \in N \cup \{\overline{v}\}$.

```
1  procedure ADAPT(r ∈ ⋃_{s∈S} R_s)
   begin
     if IDLE(r) then
       r.DISSOLVE()
     else
6      (v, w) = GETREPLICATIONTARGETS(r)
       if v ≠ v̄ ∧ w ≠ v̄ then
         r.REPLICATE(v, w)
       else
         v = GETMIGRATIONTARGET(r)
11       if v ≠ v̄ then
           r.MIGRATE(v)
         endif
       endif
     endif
16 end
```

Figure 8.5: The core adaptation algorithm.

The function ADAPT implements the core algorithm. It takes a replica r from the union of all replicas over all service types $s \in S$ and decides which adaptation is appropriate for r. Note that it may also opt not to issue any adaptation. ADAPT defines a general precedence for the rules applied in the adaptation process. Of course, testing for possible migrations or replications is useless if a replica is idle (receives no or very few requests) and, thus, is in a state that makes it a candidate for removal. If the replica is not idle, we first try to replicate it. GETREPLICATIONTARGETS() selects target nodes for the replication according to some strategy to be defined by our online distribution algorithms. If the algorithm selects valid target nodes, we execute the REPLICATE operation on the replica. We try to replicate first since this produces the necessary number of replicas quickly. If we would opt to migrate first, then the single initial replica would tend to move towards the center of request traffic and then produce replicas that move into the opposite direction. This causes unnecessary migrations and, thus, costs. If we replicate early, the individual replicas may move more directly to locations that minimize network traffic. Thus, only if we cannot replicate, we choose to migrate by calling the GETMIGRATIONTARGET() to let the distribution algorithm select a target node. If this node is valid, we issue a MIGRATE operation on the replica. Note that if neither a pair of replication targets nor a migration target is selected, the core algorithm exits without issuing any adaptation. The implementation of IDLE(), GETMIGRATIONTARGET(), and GETREPLICATIONTARGETS() specifies the strategy applied by the concrete service distribution algorithm. We will introduce these operations when we present the algorithms.

Replica Garbage Collection

Removing unused replicas is important because they still take part in reconciliations with their fellow replicas and, thus, they generate costs without a notable benefit. A replica may suddenly lose all or most of its clients when other replicas attract them or when clients move out of the replica's area. The absence of requests leaves the replica unable to adapt since it is lacking a stimulus. Therefore, we have to garbage-collect such replicas to reduce the replication costs.

IDLE() is defined such that a replica is considered to be idle if it has not received more than an α-fraction of a request per time unit on average during the past m adaptation intervals. Thus, α specifies which level of load (requests per time unit) is necessary to justify the existence of a replica. m defines the length of time we are willing to tolerate load levels that are too low. Setting $\alpha > 0$ avoids that a single client that sends sporadic requests can keep a replica alive. m defines a grace time. It is beneficial to wait before dissolving a replica since its low request rate may only be temporary.

Terminology and Notation

In the following sections, we will introduce two different concrete service distribution algorithms. The first one is called *simple algorithm* and will be denoted by $\mathcal{S}$. The second one is the *event flow tree (EFT) algorithm* which will be denoted by $\mathcal{E}$. We use $\mathcal{A}$ to denote one of the algorithms in general, i.e. $\mathcal{S}$ or $\mathcal{E}$ can be substituted for $\mathcal{A}$. We use the notation $\mathcal{A}_v$ to signify the instance of the algorithm $\mathcal{A}$ running on node v. $\mathcal{A}_v(r, t)$ is the adaptation that results from the execution of algorithm $\mathcal{A}$ on node v for replica r at time t. Thus, $\mathcal{A}_v(r, t) \in \{migrate(u), replicate(u, w), dissolve\}$ with $u, w \in N$.

8.5   Simple Algorithm

The simple service distribution algorithm $\mathcal{S}$ exploits a basic property of message flows in an ASG network. Figure 8.6 depicts a simple network with three clients and one replica. Clients c_1 and c_2 send 5 requests per time unit each while c_3 sends 15 requests per time unit. Replica r_1 can minimize the number of transmissions in the network per time unit (denoted as C_{qr} in the following) simply by moving towards c_3. It is easy to see that C_{qr} is reduced by 5 with every step r_1 takes in the direction of c_3 because the amount of transmissions flowing towards r_1 from c_3 (15) is greater than the sum of all other message flows (5+5).

More formally, $C_{qr}(t)$ is the sum of request costs and reconciliation costs at time t: $C_{qr}(t) = C_q(t) + C_r(t)$. This is the cost function that is optimized by the online algorithm. It does not contain the migration costs $C_m(t)$ for the argument presented in Section 8.4.2. Let us assume that the configurations shown in the sub-figures a, b, and c of Figure 8.6 represent the system at time indices t_1, t_2, and t_3 respectively. Then $C_{qr}(t_1) = 40$, $C_{qr}(t_2) = 35$, and $C_{qr}(t_3) = 30$. $\mathcal{S}$ minimizes C_{qr} by migrating replicas to neighbor nodes in the aforementioned way. It employs replication if it detects that request paths are longer than a specified threshold on average. Both rules enforcing this behavior are presented in the following sections.

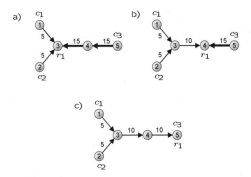

Figure 8.6: Incremental cost optimization.

8.5.1 Migration Rule

Let N_v be the set of v's neighbors in $G = (N, L)$:

$$N_v = \{w|(v, w) \in L\} \cup \{v\} \tag{8.25}$$

Note that v is in its own neighbor set. The replica r and one or more of its clients may be co-located at the same node v. Thus, the bulk of requests for r may come from v (i.e. from local clients). In this case, r must remain at v. Therefore, we need to include v itself in N_v. Let $m_v(r, w, t)$ be the number of requests that replica r, running on node v, receives via neighbor $w \in N_v$ at time t. Then

$$M_v(r, w, t_0, \Delta t) = \sum_{t=t_0-\Delta t}^{t_0-1} m_v(r, w, t) \tag{8.26}$$

is the sum of all requests received by replica r on node v via node $w \in N_v$ in the time interval $[t_0 - \Delta t, t_0 - 1]$. t_0 denotes the current time index at which the migration rule is evaluated. The fact that the request flow received via a neighbor u in the window of historic data T_h (cf. Section 8.4.2) is greater than the sum of request flows received from all other neighbors during that interval is expressed by the *simple migration condition*:

$$M_v(r, u, t_0, T_h) > \sum_{w_i \in N_v \setminus \{u\}} M_v(r, w_i, t_0, T_h). \tag{8.27}$$

We could let $\mathcal{S}_v$ migrate replica r to node u if condition (8.27) is true. However, this would eventually result in a behavior that is inherently unstable. Figure 8.7 shows an example configuration that produces an unstable behavior if we employ the migration condition (8.27) in $\mathcal{S}$.

Figure 8.7: Example of an unstable configuration for $\mathcal{S}$.

Two clients c_1 and c_2 send requests to a replica r_1. Both clients produce a constant message flow m with a small, random, time-dependent variation $\varepsilon_1 \ll m$ and $\varepsilon_2 \ll m$ over any interval $[t_0 - T_h, t_0 - 1]$. If condition (8.27) is evaluated to find out if a migration from node 2 to node 1 shall be executed at time t_0, it boils down to

$$m + \varepsilon_1 > m + \varepsilon_2 \quad \Leftrightarrow \quad \varepsilon_1 > \varepsilon_2. \tag{8.28}$$

Thus, the decision depends on the random variations in the message flows, and although r_1 should simply stay at node 2, it is migrating among the three nodes randomly. In order to avoid such an undesirable behavior, we apply a stability analysis to $M_v(r, u, t_0, T_h)$ and require that condition (8.27) must be stable. To analyze the stability of the condition, we divide the history interval $[t_0 - T_h, t_0 - 1]$ into smaller sub-intervals of length Δt with $\Delta t \ll T_h$ and $(T_h \bmod \Delta t) = 0$ and apply condition (8.27) to each of these intervals. The condition is stable if it holds for more than an η-fraction of all sub-intervals. η is called the *stability threshold*. To formalize this, we first define a function that evaluates to 1 if condition (8.27) holds in a given interval and to 0 otherwise:

$$b_v(r, u, t_0, \Delta t, I) = \begin{cases} 1 : M_v(r, u, t_0, \Delta t) > \sum_{w_i \in N_v \setminus (\{u\} \cup I)} M_v(r, w_i, t_0, \Delta t) \\ 0 : \text{otherwise} \end{cases}$$

$$\tag{8.29}$$

I is a set of neighbor nodes that shall be ignored in the analysis. We will use this feature later on. Based on this function, we can formulate the *stability condition*:

$$\frac{\Delta t}{T_h} \cdot \sum_{i=0}^{\frac{T_h}{\Delta t}} b_v(r, u, t_0 - i \cdot \Delta t, \Delta t, I) > \eta \tag{8.30}$$

The *advanced migration condition* is defined as a conjunction of (8.27) and (8.30). Let $P_m(r, u)$ be the migration predicate that is true if and only if condition (8.27) is fulfilled for r and u. Likewise, let $P_s(r, u, I)$ be the stability predicate that is true if and only if condition (8.30) is fulfilled for r, u, and I. The advanced migration condition is simply

$$P_m(r, u) \wedge P_s(r, u, \emptyset). \tag{8.31}$$

With a sufficiently high value for η, the stability condition (8.30) ensures that random fluctuations do not cause a migration. In the simulations, we typically use 20 sub-intervals and $\eta = 0.75$ for the stability analysis.

S_v migrates r to node $u \in N_v$ at time t_0 if and only if condition (8.31) holds. Please note that the first clause (condition (8.27)) can only be true for at most one node $u \in N_v$. Furthermore, if such a node u exists, it is the node contributing the greatest request flow:

$$M_v(r, u, t_0, T_h) = \max_{w \in N_v} (M_v(r, w, t_0, T_h)) \tag{8.32}$$

The migration rule is implemented in the function GETMIGRATIONTARGET (used in the core algorithm depicted in Figure 8.5) as shown in Figure 8.8.

8.5.2   Migration Rule – Discussion

The simple migration condition (8.27), as the first component of the advanced condition (8.31) implements an essential part of the feedback mechanism discussed in

```
     procedure GETMIGRATIONTARGET (r ∈ ⋃_{s∈S} R_s)
     begin
        select u from N_v
4          with M_v(r, u, t_0, T_h) = max_{w∈N_v}(M_v(r, w, t_0, T_h))
        if P_m(r, u) ∧ P_s(r, u, ∅) then
           return u
        else
           return v̄
9       endif
     end
```

Figure 8.8: Implementation of $\mathcal{S}$' migration rule.

Section 8.4.1. The overall process by which $\mathcal{S}$ finds a good (low-cost) configuration can be divided into three phases. For the sake of simplicity, we assume that there is only very little dynamics in the system.

Attraction phase (positive feedback): At the start of the process, replica r is placed in a suboptimal location with respect to the client allocation and the request pattern. For example, r might have been placed at some node v far away from clients and request hotspots. In such a suboptimal position, the flows received via the neighbors of v tend to differ in strength very widely since all requesting clients lie in the same general direction. If there is a certain distance between the client group and r, the network routing mechanism gathers the requests on one route such that they are received by r via the same neighbor. Thus, for a few consecutive adaptations, condition (8.27) finds a neighbor node u with

$$M_v(r, u, t_0, T_h) \gg \sum_{w_i \in N_v \setminus \{u\}} M_v(r, w_i, t_0, T_h) \tag{8.33}$$

that leads r towards that direction. In this phase, r is attracted very quickly by the group of requesting clients. Due to first feedback rule resented in Section 8.4.1 on page 90, this tends to attract more clients which strengthens the attraction even more.

Depletion phase (negative feedback): After some adaptations, r crosses a point at which the directions of requests start getting more diverse. As r gets closer to the group of clients, their requests come in via more than one neighbor node since the distance is too small for the gathering effect of the routing algorithm to occur. Figure 8.4 on page 91 presents a good example of this effect: In sub-figure c, the requests of c_4 and c_5 are gathered at node 11 and routed to r_2 via node 10. As r_2 moves to node 11, it starts receiving the same requests from two different nodes (12 and 13). As this directional diversity sets in, the solution to condition (8.27) becomes less obvious, which causes the strength of the attraction present in phase 1 to decrease. This is the point at which the negative feedback sets in because the force that caused the quick migration towards the group of clients is progressively depleted by the migration itself. Requests start coming in from opposite directions as r migrates into the group of clients. Thus, with every migration towards a good location, r's "motivation" to execute another migration based on condition (8.27) decreases. The speed of adaptation is reduced, and r slowly approaches a good position around the center of the group of requesting clients. This mechanism has a strong stabilizing effect.

Fluctuation phase: As r finds a good area somewhere around the center of its clients, the differences in the flows from different directions are evened out. When this has happened, the system has more or less *settled down* into a stable state, i.e. there is no distinct outside force that drives r into further adaptations. However, the degree of stability may vary in this phase. At one extreme end, r may constantly be at the edge of yet another migration, and at the other extreme, it may be far from migrating. For the sake of clarity, we will formalize this. For the brevity of notation, we define a shorter term for the right side of equation (8.27):

$$M_v(r, \overline{u}, t_0, T_h) = \sum_{w_i \in N_v \setminus \{u\}} M_v(r, w_i, t_0, T_h) \tag{8.34}$$

Furthermore, we set $M_v(u) = M_v(r, u, t_0, T_h)$ for a more compact notation. The following inequation is the general condition for an unstable system:

$$\exists u \in N_v \wedge \varepsilon \ll M_v(u) : M_v(\overline{u}) + \varepsilon > M_v(u) > M_v(\overline{u}) - \varepsilon \tag{8.35}$$

In other words, there is a node u and a small value ε such that u fulfills the migration condition if its flow increases by ε and fails to fulfill it if the flow decreases by ε. If ε is in the order of the random flow fluctuations in the system, then r may enter a series of random migrations between v, u, and possibly other nodes.

For the ability of the system to react to dynamic changes by readapting, this phase is the most important one. The system must not execute random, unproductive migrations. However, it must still be able to adapt quickly if *significant* changes occur. The stability condition (8.30) solves this problem by checking the *statistical significance* of a flow difference that fulfills the migration condition. If we set $\eta = 0$, the stability condition is effectively turned off. With $\eta = 1$ we require that condition (8.27) holds for each sub-interval before we trigger a migration. This prevents most migrations, especially in the later stages of a simulation run where differences are only marginal. We assume that when random fluctuations happen in an unstable state (cf. equation (8.35)) they result in the stability condition being fulfilled in about half of all sub-intervals Δt. Thus, appropriate values for the stability threshold η are $\frac{1}{2} < \eta < 1$.

8.5.3   Replication Rule

Replications are issued by $\mathcal{S}$ based on the average distance between the replica and all requesting clients. We assume that the distance (number of network hops) between the replica and a client can be extracted from the client's request messages. This defines a basic requirement for the middleware platform on which our algorithms are implemented.

The parameter ρ defines the so-called *replication radius*. Informally, the replication rule can be stated as follows:

For $|N_v| \geq 2$, we replicate if the neighbor u, contributing the highest request flow, averages a request path length of at least ρ. The destinations of the replication are u and the neighbor contributing the second highest stable request flow.

In order to achieve stability also in the replication process, we need to avoid that insignificant request flows with a high average path length can trigger a replication. Otherwise, a single client at the edges of the network may cause a replication into a region that does not provide sufficient volumes of requests to justify the existence of a replica. We do this simply by requiring that a replication can only be triggered by the neighbor node with the highest request flow.

For the formal definition, let $\overline{d(u)}$ be the average number of hops traveled by requests that were received via neighbor node u. Let $U_{\widehat{d}}$ be the set of neighbor nodes with the highest average distance among all neighbor nodes:

$$U_{\widehat{d}} = \{u \in N_v \mid \forall w \in N_v : \overline{d(u)} \geq \overline{d(w)}\} \tag{8.36}$$

Furthermore, let $U_{\widehat{m}}$ be the set of neighbor node with the highest message flow:

$$U_{\widehat{m}} = \{u \in N_v \mid \forall w \in N_v : M_v(u) \geq M_v(w)\} \tag{8.37}$$

Note that $|U_{\widehat{d}}| > 1$ if and only if there is more than one node whose average client distance is maximal, and $|U_{\widehat{m}}| > 1$ if and only if there is more than one node whose request flow is maximal. The *replication condition* is defined as follows:

$$|N_v| \geq 2 \ \wedge \ \exists u \in U_{\widehat{m}} \cap U_{\widehat{d}} \mid \overline{d(u)} > \rho \tag{8.38}$$

$\mathcal{S}$ chooses a node u such that condition (8.38) is fulfilled. If such a node exists, $\mathcal{S}$ chooses a second node u' such that

$$\forall w \in N_v : M_v(u) \geq M_v(u') \geq M_v(w) \tag{8.39}$$

and uses u and u' as replication targets if condition (8.39) holds stably with respect to the stability condition (8.30).

$\mathcal{S}$ implements the replication rule in the function GETREPLICATIONTARGETS (used in the core algorithm) as shown in Figure 8.9.

8.5.4   Replication Rule – Discussion

The replication radius forces a replica r to create a new replica if a notable amount of traffic is coming in from far away. If an average request comes from inside the replication radius, $\mathcal{S}$ will not replicate and try to migrate instead to optimize its distance to its current clients.

Figure 8.10 depicts an example with one replica and three clients. The replication radius is set to 1. Thus, requests that originate from nodes that are more than one hop away may potentially trigger a replication. c_3 is sending a high volume of requests from node 5 which is outside the replication radius. In this example, $U_{\widehat{d}} = \{4\}$ since the requests from c_3 have traveled two hops when they reach r_1 via node 4: $\overline{d(1)} = \overline{d(2)} = 1$ and $\overline{d(4)} = 2$. $U_{\widehat{m}} = \{1, 4\}$ since r_1 receives 15 requests per time unit from nodes 1 and 4 and only 10 requests from node 2.

```
procedure GETREPLICATIONTARGETS (r ∈ ⋃_{s∈S} R_s)
begin
    if  |N_v| < 2 then
        return  (v̄, v̄)
5   else
        calculate  U_d̂
        calculate  U_m̂
        forall  u ∈ U_d̂ do
            if  d(u) > ρ ∧ u ∈ U_m̂  then
10              select  u' ∈ N_v | ∀w ∈ N_v : M_v(u) ≥ M_v(u') ≥ M_v(w)
                if  ¬P_s(r, u', {u})  then
                    u' = v  // u'  not  stable !
                    return  (u, u')
                endif
15          endforall
            return  (v̄, v̄)  // No node u found !
        endif
end
```

Figure 8.9: Implementation of $\mathcal{S}$' replication rule.

The replication condition (8.38) is fulfilled since

$$|N_3| = 4 \geq 2 \quad \wedge \quad \overline{d(4)} = 2 > \rho \quad \wedge \quad U_{\hat{d}} \cap U_{\hat{m}} = \{4\}. \tag{8.40}$$

Thus, 4 is the first destination node for the replication. Furthermore, $M_3(4) \geq M_3(1) > M_3(2) > M_3(3)$ and, thus, according to condition (8.39), node 1 is chosen as the second destination node. Therefore, $\mathcal{S}_3$ issues the adaptation $r_1.replicate(1, 4)$. The resulting configuration is shown in Figure 8.10b. The newly created replica r_2 has only one client c_3 on node 5 and migrates to that node (Figure 8.10c). For r_1, neither the migration condition, nor the replication condition is fulfilled as it is running on node 1. The dotted lines indicate request flows that are exchanged between clients and replicas on the same node.

Controlling the Overall Number of Replicas

The replication rule forces replicas to distribute in such a way that the main stream of client requests only travels ρ hops on average. Note that there may well be clients outside this range. The replication radius ρ controls the overall number of replicas. If ρ is large, then a small number of replicas suffices to create a configuration such that the second clause in the replication condition is negated: $\left(\forall u \in U_{\hat{m}} \cap U_{\hat{d}} : d(u) \leq \rho\right)$. If ρ is small, many replicas are required to ensure that no replica receives a significant number of requests from a distance $> \rho$. At this extreme end, if $\rho = 0$, $\mathcal{S}$ will try to position a replica on each client node such that the distance traveled by requests is 0. Controlling the number of replicas is an important task in a distributed replication system like the one presented here. Therefore, we will take a closer look at the model behind this control mechanism in the following.

Figure 8.11 shows how the average number of replicas over a complete simulation run decreases as the replication radius increases (error bars indicate 95% confidence intervals). This data has been measured for networks of 50 nodes. The function that

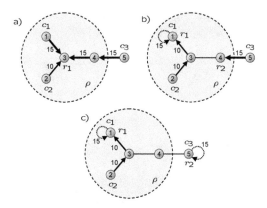

Figure 8.10: Example for the application of the replication rule in $\mathcal{S}$.

was acquired experimentally is roughly proportional to ρ^{-2}. Approximately for $\rho > 6$, there is no replication in the system. As Table 8.1 shows, the average diameter D for a network of 50 nodes is 10.35. Thus, approximately for $\rho > 1.15942 \cdot \frac{D}{2}$, replication virtually stops.

In order to explain this behavior, we adopt an idealized view of an ASG network and assume that it has a circular shape. In fact, for an average network that was created by the process presented in Section 8.3.1, this idealized view fits quite well. Figure 8.12 shows the probabilities for a node being placed on a particular cell on the simulation plane. 17800 networks were used to collect this data. Each consisted of 50 nodes placed on a plane of 70×70 grid cells. Note that we left out the probability for the center cell since this cell hosts a node in every network (nucleus). Therefore, it has a probability that is several orders of magnitude higher than that of any other cell. Figure 8.13 depicts the lines of equal placement probabilities. It shows that even the areas that have a very low probability of receiving a node ($\approx 10^{-4}$) approximate the ideal circular shape quite well.

In our idealized geometrical interpretation, each replica covers a circle with an area of $\frac{\pi}{4} \cdot (2\rho)^2$ hops. The complete network may be regarded as a circle with an area of $\frac{\pi}{4} \cdot D^2$ hops. This is depicted in Figure 8.14. The following approximation for the number of replicas ($|R|$) needed to cover the ideal network holds in this scenario:

$$\frac{\pi}{4}D^2 \approx |R| \cdot \frac{\pi}{4}(2\rho)^2. \tag{8.41}$$

Simple transformations yield

$$|R| \approx \frac{1}{4}\left(\frac{D}{\rho}\right)^2. \tag{8.42}$$

Figure 8.11 shows the number of replicas created by $\mathcal{S}$ against the replication radius ρ and the idealized ("theoretical") function resulting from Equation (8.42). Since there must always be at least one replica for each service type, the experimental data approaches 1 whereas the theoretical function converges to 0. Towards smaller values of ρ, the experimental data grows less quickly since the theoretical function assumes

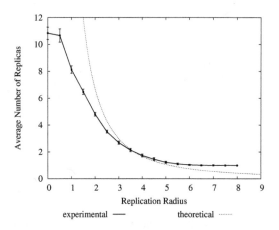

Figure 8.11: Overall number of replicas against ρ.

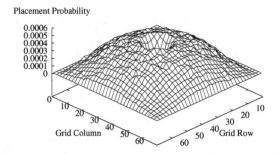

Figure 8.12: Placement probability produced by the network topology model.

that there is an infinite number of nodes on the circular plane and infinitely small replication radii are possible. Of course, the real network only has a finite number of nodes. Thus, the number of possible locations for replicas is depleted more quickly and has a cut-off point between 1 and 0. Remember that requests for a specific service type originate only from a fraction of the nodes due to the hotspot model presented in Section 8.3.2. Under these practical constraints, the experimental data represents a good match of the theoretical function which confirms that, on average, S behaves according to our idealized model.

The fact that the experimental data reaches its minimum of 1 at $\rho \approx 6 \approx 1.15942 \cdot \frac{D}{2}$ can be explained as follows. Since the replication rule is not triggered for this value, the requests received by a single replica must travel an average distance less than ρ. The client mobility model causes each client to make a random walk through the network. Thus, we can assume that (measured over a sufficiently long period of time) that clients are equally distributed over the entire network. Therefore, the single replica must cover more than half the area of the network in order to avoid replications completely since that puts more than half of the clients inside the

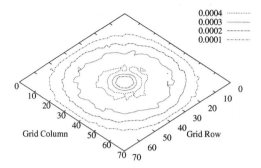

Figure 8.13: Lines of equal placement probability.

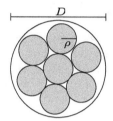

Figure 8.14: Idealized geometrical interpretation of ρ.

replica's replication radius. Thus, more than half of the requests travel less than ρ hops. Due to the circular shape of the network, the remaining requests cannot travel over paths that are long enough to compensate that and raise the average path length to a value greater than ρ. Therefore, with more than half the network covered, the overall average path length of a request is reduced to a value below ρ.

To achieve this, ρ must be large enough such that even if the replica is at the very edge of the network, it still covers more than half of the area. Geometrically, this results in the following question: At which radius ρ does a replica's coverage circle (that has its center at the edge of the network circle) cover half of the area of that network circle? The idealized geometrical version of this question is depicted in Figure 8.15. The single replica with radius r_2 is positioned on the edge of the network (smaller circle with radius r_1) and covers the area C of that circle. It is well-known that the area C may be calculated as follows:

$$
\begin{aligned}
C \;=\;& r_2{}^2 \cos^{-1}\left(\frac{d^2 + r_2{}^2 - r_1{}^2}{2dr_2}\right) + r_1{}^2 \cos^{-1}\left(\frac{d^2 + r_1{}^2 - r_2{}^2}{2dr_1}\right) - \\
& \frac{1}{2}\sqrt{(-d + r_2 + r_1)(d - r_2 + r_1)(d + r_2 + r_1)}
\end{aligned}
\tag{8.43}
$$

In our case, $d = r_1$. We are interested in the factor between the radii of both circles such that at least half of the left circle is covered. Thus, we set $r_2 = x \cdot r_1$ and try to find the unknown factor x such that $C = \frac{1}{2}\pi r_1{}^2$. If we make the necessary

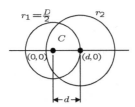

Figure 8.15: Geometrical explanation for the convergence point of $|R|$.

substitutions in (8.43), we get

$$x^2 \cos^{-1}\left(\frac{x}{2}\right) + \cos^{-1}\left(1 - \frac{x^2}{2}\right) - \frac{1}{2}\sqrt{4x^2 - x^4} = \frac{\pi}{2}. \qquad (8.44)$$

Solving this equation numerically yields $x \approx 1.15873$. This is the factor by which the replication radius ρ of a single replica must be greater than the network radius $\frac{D}{2}$ in order to cover half the network area and, thus, produce an average request path length of ρ irrespective of the placement of the replica. Since the coverage area C is monotonically increasing with x, no replication will take place in an average network for $\rho > x \cdot \frac{D}{2}$. The value of $x \approx 1.15873$ corresponds very well with the value of 1.15942 at which our simulation stopped producing any replicas.

8.5.5   Data Structures

As the preceding discussion shows, $\mathcal{S}$ only relies on the analysis of client request messages. For this analysis, two types of information are extracted from the flow of requests:

1. The flow volume: Requests received in T_h must be counted.

2. The average path length: The length of the path traveled by each request must be summed and divided by the message count (flow volume).

These are two very simple pieces of information that have to be stored on node v for each neighbor and that suffice to evaluate the migration and replication conditions. However, T_h represents a sliding time window: The flow volume at time t_0 is the sum of all requests received in the interval $[t_0 - T_h, t_0]$. This cannot be implemented with a simple counter. Instead, $\mathcal{S}$ divides T_0 into smaller time units Δt and maintains a time series holding the values for all Δt sections of $[t_0 - T_h, t_0]$. When $\mathcal{S}$ is run at t_0, all values that are older than $t_0 - T_h$ are removed from the series before the overall sum is calculated. For the calculation of the average request path length, $\mathcal{S}$ maintains two similar time series: One is holding the sum of the path lengths of all requests for each Δt sections, the other stores the number of requests received per Δt section.

8.6 Event Flow Tree Algorithm

The fact that $\mathcal{S}$ is inherently restricted to one-hop adaptations, limits the speed at which it can approximate the optimal configuration starting from the initial configuration (a single, randomly placed replica). The question arises as to whether an algorithm that may apply multi-hop adaptations can achieve a faster convergence while preserving the approximation quality, the adaptability, and the stability of $\mathcal{S}$.

In this section, we introduce the *Event Flow Tree service distribution algorithm* $\mathcal{E}$ that makes use to the complete request paths to find a good configuration faster than $\mathcal{S}$. $\mathcal{E}$ exploits the path information stored in requests to create a data structure we call *event flow tree*[5]. $\mathcal{S}$ only counts incoming requests and records the average length of the paths they traveled through the network to find a better location among the neighbor nodes. In contrast to this, $\mathcal{E}$ uses the structural information contained in the request paths to look further into the distance and find better locations for a replica more quickly.

In Figure 8.4 on page 91 we depicted a series of adaptations to explain the feedback mechanisms. If $\mathcal{S}$ was applied to this example network, it would need 5 adaptations and 4 adaptation steps (intervals) to reach the final configuration (Figure 8.4d) from the initial configuration (Figure 8.4a):

$$(1 \xrightarrow{r_1} 2); (2 \xrightarrow{r_1} 3); \{(3 \xrightarrow{r_1} 4)|(9 \xrightarrow{r_2} 10)\}; (10 \xrightarrow{r_2} 11)$$

If we allow multi-hop adaptations, an *optimal* algorithm that can predict the best configuration needs one interval and 2 adaptations:

$$\{(1 \xrightarrow{r_1} 4)|(9 \xrightarrow{r_2} 11)\}$$

But even under realistic assumptions, there is a potential for reducing the series to 3 adaptations and 2 intervals:

$$(1 \xrightarrow{r_1} 3); \{(3 \xrightarrow{r_1} 4)|(9 \xrightarrow{r_2} 11)\}$$

Thus, for an algorithm that may inspect the complete paths of client requests, it should be possible to reduce the number of adaptations and adaptation steps. $\mathcal{E}_v$ achieves this by selecting adaptation target nodes based on the number of messages flowing through them and their distance from v. The greater the message flow through a node u and the greater the distance between the final receiver v and u, the more transmissions can be saved by migrating replica r from v to u. $\mathcal{E}$ is an improved version of $\mathcal{S}$. It uses the same migration and replication rules that we specified in the preceding sections. However, the choice of target nodes for migrations and replications is different. We will first explain the concept of an event flow tree before we introduce the mechanism by which the target nodes for an adaptation are chosen based on the tree.

8.6.1 Event Flow Trees

Whenever $\mathcal{E}_v$ receives a request message m it extracts m's path $\Pi(m) \in N^l$ of length l, which has been recorded in the message as it was routed through the network. The

---

[5]In this context, "event" is a more general term for message.

paths of all messages are added to the event flow tree (EFT) $E = (N_E, L_E)$, where
N_E is the set of nodes in E and L_E is the set of links between the nodes. $(v, w) \in L_E$
if and only if w is a child of v in E. Consequently, an EFT is the spanning tree of the
sub-graph $G_C = (N_C \cup \{v\}, L_C)$ of all nodes $w \in N_C \subseteq N$ that have been sending
requests to v in the time interval of length T_h during which the tree was recorded.
The replica's node v is the root of that tree. Each node u in the tree has a weight
associated with it. This weight is simply the number of request messages that have
flowed through u. This includes all messages that originated from other nodes and
that have been relayed by u, and it includes all request messages that originated from
u itself. In other words, the weight of node u is simply the number messages that
included u in their paths. The EFT is created and updated by the algorithm shown
in Figure 8.16.

Let $|\Pi(m)|$ be the length of the path taken by message m. $\Pi(m) = (v)$ if the sending
client c and the receiving replica r are both on the same node v. If c is on node u
and r is on node v with $u \neq v$, then $\Pi(m) = (u, \omega, v)$ where ω is the list of nodes on
the path between u and v. Let $\Pi(m)_j$ be the j-th node in the path $\Pi(m) = (u, \omega, v)$
with u being at $\Pi(m)_0$.

By this definition, the last node in each path is the replica's node v ($\forall m$:
$\Pi(m)_{|\Pi(m)|} = v$), simply because all messages have been sent to r.

---

procedure INITIALIZEEFT (E)
2 **begin**
$\quad N_E = \{v\}$
$\quad L_E = \emptyset$
$\quad v.weight = 0$
end

7

procedure UPDATEEFT $(E,\ m)$
begin
$\quad$ **for** $j = |\Pi(m)|$ to $j = 0$ **do**
$\quad\quad$ **if** $\Pi(m)_j \notin N_E$ **then**
12 $\quad\quad\quad N_E = N_E \cup \Pi(m)_j$
$\quad\quad\quad L_E = L_E \cup (\Pi(m)_j, \Pi(m)_{j+1})$
$\quad\quad$ **endif**
$\quad\quad$ Let $u \in N_E$ be the node that equals $\Pi(m)_j$
$\quad\quad u.weight = u.weight + m.size$
17 $\quad$ **endfor**
end

Figure 8.16: Event flow tree update algorithm.

When $\mathcal{E}_v$ initializes the EFT, it puts the root node v into the node set. The update
algorithm goes through all nodes in the given path. If the path only contains v, then
the request was issued by a client on the replica's node v. Otherwise, the update
algorithm starts at the predecessor of the root node and goes backwards in the path.
If a node is not in the tree, it is added, and an edge is added to its successor in the
path. After updating the tree structure, the message's size is added to the weight
associated with each node.

Figure 8.17 shows a sample network (left side) with one replica and four clients. On
the right side, the paths of five exemplary request messages are depicted.

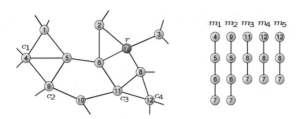

Figure 8.17: EFT update: example network and client request paths.

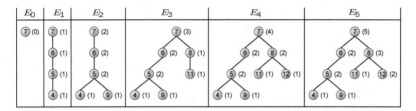

Figure 8.18: EFT update procedure.

Figure 8.18 shows how the EFT of $\mathcal{E}_7$ is updated with the message paths (node weights are given in parenthesis). E_0 is the state of the EFT after the initialization. It contains only the root node 7. After the first request m_1 comes in, the tree simply consists of the path taken by m_1. The second request was sent from node 9. Thus, node 9 is added to the tree and all nodes in $\Pi(m_2)$ that were already present in E_1 have their weights increased. m_3 adds a new subtree to the root since the request came in from a different neighbor (node 8). Each time, a node is encountered that is not present in the current tree, it is added, and, for every node that is already in the tree, the weight is increased.

8.6.2 Selection of Target Nodes

The migration and replication rules of $\mathcal{E}$ are identical to those of $\mathcal{S}$. $\mathcal{E}$ also migrates if one neighbor dominates the complete request flow entering a replica's node, and it replicates if the average path length of all requests exceeds the replication radius ρ. However, the new algorithm uses the event flow tree to select better target nodes that may also be further away from the replica's node.

For the selection process, we introduce a flow measure $\mathcal{F} : N_E \rightarrow \mathbb{R}$ that maps each node u in the tree to a real number quantifying u's contribution to the overall number of transmissions in the tree. Based on our definition of a transmission, $\mathcal{F}$ is defined as

$$\mathcal{F}(u) = d_E(u) \cdot w_E(u). \tag{8.45}$$

Where $d_E(u)$ is the depth of node u in E, and $w_E(u)$ is the weight of node u recorded in E. $d_E(u)$ has the following recursive definition:

$$d_E(u) = \begin{cases} 0 & : & \text{if } u \text{ is the root node of } E \\ d_E(v) + 1 & : & \text{if } u \text{ is a child node of } v \end{cases} \tag{8.46}$$

According to the definition of an EFT, $w_E(u)$ is the total number of requests that was sent from the subtree with root node u to the replica's node. The depth of a node u corresponds to the number of hops needed to transport a request from u to the root node hosting the replica. Therefore, $\mathcal{F}(u)$ is the number of transmissions that can potentially be saved if the replica at the root node migrated to u. $\mathcal{E}$ selects target nodes for migrations and replications based on this measure.

Selecting Migration Targets

For a migration, $\mathcal{E}_v$ first applies the simple migration condition (8.27) to find a neighbor $u \in N_v$ whose request flow dominates the overall flow. Let E' be the subtree with root node u. Then, $\mathcal{E}_v$ selects the node u' which has the greatest flow measure in E' as the migration target:

$$\mathcal{F}(u') = \max_{w \in E'} \mathcal{F}(w) \tag{8.47}$$

Figure 8.19 illustrates this for an example tree. The numbers in parenthesis for each node x are $(w_E(x), \mathcal{F}(x))$. Nodes from which clients send requests are marked. $\mathcal{E}_v$ selects the subtree E' rooted at node 8 using the migration condition since its request flow is greater than that of neighbor node 6. Node 8 would be selected as the final migration target by $\mathcal{S}$. But $\mathcal{E}$ has more knowledge. Instead of migrating r straight to node 8, $\mathcal{E}_7$ selects node 12 as the final target since its flow measure is maximal in subtree E'. If we assume that after a migration from v to u, all nodes in the tree will still use r and that all request messages will be routed to u via v, the tree on the right side of Figure 8.19 is the result of the migration.

The overall number of transmissions C_{qr} (cf. Section 8.5 on page 98) required to transport all client requests and all reconcile messages to the replica is the sum of all messages emitted by client nodes multiplied by the depth of these nodes. The number of messages emitted by node u is called the *emitted flow measure* and denote by $\mathcal{F}_e(u)$:

$$\mathcal{F}_e(u) = \left(w_E(u) - \sum_{u' \in L_u} w_E(u') \right) \cdot d_E(u) \tag{8.48}$$

with L_u being the set of children of node u:

$$L_u = \{u' | (u, u') \in L_E\} \tag{8.49}$$

Therefore, based on $\mathcal{F}_e(u)$, C_{qr} is defined as

$$C_{qr} = \sum_{u \in N_E} \mathcal{F}_e(u). \tag{8.50}$$

In our example, the client nodes that emitted requests are 4, 9, 11, and 12. For these nodes, $\mathcal{F}_e > 0$. For the remaining nodes, $\mathcal{F}_e = 0$. For the original tree (Figure 8.19, left side), $C_{qr} = 3 + 3 + 2 + 10 = 18$. For the (virtual) tree that would result if we let $\mathcal{S}$ select the migration target (Figure 8.19, middle) $C_{qr} = 4 + 4 + 1 + 5 = 14$, and for the tree produced by $\mathcal{E}$ (Figure 8.19, right side) we have $C_{qr} = 5 + 5 + 2 = 12$. Thus, in the example, $\mathcal{E}$ achieves a greater reduction with one adaptation than $\mathcal{S}$ would have achieved.

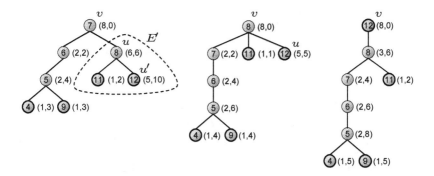

Figure 8.19: EFT target node selection (original, virtual, selected).

Note that the assumption that r will still receive requests from nodes 4 and 9 is a pessimistic one. As replica r moves, it shortens its distance to one part of its clients (denoted as $K_s \subseteq K$) while extending its distance to another part (denoted as $K_f \subseteq K$). For some clients, the distance remains the same. In our example, $K_s = \{12\}$, $K_f = \{4, 5, 6, 7, 9\}$, and $K \setminus (K_s \cup K_f) = \{8, 11\}$. Our first basic feedback rule states that clients always choose the closest replica. If $|R| > 1$ for the replica's service type, then clients may choose between several alternative replicas. Since the distance to the clients in K_s is reduced, their affinity to r is strengthened. For the clients in K_f, the converse is true. As a consequence of r's move, it is likely that some clients from K_f choose an alternative replica r' because r's move has made r' their closest replica. Thus, by moving away from K_f, $\mathcal{E}$ did not only reduce C_{qr}. It may also get rid of the clients in K_f which may be interpreted as an a posteriori approval of the decision.

If r is the only replica of its service type ($|R| = 1$), then all clients have to use r. In this case, the migration may increase the average request path length beyond ρ. In the example, the path length increases from 2.25 to 4. A replication may be triggered by which the system reduces the average distance between clients and replicas again.

Selecting Replication Targets

Just like in $\mathcal{S}$, a replication is triggered if the replication condition (8.38) is fulfilled. This is the case if there is more than one neighbor and the neighbor u contributing the greatest request flow is also the neighbor with the highest average request path length greater ρ. The selection of the two replication target nodes is depicted in Figure 8.20. The first target node is the node with the greatest flow measure in the subtree with root u. For the selection of the second target node, we remove the subtree with root u and simply check if the migration condition if fulfilled for the remaining tree. If this is the case, there is a neighbor w dominating the request flow, and we apply the selection criteria stated above to find a migration target in the subtree with root w. If the migration condition is not fulfilled, the second replica stays at the root node of E.

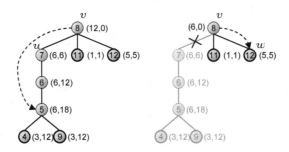

Figure 8.20: EFT target node selection (first node, second node).

8.6.3   Generalized Algorithm

Both algorithms, $\mathcal{S}$ and $\mathcal{E}$, are special cases of a more general algorithm $\mathcal{G}$ that employs the tree-based node selection with a *variable range of sight*. We introduce a new parameter ς that limits the depth of an EFT, and denote an algorithm that is limited to a depth of ς as $\mathcal{G}_\varsigma$. $\mathcal{G}_\varsigma$ may choose target nodes in the EFT up to a depth of ς. Under this definition, $\mathcal{E} \equiv \mathcal{G}_\infty$ and $\mathcal{S} \equiv \mathcal{G}_1$ hold.

In the following quantitative evaluation, we present several diagrams on different quantitative aspects of the ASG system. In these diagrams, we denote $\mathcal{S}$ with "online (d=1)" and $\mathcal{E}$ with "online (d=0)". "d" stands for distance and represents the range-of-sight-parameter used in the simulations. A value of $d = 0$ is interpreted as $d = \infty$.

8.7   Quantitative Evaluation

In this section, we first explore the behavior of the algorithms $\mathcal{S}$ and $\mathcal{E}$ under different settings of key parameters and investigate under which settings the algorithms perform best. In the second part of the evaluation, we compare the performance of the algorithms $\mathcal{S}$ and $\mathcal{E}$ with three other approaches for distributing service replicas in an ASG. These approaches include online algorithms that are applicable in practice requiring different degrees of global knowledge as well as offline algorithms that serve as a benchmark and give a good indication for the best (lowest) cost that is achievable. The comparison is based on the cost measure introduced in Section 8.2.1 and includes aspects of scalability and the behavior under different degrees of dynamics for the models introduced in Section 8.3.3. Furthermore, we investigate under which conditions, the replication and migration of service replicas is feasible. One important variable in this context is the replica size. It is intuitively clear that any mechanism that migrates programs at runtime will only be beneficial if these programs are small enough. We will show what "small enough" means in the context of the ASG by comparing the performance of our algorithms with the performance of other practical approaches for increasing replica sizes.

8.7.1 Cost Function

We evaluate all algorithms using the cost function C (Equation (8.6) on page 79). As we explained in Section 8.4.2, our online algorithms do not use the migration costs in their adaptation decisions. In the evaluation, however, we use the complete cost function (including migration costs) to compare all algorithms.

Interpretation of the Cost Function Values

The result of calculating the cost function C is a real-valued scalar that must be multiplied by the average size of a client message (requests and replies measured in bytes) to get the number of bytes transmitted throughout the entire ASG network per simulation tick. So the cost is measured in *average client messages sizes*. We chose this relative measure since it decouples our evaluation from any concrete application to a certain degree. That is, no matter how complex the application-dependent request (and reply) messages may get, the cost of a specific configuration is always the same. Moreover, this approach enables us to answer the following central question in a more general way: Up to which replica size does replica distribution at runtime really pay off? Choosing the relative measure based on the average size of client messages enables us to make a statement like: If the average size of a replica's state is below a value of x times the average client message size m_c, dynamic replica distribution is beneficial. This statement is also independent of the specific complexity in the data exchanged and stored within a certain application.

Requests Cost Calculation

During a simulation run, the online algorithm attempts to find the best possible configuration in regular intervals. The resulting series of replica distributions is recorded and compared offline with the benchmark algorithms introduced above. To execute this offline comparison, we record the client request function f_Q and the client allocation function f_C. More precisely, we record the client allocation and the request distribution generated by these functions.

Let

$$g_r : K \times [0, \infty) \to R \tag{8.51}$$

be a function that maps a client to a replica at a specific time index using the function f_{CR} (Equation (8.20) on page 81):

$$g_r(c, t) = r \in R | (c, r) \in f_{CR}(t) \tag{8.52}$$

Using g_r and the client-replica distance function d_{CR} (Equation (8.18) on page 80), we calculate the request cost as follows:

$$C_q(t) = 2 \cdot \sum_{c \in K} f_Q(c, t, f_C(c, t)) \cdot d_{CR}(c, g_r(c, t), t) \tag{8.53}$$

$f_Q(c, t, f_C(c, t))$ is the number of requests issued by client c at node $f_C(c, t)$ at time t and $d_{CR}(c, g_r(c, t), t)$ is the distance (network hops) between c and the replica chosen by c. Since we need to count requests and responses, we introduce a factor of 2.

Replication Cost Calculation

In order to calculate the replication cost $C_r(t)$, we first define the replication distance
for replica r

$$d_{Rep} : R \times [0, \infty) \rightarrow \mathbb{N} \qquad (8.54)$$

as the sum of all shortest paths to all fellow replicas of r (replicas of the same service
type):

$$d_{Rep}(r, t) = \sum_{r' \in R} d(f_M(r, t), f_M(r', t)) \qquad (8.55)$$

If r reconciles with its fellow replicas, it needs to send a certain amount of data
to its fellows via the routes considered by $d_{Rep}(r, t)$. The replication cost $C_r(t)$ is
calculated a follows:

$$C_r(t) = w_e \cdot \sum_{c \in K} f_Q(c, t, f_C(c, t)) \cdot d_{Rep}(g_r(c, t), t) \qquad (8.56)$$

The consistency protocol that will be presented in Chapter 10, generates a certain
amount of reconciliation traffic per byte of data written by a client at some replica.
Clients may submit read and write operations (also called "Reads" and "Writes")
to a replica. The write ratio $w = \frac{\#Writes}{\#Reads + \#Writes}$ specifies how many Writes a
client submits in proportion to the overall number of operations submitted by the
client (Reads and Writes). Thus, if $w = 0.1$ every tenth operation (on average)
submitted by a client is a Write. w is a simulation parameter that can be set. If a
replica r receives a series of operations and the amount of bytes needed to transmit
the messages containing these operations is b, then $w \cdot b$ bytes must potentially be
transmitted to all its fellow replicas. Since the consistency protocol is optimized to
save as much bandwidth as possible, the effective number of bytes is $w_s \cdot w \cdot b$. w_s is
the number of bytes sent per Write byte and the *effective write rate* is $w_e = w_s \cdot w$.

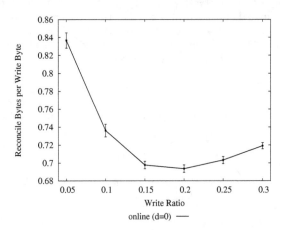

Figure 8.21: Number of effective bytes for one Write byte against w.

Figure 8.21 depicts how w_s depends on w. As the write ratio is increased, w_s drops
until it reaches a minimum at about $w = 0.2$. The reason for this decrease of w_s

is the fact that the consistency protocol relies on collecting a number of Writes and transmitting them together in one message in a specific order that minimizes the traffic. Transmissions are triggered when a certain number of Writes have been collected or when a timeout occurs (whatever comes first). Thus, for a low write ratio, reconciliations will mostly be triggered by the timeout. Therefore, the overhead is higher since more messages are needed to transmit the same number of Write operations. As w increases beyond 0.2, transmissions tend to be triggered more often since the allotted number of Writes have been received. Thus, the time interval between reconciliations gets shorter. The consistency protocol takes an optimistic approach concerning conflicts that may occur between concurrent reconciliations triggered by two fellow replicas. Therefore, such reconciliations may result in conflicts that lead to messages being dropped. Therefore, w_s increases for values higher than 0.2 since more conflicts occur and messages containing a series of Writes are sent in vain.

For the write ratio of $w = 0.15$ used in our experiments, $w_s \approx 0.7$ and, thus, $w_e = w_s \cdot w \approx 0.7 \cdot 0.15 \approx 0.1$.

In Equation (8.56), we assume that a w_e-fraction of all requests sent by a client c to a replica r is transmitted to all fellows of r. Thus, we multiply the number of requests with the replication distance and sum over all clients.

Migration Cost Calculation

The cost for the migration of a replica from node u to node v is simply

$$C_m(t) = \sigma \cdot d(u, v). \tag{8.57}$$

In this equation, σ stands for the average size of a replica's state measured in average client messages. If m_c is the size of an average client message (measured in bytes), then $\sigma \cdot m_c$ is the amount of bytes that needs to be transmitted per hop if a replica migrates. This is in line with the interpretation of cost function values stated above. Let us assume that the state of a replica consists of some sort of database and that clients read and write records in this database. Then σ might roughly be viewed as the average number of data records that reside in a replica's database. σ is a tunable simulation parameter.

8.7.2 Approximating the Best Parameter Setting

The following parameters influence the performance of our algorithms:

- The adaptation interval T_a is the fixed time interval between two consecutive adaptations. This is a system-wide, constant value. Each instance of an online algorithm is run every T_a simulation ticks.

- The window of historic data T_h is a sliding time window for which historic data is collected and used by the online algorithms.

- The stability threshold η limits the reactivity of the online algorithms to cases in which the migration rule is triggered by a stable behavior. This shall prevent erratic adaptations due to purely stochastic request patterns.

- The replication radius ρ is the radius (number of network hops) of the area that shall be served by a single replica. If the average request path length perceived by a replica exceeds ρ, a replication is triggered.

- The depth (or range of sight) ς used by the generalized algorithm $\mathcal{G}$, controls how far ahead (measured in network hops) $\mathcal{G}$ may look towards the direction of client requests. It also controls the maximum distance for a migration or a replication.

This represents a relatively small set of relevant parameters to which our algorithms are sensitive. Nevertheless, the parameter space that is created by these dimensions is rather large. In addition, a number of external factors, like network size and number of clients, that may influence the best choice of parameters, need to be considered. This prohibits a complete search for the optimal setting. A reasonable parameter setup was found over the course of a large number of experiments conducted during the implementation and testing phase. Starting from this setup, we study each parameter in isolation. We keep all values fixed, except for one parameter that is varied over a certain range to find an optimal setting. This methodology is not guaranteed to find the overall optimal parameter setup. However, it represents a good compromise.

Adaptation and History Interval

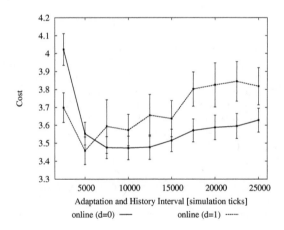

Figure 8.22: Cost for increasing adaptation and history intervals.

Figure 8.22 depicts the average cost produced by $\mathcal{S}$ (denoted by "online (d=1)") and $\mathcal{E}$ (denoted by "online (d=0)") for increasing values of T_a and T_h. Note that we always set $T_a = T_h$. Whether $T_a > T_h$ or $T_a < T_h$ would be more beneficial remains to be investigated in further experiments.

For both algorithms, the graph shows a clear minimum. Small values make the algorithms too sensitive to noise and tend to cause overreactions. High values make it too insensitive to relevant changes and prevent useful adaptations. The effects of overreactions for $\mathcal{E}$ are potentially worse than for $\mathcal{S}$ since $\mathcal{E}$ may apply more radical changes and produce higher migration costs in a single adaptation. Therefore, $\mathcal{E}$ favors an interval of 10000 ticks, whereas $\mathcal{S}$ works best at 5000 ticks. The simulations for this experiment were conducted with sudden change dynamics and an interval of 50000 ticks between the changes in request patterns. Whether the concrete setup of the dynamics influences the optimal value for T_a and T_h, remains to be studied.

Stability Threshold

Figure 8.23 displays the behavior of the online algorithms as the stability threshold η is increased from 0 to 1. At $\eta = 0$, the stability check (Equation (8.30) on page 100) is effectively turned off. At $\eta = 1$, migrations are only triggered if the migration condition holds for all subintervals of T_h. Without any stability check, the algorithms should produce considerably more adaptations and tend to oscillate between a small set of acceptable replica placements as request patterns fluctuate randomly. If we require complete stability, many useful adaptations are prevented because request flows are rarely absolutely stable. In both extreme cases, the cost produced by the online algorithms should be higher than the optimum, and there should be a minimum somewhere between the two.

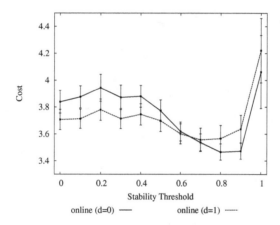

Figure 8.23: Cost for increasing stability threshold η.

Figure 8.23 confirms this hypothesis. Interestingly, the graphs show an increase in cost between 0 and 0.2. This can be attributed to the fact that such a low threshold essentially has no stabilizing effect. It does not discriminate the useful adaptations from the rest, and it only filters out random adaptations, some of which may have been useful. Thus, enforcing a very small threshold, actually raises the cost slightly. The stabilizing effect sets in for values that are higher than 0.2 and reaches its maximum (minimum cost) between 0.7 and 0.9. The more radical algorithm $\mathcal{E}$ profits more from the stability condition than $\mathcal{S}$. $\mathcal{S}$ already has a certain degree of stability "built in" since it may only take small adaptation steps. $\mathcal{E}$ actually requires the stability check to realize its full potential and outperform $\mathcal{S}$ for $\eta \geq 0.65$. In addition, the optimal threshold value for $\mathcal{E}$ is higher than for $\mathcal{S}$. Ill-advised

adaptations executed by $\mathcal{E}$ may be much more harmful due to the arbitrary range
they may cover.

Replication Radius

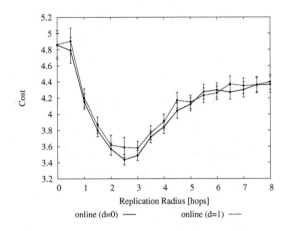

Figure 8.24: Cost for increasing replication radius ρ.

The replication radius ρ essentially defines the number of replicas that are needed to
create a stable replica placement that covers a network of a specific size. The relation
between ρ and the number of replicas in the system was examined in detail in Section
8.5.4 were we found that, for a fixed network diameter, $|R| \sim \rho^{-2}$ holds. If ρ is close
to 0, then a large number of replicas is distributed in the network. As ρ grows, this
number converges to the minimum of 1 replica. At both extremes, we expect the
cost produced by the online algorithms to be suboptimal. Figure 8.24 shows that,
for the setup chosen in this experiment, the best value for ρ is between 2.5 and 3.0.
To the left of this point, the number of replicas gets too high. The replication cost
grows and starts to dominate the overall cost. At the same time, the request cost
is not reduced significantly beyond a certain number of replicas. To the right of the
optimum, the number of replicas gets smaller. The request cost starts to dominate
while the replication costs vanishes as the minimum of one replica is reached (around
$\rho = 6$). Thus, the overall cost converges. Apart from the fact that $\mathcal{E}$ performs better
than $\mathcal{S}$ in general, the two graphs are quite similar.

Event Flow Tree Depth

As we have seen, $\mathcal{S}$ and $\mathcal{E}$ are two special cases of a more general online algorithm
$\mathcal{G}_\varsigma$ with variable tree depth ς. Figure 8.25 shows how the cost produced by $\mathcal{G}$ is
influenced by the tree depth. The "startup phase" graph depicts the behavior of
the algorithm from tick 0 to tick 100000 of a simulation that ran for 500000 ticks in
total. At the very start of a simulation, a single replica is positioned at some randomly
chosen node. Thus, in the early simulation phase the algorithm must quickly find

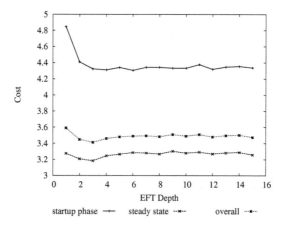

Figure 8.25: Cost for increasing tree depth.

a good replica placement starting from a rather sub-optimal configuration. During this phase, the depth has a notable influence on the algorithm performance.

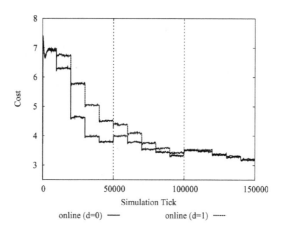

Figure 8.26: Cost development at startup against simulation time.

This is also confirmed in Figure 8.26 which presents the first 150000 ticks of two experiments with $\varsigma = 0$ (infinite tree depth) and $\varsigma = 1$. The infinite depth lets the algorithm converge to a placement with a low cost much quicker. After the initial phase, however, both algorithms maintain very similar cost levels. Consequently, the cost difference for varying ς is only marginal for the latter stage of a simulation run (ticks 100000 to 500000). During this interval, $\mathcal{G}_\varsigma$ performs best for $\varsigma = \rho$. In the simulation runs of this experiment, the replication radius ρ was set to 3. Note that ρ defines the area from which the bulk of request traffic is sent to a replica when the system is in a stable state. If the request pattern changes and the majority of

requests come from outside this area, then the replication rule is triggered and brings
the system back to a stable state. The state of the system is called "stable" if no
distinct force to replicate or migrate is applied to any replica by request flows. If $\mathcal{G}_\varsigma$
is allowed to look ahead ρ network hops, then it may promptly react to all relevant
changes within this area without necessarily disturbing the global placement (see
Figure 8.27(a)). Looking ahead further into the distance may cause a replica to react
to minor requests flows further away than ρ. If the flow measure of such a request
flow is high enough to attract the replica r, then the stable overall replica placement
is disturbed since the clients in r's former replication radius bind to other replicas and
the resulting unbalance enforces changes on a more global level (see Figure 8.27(b)).
Other replicas have to adapt to fill the gap left by r.

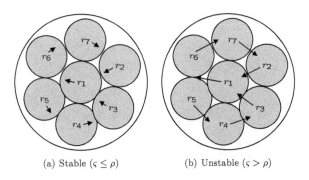

(a) Stable ($\varsigma \leq \rho$)   (b) Unstable ($\varsigma > \rho$)

Figure 8.27: Global types of adaptations.

If, on the other hand, ς is smaller than ρ, then a replica may need more adaptation
steps to react to relevant changes within its area. Therefore, the cost rises for $\varsigma > \rho$
and $\varsigma < \rho$ and has its minimum at $\varsigma = \rho$. However, with the setup used in this
experiment, this effect is rather small. Whether it becomes more significant if the
network size and ρ is increased, remains to be investigated.

Figure 8.26 illustrates the advantage that $\mathcal{E}$ $(\mathcal{G}_\infty)$ has over $\mathcal{S}$ $(\mathcal{G}_1)$: $\mathcal{E}$ converges to
a good replica placement much quicker than $\mathcal{S}$. The ability the make adaptations
that span more than one hop, enables $\mathcal{E}$ to enforce a placement in one step for which
$\mathcal{S}$ needs multiple steps and, thus, more time. Figure 8.26 clearly shows how both
algorithms adapt each 10000 ticks and that the cost exhibits a sharp drop between
adaptation intervals. Inside each interval, the cost remains at a constant level. We
ran 1000 simulations with the sudden change dynamics model and a change interval
of 50000 ticks per algorithm (indicated by the grid).

8.7.3   Benchmark Algorithms

For our evaluation, we compare our algorithms with three other approaches that are
explained in the following.

Optimal Static Placement

The ultimate benchmark for a heuristic algorithm like the ones introduced in this book is the optimal solution. Of course, calculating this optimal solution is a problem in itself, because even if we are in an offline situation with global knowledge in time and space, finding the optimal solution is too difficult due to the computational complexity of our problem. Therefore, the "optimal" algorithm used to get a lower bound for the cost achievable by our algorithms only calculates an approximation of this lower bound rather than the "real optimum".

The problem of employing migration costs in the placement decisions that we discussed in Section 8.2.1 also represents a major problem for our approximation of the optimal solution. Therefore, we constrain our approximation to a single static placement that remains immutable over the complete simulation interval. Of course, a dynamic solution that can choose different replica placements for one simulation run would yield better solutions. However, this would increase the complexity of finding a good solution considerably to a point where it becomes impractical. The problem of finding a replica placement that minimizes the number of messages transmitted in the network over a given period of time is NP-hard. Consider an algorithm for finding a series of k replica placements $\{a_{rn}(t_1), \ldots a_{rn}(t_k)\}$ where the interval $[t_{i-1}, t_i]$ is not fixed but chosen such that the migration costs $C_M(a_{rn}(t_i - 1), a_{rn}(t_i))$ amortize optimally in that interval. Such an algorithm is not only faced with the problem of solving the NP-hard problem of finding optimal placements k times independently. Instead, it would be required to find the best series of placements that are depending on each other through the amortization of migration costs. While the first problem has a complexity of $k \cdot C_p$, the latter problem has a complexity of $C_p{}^k$, where

$$C_p = \frac{|N|!}{m!(|N| - m)!} \tag{8.58}$$

is the complexity of using exhaustive search for placing m replicas on $|N|$ nodes. Moreover, k is not fixed. The optimal series of replica placements may have a different length for different networks and random client behaviors. If we assume that k_{opt} is the optimal value for k and that we have no prior hint on a good value for k_{opt}, an exhaustive search algorithm would have a complexity of $\sum_{k=1}^{k_{opt}} C_p{}^k$. With $|N| = 50$, $m = 5$, and $k_{opt} = 20$, which is realistic for the networks we investigate, this results in $3.3 \cdot 10^{126}$ possible solutions that need to be tested. Even if we reduce this number by several orders of magnitude by employing a heuristics for approximating a good solution, this still remains an impossible task. Furthermore, it is not sufficient to find such a solution for 1 network. To achieve statistically relevant results, we ran about $5 \cdot 10^4$ experiments for the results presented in this book alone. The overall number of experiments run in order to implement, test, and improve the ASG simulation was in the order of 10^5.

To be able to calculate reasonably good approximations of the optimal solution for a large number of different networks, we decided to calculate a single static solution. Thus, we constrain the "optimal" offline algorithm to $k = 1$. This algorithm uses simulated annealing to find a single good solution a_{rn} for a given network graph G and a series of request distributions $Q = \{q(0), \ldots q(T)\}$. We run the simulated annealing algorithm 100 times for each such configuration (G, Q) staring with randomly chosen replica placements and select the best of the 100 solutions. This process is run for each m (number of replicas) in $\{1, \ldots, m_{opt} + 1\}$ to find m_{opt}. We assume that there is a unique m_{opt} for each (G, Q) since the request costs C_Q decrease as more replicas are produced. At the same time, the reconciliation costs C_R increase with the number of replicas. Thus, as the number of replicas is increased, the overall costs decreases first since the request costs dominate, and at some point it starts increasing again as the reconciliation costs start to dominate. Therefore, the optimal number of replicas can be found simply by finding the best solution for $m = 1, 2, 3, \ldots$ until the costs start rising again at $m_{opt} + 1$.

Average Random Placement

The average random placement algorithm also generates a single static replica placement. It distributes m_{opt} replicas randomly inside the network G 100 times and averages the overall costs for all trials. This algorithm mimics an ad hoc approach that would be taken in practice if no knowledge about the network and the behavior of the clients can be assumed. Note that the algorithm knows m_{opt}. Thus, it has an advantage over a completely random placement that has to guess m_{opt}. In practice, the operator responsible for distributing replicas may only have an educated guess about m_{opt}. Moreover, a single random solution as it would be applied by such an operator may be considerably worse than the average case.

The random algorithm represents the main opponent of our online algorithms. Our aim is not to beat the static optimal solution, but the average random algorithm.

Greedy Heuristics

Qiu et at. present a widely cited algorithm for placing M web server replicas in a Content Distribution Network (CDN) of N nodes such that the cost of all requests is minimized [136]. This algorithm takes a greedy approach by choosing one replica at a time and placing it at an appropriate node. More precisely, in the first iteration, each of the N potential sites is evaluated individually to determine its suitability for hosting a replica. The costs of this placement are computed under the assumption that all requests are directed to that replica. The second replica is placed by evaluating the costs in conjunction with this first replica assuming that each client chooses its closest replica. This process is iterated until all M replicas are placed. The greedy algorithm by Qiu et al. has been shown to produce very good placements and, thus, is also used by other researchers as a benchmark for evaluating their work (e.g. [162, 92, 139]) and has inspired subsequent development of similar approaches (e.g. [30]).

It should be noted that unlike our algorithms, this greedy algorithm assumes global knowledge. It is an online algorithm since it operates on a window of past data (e.g. the last 24 hours) and has no knowledge about the future. However, it requires knowledge about all requests posted throughout the network in the given time window and about the network topology. Furthermore, the algorithm is run on a central node. Throughout the following evaluation, the reader should keep in mind that, in contrast to this, our algorithms are run in a fully distributed fashion and require only partial knowledge about client requests and network topology that can be extracted from the requests. Thus, no additional mechanism for collecting that data on a central node is required.

In our simulation, the greedy algorithm by Qiu et al. is run at the same intervals as the online algorithms and has the same window of past client requests. We assume that a replica allocation $a_{rn}(t_i)$ found by the greedy algorithm is produced from the previous allocation $a_{rn}(t_i-1)$ by migrating existing replicas and (possibly) replicating new ones such that the overall number of hops needed for all migrations is minimal.

8.7.4 Experimental Results

Varying Replica Size

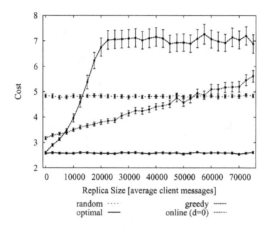

Figure 8.28: Cost for increasing replica size.

Figure 8.28 shows the behavior of the algorithms as the relative replica size is increased. The optimal and the random algorithm both remain at a constant cost level since they do not migrate any replicas. Both choose static solutions that are not altered during a simulation run. Therefore, they are independent of the replica size. The important result that can be derived from the graph is the point at which the cost of our online algorithm grows beyond that of random placement. This is the case at a replica size of about 50000. What does this mean in practice? Assume that we run a service that sells CDs. Its database contains a record for each CD that is available. A client request is a template that consists of a CD record possibly containing wildcards. A reply contains a list of records matching the query. Let us further assume that there are other types of requests that contain less data than a complete CD record, for example login or order requests. For such a service it may be plausible that the average size of all client messages is about the size of a single CD record since a reply contains several records while some requests and replies are smaller than one record. For such a CD selling service, dynamic service distribution pays off as long as each replica stores less than 50000 CD records. This number seems adequate to render this sort of service useful.

Keep in mind that this is a rather pessimistic approximation since the random algorithm knows the optimal number of replicas m_{opt}. A random algorithm that has to guess the best number of replicas in some way would produce an even higher cost. The cost produced by the online algorithm grows at a rate of approximately 0.074 points per 2500 points increase in replica size. This data indicates that even if a more realistic random algorithm would increase the cost only by 10% over the one used in this measurement, the point up to which dynamic replica distribution is beneficial raises by approximately 32% to an absolute value of about 66000.

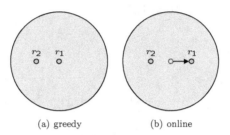

(a) greedy   (b) online

Figure 8.29: Geometrical explanation for the superlinear growth in cost for the greedy algorithm by Qiu et al.

The second important result presented in Figure 8.28 is the fact that the growth in cost of the greedy algorithm is superlinear at first and reaches a state of saturation at about the 20000 mark. The greedy algorithm is superior to our online algorithm only for rather small replica sizes. The explanation for this behavior is depicted in Figure 8.29 where the large circles represent a network with uniformly distributed client requests. The basic approach of the greedy algorithm is to position each replica optimally with respect to the previous allocation and keep all previous positions fixed while the next replica is placed. At the left side of Figure 8.29, r_1 has been put at the center of the circular network and remains there as r_2 is placed. Therefore, the placement of r_2 by the greedy algorithm has only limited benefits since it only shortens the request paths for the clients in the left half of the network. The online algorithm is allowed to move replicas in reaction to changes in the request patterns. In particular, such changes are stimulated when an additional replica is placed. The right side of Figure 8.29 shows how r_1 moves to the right as the new replica r_2 is placed to the left of it since r_2 now takes away requests coming from the left and creates an unbalanced state that forces r_1 to move. The consequence is that the greedy algorithm produces fewer replicas as the replica size increases because the limited benefits of having more replicas is outweighed by the additional cost of placing them (migration). At a replica size of 20000, the greedy algorithm stops replicating completely and converges to a configuration with a single replica. In contrast to this, the online algorithm can benefit from creating new replicas since existing ones may react by moving to better positions.

Varying Write Ratio

Figure 8.30 shows how the algorithms perform under an increasing write ratio. At a write ratio of 0, no Writes are produced by clients. Thus, the replication cost component is also 0 and only requests and migrations contribute any cost. At a write ratio of 1, every operation submitted by a client is a Write and the replication cost reaches its maximum. The optimal algorithm starts out at a cost of 2 and converges to about 4 after a steep rise at the beginning. As the write ratio is slowly increased, the optimal algorithm produces less and less replicas since maintaining a larger number of replicas gets more and more expensive and looses its benefits. As w approaches 1, only one replica is used by the optimal algorithm per service type. As the number of replicas distributed on average approaches the boundary of 1, the graph converges since the replication cost gets less significant and vanishes with one replica.

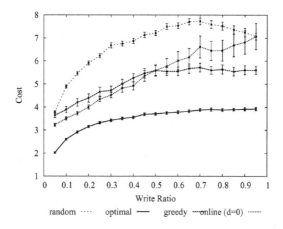

Figure 8.30: Cost for increasing write ratio w.

The random algorithm starts out in a similar fashion, albeit at a much higher cost level. The similar development can be attributed to the fact that this algorithm uses the same number of replicas as the optimal algorithm, as explained in Section 8.7.3. Approximately at $w = 0.7$, the cost produced by the random algorithm starts falling again. As the number of replicas used approaches 1, the relative positioning of the replicas looses its influence. Before, the unoptimized, possibly large distance between the replicas had a large negative effect as w was increased.

The greedy algorithm exhibits a linear increase below $w = 0.5$ and remains constant after that. Like all other algorithms, the greedy one starts off without producing notable replication costs. Thus, it uses more than one replica per service type. As we explained, the greedy algorithm has limited possibilities for placing replicas since it does so iteratively keeping allocated positions fixed (see Figure 8.29). Therefore, it cannot reduce the number of replicas as gradually as the optimal algorithm. As a consequence, its cost grows linearly at the beginning until it persistently finds that a single-replica solution has the lowest cost. This is the case at $w = 0.5$. From that point on, it sticks with a single-replica solution and produces constant costs. The difference in the cost level compared to the optimal algorithm is caused by the fact that the greedy algorithm takes its decisions online. That is, it uses past information and finds the best single-replica placement for the next interval. Thus, these decisions may be sub-optimal in the interval in which they actually take effect. Furthermore, the greedy algorithm produces migration costs in contrast to the optimal algorithm. The optimal algorithm does not have these difficulties since it works offline. Therefore, it produces much a lower cost.

The online algorithm does not choose its number of replicas based on the overall cost. Since it is distributed in nature, it has no means for taking a global decision about the number of replicas. Instead, it uses the replication radius ρ to take that decision locally. Therefore, it always chooses about the same number of replicas based on ρ and indirectly on the diameter of the network which was fixed throughout the experiments. The general increase in reconciliation traffic for a growing a write ratio shown in Figure 8.21 is counteracted by the fact that the replication distance d_{Rep} decreases. The set of replicas tends to stay closer together if the reconciliation traffic increases since this is also a part of the message flows evaluated by the online algorithm. As a result, the cost produced by the online algorithm increases linearly with the write ratio.

Varying Dynamics

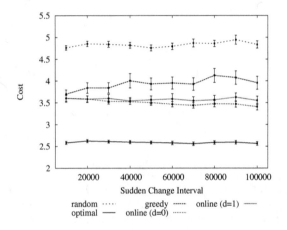

Figure 8.31: Cost for decreasing sudden change dynamics.

In Figures 8.31, 8.32, and 8.33 the behavior of all algorithms is depicted for varying degrees of dynamics in the three dynamic request pattern models introduced in Section 8.3.3. These graphs basically show that the online algorithms exhibit a stable performance under all three forms of dynamics and for the complete range of dynamics. This seems counterintuitive at first, as one would expect a more vivid reaction to radical increases in the degree of dynamics. The insensibility to dynamics can be explained by the effect of the adaptation history interval T_h (cf. Section 8.4.2). As the degree of dynamics is raised, changes take place with an increasing frequency. If this frequency gets too high, the simple low-pass filter introduced by averaging over the interval T_h takes effect. At high frequencies, the online algorithms do not realize that request patterns change. Instead, the algorithms see a more or less uniformly distributed flow of requests from different directions.

For the moving change model, this observation is confirmed in Figure 8.34: When there is no dynamics in the system, $\mathcal{E}$ executes the highest number of adaptation

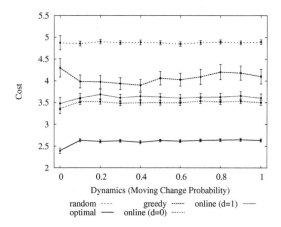

Figure 8.32: Cost for increasing moving change dynamics.

actions per adaptation interval. This is because $\mathcal{E}$ is able to detect the directions from which the dominant request flows come in, very clearly. Note that the cost depicted in Figure 8.32 has its minimum at this point. As the degree of dynamics increases, the number of migrations and replications drop considerably since the averaging effect makes the decision for the right adaptation less clear for $\mathcal{E}$. The number of migrations continues to drop as request flows appear to come in more uniformly from all directions. The number of replications rises again for higher dynamics. As request flows appear more uniformly, it becomes more likely that a request flow whose average path length exceeds ρ is also the maximum flow. Thus, the replication condition (8.38) is fulfilled more often and more replications take place.

The fact that the online algorithms lose their ability to discriminate changes in request patterns at a high frequency prevents them from overreacting. Thus, the trivial predictive mechanism introduced in Section 8.4.2 does work as expected. An increase in dynamics leads to a slight raise in the cost, but very quickly, the algorithm stabilizes at a very good cost level and sustains it even for extremely high degrees of dynamics. The fact that the optimal algorithm experiences a similar initial increase in cost (for the moving change model) indicates that this behavior is inherent to the system.

For all three dynamics models, the cost of the online algorithms shows the same characteristics as the cost of the optimal algorithm. It seems that the respective graphs are only shifted. In fact, a closer look at the average cost values over the whole range of dynamics reveals that this shift is caused by the migration cost component. Figure 8.35 shows the average cost for the online algorithm $\mathcal{E}$ ("online") and the optimal algorithm ("optimal"), the cost difference between the two ("diff."), the migration cost produced by the online algorithm ("online migr."), and the cost difference between the two algorithms if the migration cost is ignored ("net diff."). It is evident that the difference in the overall cost between the optimal and the online algorithm is caused by the migration cost component. In other words, the quality of

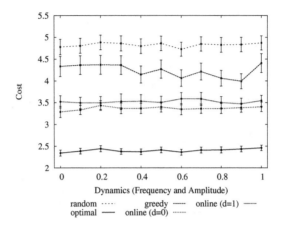

Figure 8.33: Cost for increasing oscillating change dynamics.

the configurations found by the online algorithms is approximately the same as that of the optimal algorithm. For the sudden change and oscillating change models it is slightly better. Remember that the optimal algorithm finds a single replica distribution for an entire simulation run whereas the online algorithm may adjust the replica distribution each adaptation interval. Obviously, the online algorithm exploits this advantage and finds better distributions.

Scalability

To study the scalability of the ASG service distribution algorithms, we measured the cost produced by all algorithms

1. for an increasing number of network nodes (Figure 8.36) and

2. for an increasing number of clients (Figure 8.37).

It is important to note that in the first experiment, we did not merely increase the number of network nodes but also the number of clients. The motivation behind this is that an operator would scale the network according to the number of clients that use it. Thus, in a realistic scenario, the network size is depending on the number of clients. In the simulation, we model this by letting the number of clients $|K|$ grow proportionally to the number of network nodes $|N|$: $|K| = c_n \cdot |N|$. In the first scalability experiment, we set c_n to a value of 0.5 for all measurements.

Figure 8.36 shows that for all algorithms, the cost grows non-linear as the number of nodes is increased. This is mainly caused by the replication cost component (cf. Equation (8.56)): The number of requests is proportional to $|K|$ and, thus, it is also proportional to $|N|$. This is multiplied by the replication distance which in turn is the product of the average distance between the replicas and of the number of replicas. Both of these quantities are, likewise, proportional to $|N|$. The resulting overall cost function is in $O(|N|^3)$.

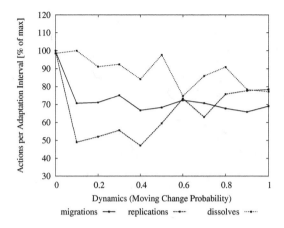

Figure 8.34: Relative number of adaptation actions performed by $\mathcal{E}$.

As expected, the optimal algorithm exhibits the best scalability and the random algorithm has the worst scalability, in terms of the growth rate. The online algorithms $\mathcal{S}$ and $\mathcal{E}$ as well as the greedy algorithm lie between these two. An interesting result of this experiment is that the greedy algorithm is more scalable than the online algorithms. It is important to note that the greedy algorithm was originally designed for wide area networks with a size that is several orders of magnitudes bigger than an average ASG network. Therefore, it outperforms our online algorithms as the number of nodes grows beyond 100. The online algorithms were not designed for large networks. Instead, they are explicitly targeted towards medium-scale networks. We deliberately trade off scalability to render our algorithms as decentralized and self-organizing as possible. Nevertheless, within the relevant range of network sizes, they may compete with the greedy approach.

Figure 8.37 depicts the second scalability experiment in which we used a fixed network size of 50 nodes and increased the number of clients from 10 to 100. For all algorithms, the cost scales linearly with the number of clients because the number of requests is proportional to the number of clients. Again, the optimal algorithm displays the best scalability and the random algorithm scales worst. The online and the greedy algorithms are close together with the greedy approach performing better for large networks.

8.8 Qualitative Evaluation

In the previous section, we have shown that despite their distributed control mechanisms, our algorithms perform well under different conditions. This quantitative evaluation proves that our concepts are valid and achieve the original task. In this section, we evaluate our algorithms from a qualitative perspective. We show that they do exhibit self-organizing behavior and adapt to their environment. We also take a look at the emergent properties displayed by the overall system.

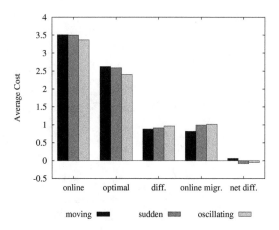

Figure 8.35: Impact of migration cost on the online algorithms' overall cost.

8.8.1 Why is it Self-Organizing?

In the following, we apply the classification methodology introduced in Chapter 4 to show that our replica placement algorithms are in the class of self-organizing software systems. We start by giving a proper description of the relevant elements of the system within the boundaries set in Section 4.6. Subsequently, we show that, according to this description and Definition 4.2, our system is self-organizing.

Defining the Key Elements of the Overall System

The description on which we base our classification is the following:

- **The system,** for which we would like to show that it is self-organizing, consists of the set of service replicas and the Serviceware that runs the distributed placement algorithm $\mathcal{A}$ on each node.

  In Section 8.4.2, we have stated that the distributed placement algorithm actually runs in the Proxy Agents which are statically placed on each node. The reason for this choice is that this makes service replicas more light-weight and less complicated. In principle, it really makes no difference whether the adaptation algorithm runs inside each replica or in the Serviceware on the Service Cubes. Thus, for the purpose of this discussion, we ignore this distinction and assume that the adaptation algorithm belongs to the replicas. Analogous to the two different descriptions of an ant colony stated in Section 4.4, one may decompose our system horizontally into the replicas and the adaptation algorithm. However, we argue that one component of the system should rather be defined as consisting of a replica and its adaptation algorithm as this captures the system's essence much better.

- **The environment** that this system shall adapt to, comprises (i) the dynamic request patterns manifested by the clients' requests, and (ii) the client-replica

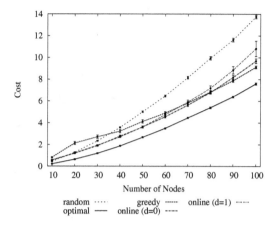

Figure 8.36: Overall cost for an increasing number of nodes.

allocation defined by f_{CR} (Equation (8.20)). The request patterns may be changing over time according to the dynamics models introduced in Section 8.3.3. The client-replica allocation changes as clients move and in reaction to changes in the replica placement.

- **The self-organizing system's internal structure** is given by the replica placement. More formally, the time-dependent mapping of the set of replicas to the network nodes, given by the migration function f_M (Equation (8.12)), defines the system's internal structure that is changed to adapt to changes in the environment.

- **Good versus bad organization:** A good organization is a replica placement, for which the value of the cost function C is within a predefined constant factor of the cost produced by the optimal algorithm. The criterion of acceptability W in Zadeh's adaptivity model (cf. Section 4.3) is defined accordingly in the following.

Structuring

To provide evidence of a structuring process, we need to define the system's state space first. We select two measures to represent the state at time t:

- the number of replicas active at t and

- the average distance between these replicas.

This choice can be motivated as follows: The trade-off between minimizing the request cost and the replication cost, should force the system to choose the number of replicas with care. Too many replicas may reduce the request cost but the increased replication cost nullifies this positive effect. On the other hand, a low number of replicas is good for reducing the replication cost but results in a high request cost as

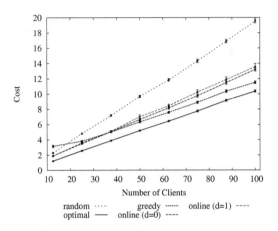

Figure 8.37: Overall cost for an increasing number of clients.

the average distance between the clients and their nearest replica is high for a low number of replicas. Therefore, there must be some optimal number of replicas for any given setup (network size, client number etc.). Thus, we would expect a useful replica placement system to constrain itself to a certain number of replicas such that not any arbitrary number of replicas is possible for the system.

The distance between the replicas should also be constrained since the system should try to cover the whole network with a limited number of replicas. Thus, we expect the replicas not to be arbitrarily close to each other, but also not arbitrarily far apart.

We normalize the number of replicas $|R|$ by dividing it by the network size $|N|$. We assume that each node may run at most one replica of a specific service. Thus, $r = \frac{|R|}{|N|}$ is the first dimension of our state space. Likewise, we normalize the average distance $\bar{d}$ between the replicas by dividing it by the network diameter D. Therefore, $d = \frac{\bar{d}}{D}$ becomes our second state space dimension. A state is a tuple $(r, d) \in [0, 1] \times [0, 1]$. To get a discrete state space with a finite number of different states, we divide each dimension into 10 categories of width 0.1. Each value measured for r and d is rounded to the nearest tenth. This creates a space of 100 (10×10) possible states. If our replica placement system really creates structures with low costs, then it should reside only in a small subset of these states.

In order to verify this, we measured r and d for both algorithms. We ran $\mathcal{S}$ and $\mathcal{E}$ 1000 times each with the sudden change dynamics model and a change interval of 50000 ticks. Then we used the entropy measure to calculate the uncertainty about the system's state over all 1000 runs each 1000 ticks. That is, for each tick $t \in (10^3, 2 \cdot 10^3, \ldots, 50 \cdot 10^3)$, we measured r_t and d_t in each of the 1000 simulation runs. The result is a 2-dimensional random variable (r_t, d_t) with 1000 experiments (one for each simulation run) for each t. Subsequently, we computed the 2-dimensional probability distribution P_t for each (r_t, d_t). Based on the distribution P_t, we were able to compute the entropy for time t and, thus, plot the uncertainty about the state of the system against the simulation time. The resulting graph for both algorithms is shown in Figure 8.38.

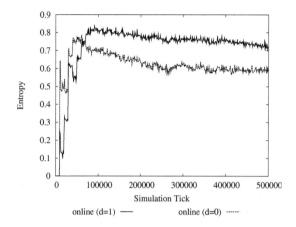

Figure 8.38: The structural entropy of replica placement.

The entropy was calculated using the logarithm to base of 10. Thus, a completely unstructured system for which each of the 100 states has equal probability would exhibit an entropy of 2 ($\log_{10} 100$). Any values less than 2 indicate that the system is structured. As can be seen in Figure 8.38, both algorithms have an entropy that is considerably lower than the theoretical maximum. The entropy at the end of the simulations is about 0.7 for S and 0.6 for $\mathcal{E}$. This means that S is constrained to about 5 ($10^{0.7}$) of the 100 states, whereas $\mathcal{E}$ resides only in about 4 ($10^{0.6}$) different states.

What is striking about the entropy graphs is that the uncertainty about the system's state seems to increase initially. This seems to be counter-intuitive as we would expect the system to create a higher degree of order as time progresses. That is, one would expect that the system comes from an unstructured state and converges to an increasingly structured state over time. The strange decrease in structure can be explained by the fact that we start every simulation run with one initial replica for each service type. This number as well as the average distance between the set of replicas are completely determined during the first adaptation interval. The state is $r = 1$ and $d = 0$ in each of the 1000 runs. Thus, the uncertainty about this state is zero. As new replicas are created over the first few adaptation intervals, the uncertainty starts to grow, simply because the number of possible different states grows. After a certain number of ticks, however, the increase in entropy stops and both graphs start to converge. As the algorithms have reached their optimal number of replicas through replication, they gradually increase the degree of structure (entropy decreases). $\mathcal{E}$ enters this phase quicker since it is allowed to take larger steps. What is more interesting, though, is that $\mathcal{E}$ also produces less uncertainty in the later stages of the runs. The reason for this is that $\mathcal{E}$ tends to produce a smaller range of different numbers of replicas when observed at the same time t over the 1000 simulation runs.

We conclude that a definite structuring process is observable in our replica placement system. The degree of uncertainty (the entropy) is considerably lower than the maximum of 2 since the algorithms constrain the system to a mere $4 - 5\%$ of the possible state space. Thus, the system structures itself.

Adaptivity

Definition 4.2 states that every self-organizing system is also an adaptive system. It (re)organizes itself in order to adapt to a changing environment. Therefore, we first prove that the system is adaptive. We do this by mapping our system to the elements found in Zadeh's definition (Definition 4.4 on page 39) and by showing that this valid mapping fulfills the requirements for an adaptive system.

Let $\mathfrak{S}_{\mathcal{A}}$ be the system as defined above running the replica placement algorithm $\mathcal{A}^6$. The set of time-dependent input functions $\{S_\gamma\}$ contains all possible request distributions $q(t)$ generated by f_Q (Equation (8.10) on page 79). Since we assume a fixed client mobility model (see Section 8.3.2), the characteristics of a request distribution is only given by the dynamics model (see Section 8.3.3).

Let D_x denote the dynamics model, where $x = s$ for the sudden change model, $x = m$ for the moving change model, $x = o$ for the oscillating change model, and $x = n$ for static model that produces no change. Since each model (except for D_n) needs to be parameterized, we define the following sets of parameterized dynamics models:

$$
\begin{aligned}
D_s &= \{d_s(x)|0 < x \leq T\} \\
D_m &= \{d_m(x)|0 < x \leq 1\} \\
D_o &= \{d_o(x)|0 < x \leq 1\} \\
D_n &= \{d_n|d_n = d_s(x \geq T) \\
&= d_m(0) = d_o(0)\}
\end{aligned}
\tag{8.59}
$$

These are the sets of all possible parameterized dynamics models that may occur in our environment and that our model shall adapt to. Therefore, according to Zadeh's model, γ corresponds to a specific parameterized model, and we have

$$
\Gamma = D_s \cup D_m \cup D_o \cup D_n.
\tag{8.60}
$$

For example, if $\gamma = d_m(0.5)$, then $\{S_\gamma\} = \{S_{d_m(0.5)}\}$ and each simulation run under this setting produces a different request distribution $q(t) \in \{S_{d_m(0.5)}\}$. However, all $q(t) \in \{S_{d_m(0.5)}\}$ display the same characteristics generated by the parameterized dynamics model $d_m(0.5)$ (moving change dynamics with a move probability of 0.5).

The performance function $P(\gamma)$ is simply our cost function C. We denote the time-dependent cost produced under a parameterized dynamics model γ by a system $\mathfrak{S}_{\mathcal{A}}$ (running algorithm $\mathcal{A}$) as $C_\gamma^{\mathcal{A}}$ and define:

$$
\forall \gamma \in \Gamma : P(\gamma) = C_\gamma^{\mathcal{A}}
\tag{8.61}
$$

The only thing that is left to complete our mapping to Zadeh's model is the definition of the criterion of acceptability, W. We define a simple criterion by stating that the system's performance must be within a constant factor c of the optimal algorithm's

---

[6] According to the notation introduced in Definition 4.7, we should rather define a description $\mathfrak{D}_{\mathcal{A}}$ that employs algorithm $\mathcal{A}$. The proper notation for the system would then be $\mathfrak{S}_{\mathfrak{D}_{\mathcal{A}}}$. We avoid this for the sake of readability.

performance $C_{opt}(t)$ in order to be acceptable. If the system fulfills this criterion after a finite time, we say that it is *c-adaptive*. Thus, we define W_c as

$$W_c = \{f(t) \mid \exists t' : \forall t \geq t' : f(t) \leq c \cdot C_{opt}(t)\} \tag{8.62}$$

and say that $\mathfrak{S}_\mathcal{A}$ is c-adaptive if

$$\forall \gamma \in \Gamma : C_\gamma^\mathcal{A} \in W_c. \tag{8.63}$$

In reference to Zadeh's definition (Definition 4.4), we can also say that $\mathfrak{S}_\mathcal{A}$ maps Γ into W_c. We denote the time-dependent upper bound on the factor $x(t) = \frac{C_\gamma^\mathcal{A}(t)}{C_{opt}(t)}$ between the cost produced by the placement algorithm $\mathcal{A}$ under the dynamics model γ and the cost of the optimal algorithm as

$$b_\gamma^\mathcal{A}(t) = \min\left\{x \mid \forall t' \geq t : \frac{C_\gamma^\mathcal{A}(t')}{C_{opt}(t')} \leq x\right\} \tag{8.64}$$

and note that

$$\left(\exists t : b_\gamma^\mathcal{A}(t) \leq c\right) \Rightarrow \left(C_\gamma^\mathcal{A} \in W_c\right). \tag{8.65}$$

Furthermore,

$$\left(\exists t : \max_{\gamma \in \Gamma} \left(b_\gamma^\mathcal{A}(t)\right) = c\right) \Rightarrow \mathfrak{S}_\mathcal{A} \text{ is c-adaptive.} \tag{8.66}$$

In Table 8.2 (on page 138), we have collected the values for $b_\gamma^\mathcal{A}(t)$ for both online algorithms. The table lists all parameterized dynamics models that we have run simulations for and depicts $b_\gamma^\mathcal{A}(t)$ for four different values for t. Of course, the tested models are only a subset of Γ. However, the data does not indicate that other models behave differently. We give the data for different points in time to show informally that $\mathfrak{S}_\mathcal{S}$ and $\mathfrak{S}_\mathcal{E}$ need some time to adapt and reach their best performance towards the end of the simulation runs. The simulations have been run for 500000 ticks. We took the last measure of $b_\gamma^\mathcal{A}(t)$ at tick 300000 since with less ticks left to the end of the simulation run, $b_\gamma^\mathcal{A}(t)$ shows less statistical reliability.

The last row in Table 8.2 lists the maximum values over all measured models for the specific time t. According to this data and to Equation (8.66), $\mathfrak{S}_\mathcal{S}$ is 1.415-adaptive and $\mathfrak{S}_\mathcal{E}$ is 1.356-adaptive. It is important to note that these are only upper bounds on the adaptivity of the algorithms. These values could improve if the simulations were run longer. Thus, despite the constant changes in the environment, our algorithms continuously reduce the gap to the performance of the optimal algorithms.

Decentralized Control

To show that the replica placement system $\mathfrak{S}$ has no central controller, we proceed according to our Decomposition Theorem (Theorem 4.1). As our system definition and the preceding sections clearly indicate, the system consists of homogeneous components, similar to an ant colony. There is no single component that is dedicated to any higher-level control task. Any decomposition, therefore, results in two subsystems of homogeneous components $\mathfrak{S}_1$ and $\mathfrak{S}_2$. There are essentially three possible decompositions:

model γ	$b^S_\gamma(t)$ for $t =$				$b^E_\gamma(t)$ for $t =$			
	10000	50000	150000	300000	10000	50000	150000	300000
$d_m(0.0)$	2.860	1.723	1.415	1.355	2.565	1.510	1.369	1.342
$d_m(0.1)$	2.699	1.669	1.368	1.306	2.345	1.460	1.315	1.287
$d_m(0.2)$	2.794	1.722	1.366	1.312	2.499	1.459	1.328	1.286
$d_m(0.3)$	2.632	1.674	1.336	1.289	2.377	1.471	1.324	1.264
$d_m(0.4)$	2.725	1.701	1.345	1.300	2.357	1.477	1.318	1.285
$d_m(0.5)$	2.729	1.706	1.345	1.280	2.368	1.455	1.323	1.277
$d_m(0.6)$	2.751	1.662	1.319	1.281	2.382	1.478	1.302	1.272
$d_m(0.7)$	2.719	1.648	1.337	1.292	2.316	1.483	1.279	1.279
$d_m(0.8)$	2.702	1.651	1.334	1.302	2.297	1.490	1.313	1.274
$d_m(0.9)$	2.646	1.695	1.348	1.294	2.320	1.453	1.309	1.265
$d_m(1.0)$	2.706	1.668	1.347	1.280	2.362	1.424	1.294	1.266
$d_o(0.0)$	2.960	1.751	1.400	1.363	2.577	1.513	1.361	1.341
$d_o(0.1)$	2.882	1.753	1.407	1.355	2.558	1.496	1.359	1.337
$d_o(0.2)$	2.893	1.779	1.414	1.372	2.417	1.517	1.377	1.331
$d_o(0.3)$	2.898	1.749	1.421	1.389	2.537	1.508	1.400	1.353
$d_o(0.4)$	2.985	1.796	1.433	1.373	2.558	1.504	1.397	1.356
$d_o(0.5)$	2.950	1.771	1.438	1.392	2.544	1.530	1.364	1.332
$d_o(0.6)$	2.943	1.812	1.456	1.415	2.522	1.502	1.399	1.356
$d_o(0.7)$	2.874	1.804	1.422	1.377	2.510	1.494	1.370	1.323
$d_o(0.8)$	2.938	1.759	1.385	1.343	2.486	1.509	1.368	1.336
$d_o(0.9)$	2.898	1.774	1.403	1.369	2.555	1.472	1.363	1.330
$d_o(1.0)$	2.828	1.746	1.401	1.346	2.520	1.450	1.361	1.335
$d_s(10^4)$	2.681	1.692	1.344	1.306	2.470	1.548	1.345	1.345
$d_s(2 \cdot 10^4)$	2.627	1.656	1.311	1.294	2.359	1.522	1.351	1.299
$d_s(3 \cdot 10^4)$	2.686	1.680	1.363	1.309	2.420	1.514	1.337	1.298
$d_s(4 \cdot 10^4)$	2.589	1.660	1.336	1.286	2.285	1.487	1.364	1.320
$d_s(5 \cdot 10^4)$	2.677	1.753	1.368	1.286	2.338	1.588	1.373	1.336
$d_s(6 \cdot 10^4)$	2.755	1.652	1.331	1.322	2.346	1.565	1.358	1.321
$d_s(7 \cdot 10^4)$	2.711	1.617	1.375	1.312	2.347	1.525	1.377	1.325
$d_s(8 \cdot 10^4)$	2.630	1.648	1.414	1.349	2.283	1.516	1.372	1.336
$d_s(9 \cdot 10^4)$	2.794	1.664	1.357	1.336	2.393	1.515	1.383	1.320
$d_s(1 \cdot 10^5)$	2.676	1.631	1.370	1.352	2.383	1.457	1.385	1.311
max	2.985	1.812	1.456	1.415	2.577	1.588	1.400	1.356

Table 8.2: Adaptivity of S and E for all dynamics models.

1. $\mathfrak{S}_1 = \mathfrak{S}$ and $\mathfrak{S}_2 = \emptyset$,

2. $\mathfrak{S}_1 = \emptyset$ and $\mathfrak{S}_2 = \mathfrak{S}$, and

3. $\mathfrak{S}_1 \neq \emptyset$ and $\mathfrak{S}_2 \neq \emptyset$ and $\mathfrak{S}_1 \cup \mathfrak{S}_2 = \mathfrak{S}$.

Under the first two decompositions, either $\mathfrak{S}_1$ (in case 1) or $\mathfrak{S}_2$ (in case 2) can take over the function $f_\mathfrak{S}$ as they are equivalent to $\mathfrak{S}$. The placement system consisting of the distributed replicas that run the placement algorithm has no critical mass. That is, even with a single replica (if we prohibit replications), it still achieves a reduction in communication cost since that single replica may migrate to the best single-replica location. This basic function is also preserved as we increase the number of replicas, which is what the algorithm naturally does. An important property of our system is that replicas do not communicate directly. That is, they do not rely on the fact that any specific number of replicas is present in the system. Therefore, the replicas do their job irrespective of their number.

The only case in which a sensible reduction of communication cost is difficult is if we have too many replicas in the system. Then, the replication cost component would be overwhelmingly high and a useful reduction would not be possible.

Thus, if we assume that there are not too many replicas in the system, then any decomposition of the existing group of replica preserves the system's function $f_\mathfrak{S}$. Moreover, any group of replicas that is too large would converge to a smaller group by dissolving replicas, and, conversely, any group that is too small increases in size by replicating. This behavior inherently belongs to the algorithm.

Thus, a destructive decomposition is not possible which implies that there is no central controller in the system.

Global Knowledge and Local Interactions

None of the replicas has information on the global placement scheme. In fact, a replica does not know how many fellow replicas it has or even whether there are other replicas at all. There is also no reference to some global pattern with respect to the network topology or the client behavior. The sole information, that a replica using algorithm $\mathcal{S}$ has, consists of the following:

- A list of neighbor nodes stored locally on the network node occupied by the replica,

- the message flows received via each of the neighbors,

- the length of the paths traveled by messages.

Apart from the hop counters in messages, all of these items are strictly local in nature. The hop counter, too, does not transport any significant structural information to the replica.

Under algorithm $\mathcal{E}$, a replica may additionally access the paths taken by messages. One may argue that this represents non-local information about the network topology. However, this information only pertains to a small region of the network. Only in the very beginning, with a single replica, the path information may span a larger part of the network. However, even at this stage, it only represents partial information as only the routes are covered and not the topology graph. Furthermore, this does by no means represent the global structure since it does not contain any information about the placement of the other replicas. Thus, replicas have partial knowledge that covers increasingly less of the network as time progresses and that contains no information on the structure that is created. Therefore, we conclude that there is no global knowledge involved in running the distributed placement algorithm.

The interaction among replicas is restricted to the exchange of update messages for achieving data consistency. This communication is also partial in nature as replicas can reconcile in groups of arbitrary size irrespective of the actual global number of replicas (see Chapter 10). Moreover, this communication bears no information concerning the placement. Instead, update messages are used independent of their content in order to calculate message flows. Thus, there is no direct communication among replicas for the purpose of coordinating their global placement.

Conclusions

This completes our line of arguments and our classification. We showed that the replica placement system is self-organizing since it creates structure, it adapts to changes in client behavior, it has no central control, it has no reference to the global structure, and its components interact only locally.

On the Usefulness of Our Definition

It is worthwhile testing whether our definition of self-organization is really useful. The usefulness of a definition is given by its discriminating power. We have shown that our system lies within the set of systems covered by the definition. However, are there also systems that lie outside? And what would such systems look like? One variant of our own replica placement system that violates an important part of the definition would use a single replica placement that is not changed over time but that adapts nevertheless. Such a fixed-placement system could, for example, increase a globally defined time period after which a new reconciliation is executed between the existing replicas. This change of a global scalar value is no structural change according to our definition. Common definitions of the terms structure and organization [11] as well as our intuition also indicate that a single scalar value does not exhibit any form of organization at all. Therefore, we have created a system that is adaptive according the Zadeh's definition but does not change its structure and, thus, is not self-organizing.

Another example of a placement system that lies outside the definition of self-organization is the greedy algorithm. It adapts and changes its structure, but it does so with reference to the global pattern and in a centralized way.

8.8.2   Emergent Properties

In this section, we take a closer look at some of the interesting emergent properties of the replica placement system. These are features that may not be obvious from an analysis of the algorithms we presented. However, they can either further our understanding of the way in which the system functions, or they represent additional benefits that were not directly targeted during the design phase.

Replica Placement Patterns

The collective adaptation process of all replicas creates a global pattern consisting of the cells of a Voronoi decomposition. This is simply a consequence of the first feedback rule introduced in Section 8.4.1 which states that clients always use the closest replica. In each cell, a replica serves all requests being issued inside the cell. The replica placement algorithm replicates and migrates the set of replicas such that a stable configuration is reached that minimizes the network load. This process partitions the network into the Voronoi cells. An interesting emergent property of the system is the interaction between the replicas. They do not communicate directly with one another in order to coordinate their actions in the creation process of the cell pattern. Nevertheless, they interact. However, this interaction is indirect.

Figure 8.39 depicts how the cell structure changes if the replica configuration is changed. Figure 8.39(a) shows a stable Voronoi cell pattern with three replicas: Each replica is placed at about the center of its cell and, thus, the forces applied by client requests are about the same in all directions[7]. Let us assume that, due to some disturbance in the request patterns, a new replica r_4 is created between r_2 and r_3. The resulting Voronoi diagram is shown in Figure 8.39(b). This disturbance

---

[7]Note that we assume that clients are uniformly distributed on the plane in this example.

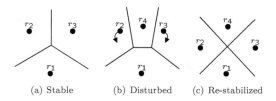

(a) Stable   (b) Disturbed   (c) Re-stabilized

Figure 8.39: Pattern formation in a system with multiple replicas.

causes a change in the cells of r_2 and r_3 which results in a configuration where these replicas are close to the borders of their Voronoi cells. As a consequence, they start receiving an unbalanced flow of requests since the requests coming from the upper part of the plane are redirected to the new replica r_4. According to the migration rule, r_2 and r_3 are forced to move to a position where the flows are in balance again. The resulting four-cell setup is depicted in Figure 8.39(c). Thus, a reconfiguration on a global scale is caused by a local disturbance without any direct communication taking place between the replicas.

This is clearly a stigmergic effect (cf. Section 3.4.1 and [61, 46]). We may consider the partitioning into cells as the subject of the replicas work. Each replica observes its own cell and tries to find a location where the request flow forces are in balance. If one replica significantly changes its location, the shape of its own cell changes as a result. This also influences the neighboring cells. They change in size and/or shape. These changes, in turn, stimulate the replicas covering these cells to find new locations and restore the balance of request flows again. Thus, the replicas interact indirectly via the cell structure. By doing so, they coordinate on a global scale and reestablish a stable global placement scheme. Of course, this behavior is not present in the specification of a single replica and its placement algorithm. It emerges as soon as two or more replicas partition the network into cells.

Reduction in Overall Network Load

Another very important emergent effect is the global reduction in network traffic. The placement algorithm does not contain any statement about minimizing the global network load. It merely specifies that a replication has to be executed if requests come from too far away, and a migration is necessary if one incoming request flow dominates the others. Obviously, the overall system that is composed of replicas applying these simple rules achieves a reduction of the network load. Thus far, we implicitly considered the replicas in combination with the placement algorithms as the lower-level components of the system. However, at a different level of abstraction, we may also say that the placement system is composed of our two feedback rules:

1. Clients always use the closest replica and

2. Replicas try to get closer to clients (implemented by a composition of the replication rule and the migration rule).

Obviously, if any of these two rules was missing, the remaining rule could not achieve the reduction in network load: In a system with a fixed static set of replicas (second rule not present), the fact that clients use the closest replica would keep the network load at about the same level. However, the load would not be reduced. If, on the other hand, clients would not be sending requests to their closest replica (first rule not present), then any adaptation effort of the replicas would be in vain because clients may actually also use the replica that is furthest away. Thus, the composition of these two rules results in the system having the emergent property of reducing the overall network load.

Balancing Message Flows

The migration rule leads to the placement of replicas at positions where message flows are balanced. Thus, for each replica, there is no single incoming flow that outweighs the remaining flows. This does not only reduce the global network load, but it also leads to a more balanced usage of the network links since the same quantity of messages is distributed more evenly over the incoming links of a replica's node. If the flows entering a replica are not balanced, then one link may receive much more traffic than the others. This may lead to congestion on this link while the capacity of the others is not fully used. Figures 8.6 and 8.10 depict examples of this effect.

Number of Replicas Created

The number of replicas created by our placement algorithms is not directly part of the algorithms' specification. Instead, it is implicitly given by the replication radius ρ and the network diameter D, as has been shown in Section 8.5.4 (see Figure 8.11). As long as the existing replicas do not cover the network, there is still a force to create more replicas. At some point in time, there are enough replicas such that each of them serves a flow of requests with an average path length of $\leq \rho$. This ends the replication process and enables the system to enter a stable configuration. The number of replicas grows when the network gets larger and when ρ is decreased.

Balancing the Processing Load

Besides the reduction in network load, the placement system also balances the processing load that is required for serving all client requests. This is a direct consequence of the replication. Thus, it may not be surprising, but it is an emergent property since the concept of load balancing is also not present in the system's description.

It should be noted that the processing load is not necessarily distributed equally over all replicas. This was no immediate design goal. It may be that one replica serves high volumes of requests while another one has only a light processing load. This depends on the volume of requests produced in each replica cell. However, the processing load is still distributed over multiple nodes and, thus, load peaks are reduced.

We have experimented with a load balancing scheme that explicitly tries to divide the load more equally between the replicas. To do this, we exploited the extended features of our service lookup system that is introduced in the next chapter. This system is able to disseminate information about the current load experienced by each replica throughout the network. Thus, this information can be made available to clients and they can decide to use the replica with the lowest load. The results of these experiments where rather disappointing since they lead to erratic and oscillating behavior. The problem lies in the fact that clients opting for the replica with the lowest load have to violate our first feedback rule since the replica with the lowest load is not always the closest one. This disturbs the core mechanism of our system. Even if we combine the lowest-load rule with the original lowest-distance rule in some way, we get unsatisfactory results as this leads to inherently unstable configurations: Suppose a client c used replica r_1 and then chooses a less heavily loaded replica r_2. c starts directing its requests to r_2 which leads to an increase in load at r_2 while the load at r_1 decreases. This increases the attractiveness of r_1 which may result in c switching to r_1 again. The consequence is an oscillating behavior that forces replicas to adapt constantly since the set of clients that send requests to one replica changes periodically.

8.8.3 Applicability to Different Service Categories

An important issue that we have already touched in our quantitative evaluation is the appropriateness of our approach for different classes of services. Since we propose a system that replicates and migrates services at runtime, it is intuitively clear that this sets some limits to its applicability. Obviously, the key factors in this context are

1. the requirement to keep a number of replicas (more precisely the data they hold) consistent with each other, and

2. the fact that we have to transmit a replica's state for a migration.

A consistency protocol that is used to transfer updates between the replicas forces them to stay closer together if the write ratio increases. There is a point at which the creation of replicas is not beneficial anymore because the high reconciliation traffic between them outweighs the reduction in request traffic. A similar argument can be made for the migration cost induced by the size of a replica's state: Depending on the choice of the adaptation interval, there is a certain value for the state size at which migrations do not amortize anymore over the next interval. At this size, the network load caused by migrations exceeds the amount of request traffic that may be saved by migrating replicas.

Thus, the set of conditions, under which runtime replication and migration is beneficial, critically depends on the write ratio w and on the average replica size σ. But what does "beneficial" actually mean? As we stated in the discussion on the benchmark algorithms that we compared our algorithms against, the random algorithm is really the only realistic contestant. The other algorithms use global knowledge, either in space (greedy algorithm) or in time and space (optimal algorithm). Furthermore, the random algorithm, as we have defined it, has an advantage over a *real* random algorithm in that it knows the optimal number of replicas. Based on these facts, we choose two algorithms as a yardstick for measuring the applicability of our approach depending on w and σ:

1. The random algorithm as we have defined it (called $\mathcal{R}$ hereafter), and

2. an additional algorithm that we call *random single* (called $\mathcal{Q}$ hereafter).

The *random single algorithm* has no information at all. It does not know the optimal number of replicas. Therefore, it is very conservative and chooses to place a single replica only. Since it also has no information on the request patterns in the network, it places its sole replica randomly. Note that if an algorithm has no information on the number of replicas that is appropriate, then any number $|R| > 1$ may either be beneficial or counterproductive, depending on the request patterns.

Defining Applicability

We say that our system is applicable for a pair (w, σ), if the cost $C^{\mathcal{A}}(w, \sigma)$ produced by online placement algorithm $\mathcal{A}$ lies below the cost $C^{\mathcal{R}}(w, \sigma)$ of the random algorithm and $C^{\mathcal{Q}}(w, \sigma)$ of the random single algorithm respectively.

We evaluate the applicability of $C^{\mathcal{E}}$ based on the data presented in Figures 8.28 and 8.30. These graphs show that $C^{\mathcal{E}}$ grows linearly with w and with σ. A linear regression yields the following linear equations:

$$C^{\mathcal{E}}(w) \;=\; a_1 + b_1 \cdot w \qquad\qquad (8.67)$$
$$C^{\mathcal{E}}(\sigma) \;=\; a_2 + b_2 \cdot \sigma \qquad\qquad (8.68)$$

with

$$a_1 = 3.229, \; b_1 = 4.282, \; a_2 = 3.189, \; \text{and} \; b_2 = 3.048 \cdot 10^{-5}. \qquad (8.69)$$

To simplify the derivation of $C^{\mathcal{E}}(w, \sigma)$, we assume that both y-intercepts are equal to their arithmetic mean: $\bar{a} = a_1 = a_2 = 3.21$. This introduces only a very small offset of about 0.02 and -0.02 to the actual curves. Now, the cost produced by $\mathcal{E}$ for any combination (w, σ) is given by

$$C^{\mathcal{E}}(w, \sigma) \;=\; \bar{a} + b_1 \cdot w + b_2 \cdot \sigma \qquad\qquad (8.70)$$

$C^{\mathcal{R}}(w, \sigma)$ can be deduced from the data presented in Figures 8.28 and 8.30. Since $C^{\mathcal{R}}(w, \sigma)$ is independent of σ (no migrations in the random algorithm) and, thus, constant for all values of σ, we simply have $C^{\mathcal{R}}(w, \sigma) = C^{\mathcal{R}}(w)$ (depicted in Figure 8.30). Since the random single algorithm is independent of the replica size σ (no migrations) and also of w (no replication), $C^{\mathcal{Q}}(w, \sigma)$ has a constant value. Experiments yielded $C^{\mathcal{Q}}(w, \sigma) = 6.97$ with a 95% confidence interval of 0.02.

$\mathcal{E}$ is applicable versus $\mathcal{R}$ for (w, σ) if and only if $C^{\mathcal{E}}(w, \sigma) \leq C^{\mathcal{R}}(w, \sigma)$. The same statement can be made for $\mathcal{Q}$. We call this the *applicability condition*.

Applicability Analysis

Figure 8.40 depicts the results of the applicability analysis. Note that these graphs do not imply some functional dependency between σ and w. They show the regions of the parameter space spanned by w (x-axis) and σ (y-axis) that represent combinations of w and σ for which our applicability condition holds with respect to $\mathcal{Q}$ (Figure 8.40(a)) and $\mathcal{R}$ (Figure 8.40(b)). Thus, the figures present classifications of points in the space spanned by the two parameters. For the combinations of w and σ that lie inside the shaded area in Figure 8.40(a), $C^{\mathcal{E}}(w, \sigma) \leq C^{\mathcal{Q}}(w, \sigma)$ holds. For the shaded area in Figure 8.40(b), $C^{\mathcal{E}}(w, \sigma) \leq C^{\mathcal{R}}(w, \sigma)$ holds.

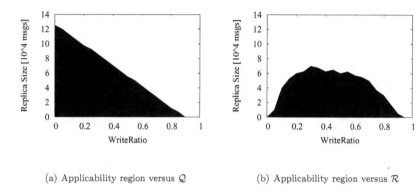

(a) Applicability region versus $\mathcal{Q}$ (b) Applicability region versus $\mathcal{R}$

Figure 8.40: Applicability regions in the space spanned by w and σ.

Figure 8.40(a) simply separates the points on the cost plane defined by Equation (8.70) into the ones that have a cost smaller than the constant value of $C^{\mathcal{Q}}(w, \sigma) = 6.97$ and those whose cost is higher. Since the cost $C^{\mathcal{E}}(w, \sigma)$ increases linearly towards the right and towards the top of the graph, the result is a linear separation: For higher values of the write ratio w, the acceptable replica size σ decreases (and vice versa). $C^{\mathcal{R}}(w, \sigma)$ is not constant, as can be verified in Figure 8.30. As the write ratio increases, $C^{\mathcal{R}}(w, \sigma)$ first increases and then, for values higher than $w = 0.7$, it decreases again. As a result, we have no simple linear separation of the parameter plane. Due to the low cost of the random algorithm for a low write ratio, the acceptable replica size is small for small values of w. Then it increases and decreases again analogously to $C^{\mathcal{R}}(w, \sigma)$ in Figure 8.30.

Note that the depicted classification is only valid if all parameters of the algorithms have the fixed values found in Section 8.7.2. If, for example, the adaptation interval is increased, then the general level of replica sizes that are acceptable rises as the migration cost has more time to amortize. As a result, both classification regions in Figure 8.40 are shifted upwards and the class of settings for which our algorithms are applicable is increased. Of course, a larger adaptation interval also means that the algorithms need longer to converge to a stable, low-cost configuration.

Applying the Applicability Measure

We deliberately refrain from specifying a list of services to which our online placement algorithms are applicable. The compilation of such a list would be based on overly restrictive and arbitrary assumptions. Instead, the methodology for the applicability analysis given above can be used to test whether a given service with known properties may profit from the self-organizing placement system. Assuming that one has a good estimation of w and σ for the service in question, one can use the classification diagrams presented in Figure 8.40 (or variants thereof for other alternative placement algorithms and parameter settings) and quickly find out whether the service should be distributed dynamically using our placement algorithms or not.

In general, we conclude that a replica size in the order of 10^4 times the size of an average client request message and write ratios of well beyond 20% should cover some useful services. Remember that σ may be interpreted as the number of data records stored by a replica.

8.9 Discussion

In this chapter, we have presented a detailed discussion of our self-organizing online replica placement system for the Ad hoc Service Grid infrastructure. We have shown that the respective algorithms that we have developed are able to adapt to changes in request patterns using only local information, simple rules, and no inter-replica communication. By using request flows as stimuli and through indirect interactions via their environment, our placement algorithms outperform an established alternative algorithm that is allowed to use global knowledge and centralized control. Moreover, it performs significantly better than the ad hoc alternative of random placement.

We have also presented a detailed qualitative evaluation in which we have shown that our algorithms are adaptive and self-organizing. In order to enable the reader to evaluate our claim and our evidence, we presented a concise definition of all relevant elements of our system. Similar to naturally occurring self-organizing systems, our system follows two basic, simple rules (cf. Section 8.4.1) that introduce positive and negative feedback in the placement process. This leads to a quick build-up of structure (positive feedback) and, eventually, to a stable configuration that does not change significantly as long as the request patterns sustain (negative feedback). This represents an important contribution to the design of self-organizing systems in the domain of computer science since it shows how the concepts of complex systems (e.g. feedback) can be used in a more abstract way. Most computer science projects that claim to produce self-organizing software or hardware systems, adopt rather obvious approaches observable in nature. The overwhelming part of these projects is targeted on designing systems based on the metaphor of social insects (ants, termites, wasps etc.). We did not take that same research path, by employing the obvious phenotypical design patterns (ants, pheromones, trails etc.). Instead, we have employed the concepts found in these and other systems in a more abstract way. The key elements that we identify for a more general design process of such systems are:

- An interplay between positive and negative feedback: Self-organizing systems create structure quickly (by positive feedback) and explicitly accept solutions that may not be optimal but pretty good. More importantly, such structures are stabilized as an effect of negative feedback.

- The usage-driven, reactive nature: External stimuli (in our case the client requests) are used to structure the system in order to adapt to these stimuli.

- Simple, robust mechanisms: Our system does not employ any mechanisms that are overly complex by themselves. A good example is the trivial predictive mechanism employed to infer some information about the future. This mechanism seems inadequate at first glance. However, the performance of our system even under dynamic request patterns shows that it works very well. Simplicity and robustness go hand in hand in self-organizing system: An elementary mechanism that can be understood and verified quickly is more robust than a sophisticated mechanism since the variety of ways in which it may fail or misbehave is much smaller. This is even more important as the interaction of a number of such mechanisms introduces a higher level of complexity that still needs to be manageable.

- Indirect, stigmergic interaction: It seems that stigmergic interaction is almost a by-product of our system. Indeed, it seems inevitable that a group of lower-level components that autonomously manipulate their environment also interact via that environment. In classical computer science, such *side effects* are in most cases considered undesirable since they tend to be uncontrollable (e.g. in software engineering). In complex adaptive system, however, they are the *glue* between the components. It seems that explicitly modeled complex interaction patterns (protocols) between the components of a computer system tend to produce a multitude of unwanted side-effects like deadlocks and race conditions. These effects need to be detected or explicitly prevented which makes such systems brittle and prone to failure. In natural self-organizing systems, the relation between effect and side effect is completely different: Explicit interactions are rather simple and sometimes there is no explicit interaction at all. The desirable effects produced by such systems seem to stem from the side effects of the components' actions. As a message for the design of artificial self-organizing systems, we conclude that we should rather try to design the side effects of much simpler direct interactions.

Finally, we presented a method for analyzing the applicability of our system to a specific service with known properties. This enables a general classification of all possible services into two classes:

1. The class of services that can benefit from the advantages offered by our dynamic service placement system, and

2. the complement of that class, for which other, more conservative placement strategies (*random* or *random single*) would be advisable.

Based on the data resulting from the applicability analysis, we conclude that the set of useful services in the first of these classes is non-empty.

Chapter 9

Service Lookup and Discovery

Contents

The Ad hoc Service Grid environment is highly dynamic by its very nature. The fact that services may replicate and migrate at runtime is positive in terms of quality of service and load balancing. However, it has a negative effect on the clients' ability to discover a service and find an appropriate replica for their purposes. The core service that is responsible for this is called the *ASG Lookup Service* [75]. This service accepts registration requests from newly created *value-added service replicas* (replicas of services that provide some function to users) and can be queried by clients to find

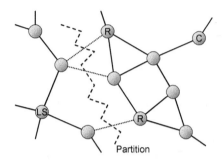

Figure 9.1: Isolated Lookup Service problem.

the *most adequate* replica. The most obvious choice for implementing such a Lookup Service would be a single centralized instance that runs under a well-known address in the network. Such a centralized service would not require any lookup itself and would always have consistent information about service replicas. However, the distributed and dynamic nature of the ASG makes a centralized Lookup Service infeasible. A single Lookup Service for an entire ASG would decrease its availability, especially, if partitions occur. In this case, some clients may theoretically be able to access replicas of a desired service that are positioned in their own partition. However, if the central Lookup Services is outside their partition, these clients are unable to get up-to-date information on the replicas' current positions. This problem, resulting from an isolation of the Lookup Service, is depicted in Figure 9.1. Moreover, the mobility of client devices can be expected to be much higher than that of service replicas. If we assume that a client is interested in interacting with the nearest replica in order to minimize the service's response time, then a client will regularly have to query the Lookup Service to get the position of the nearest replica. Thus, the network traffic caused by replicas updating the Lookup Service with their new position is much lower than the traffic caused by client queries. Therefore, distributing the Lookup Service and positioning instances of it as close to clients as possible is beneficial, as it reduces query traffic throughout the whole ASG network. On the other hand, the additional traffic introduced by updating the distributed Lookup Service instances can be minimized by applying intelligent updating strategies, as we will show in the discussion of our *lazy reply-driven update mechanism*.

For these reasons, the Lookup Service in the ASG is distributed. In this chapter we introduce its structure and architecture. We explain how the information about replica positions is distributed in a self-organized way. This update mechanism exploits the knowledge about client activity that is implicitly given by the flow of client requests, to disseminate replica positions only to those Lookup Service instances that are actively involved in resolving client queries. This is done in a lazy fashion to avoid unnecessary updates as much as possible.

The maintenance of replica location information is a continuous, collective achievement of the distributed Lookup Service instances. The algorithms proposed in Chapter 8 heavily rely on correct information about the distance between clients and all available replicas. Clients must be assigned an appropriate replica that is closest to their current position. Therefore, the Lookup Service instance used by a client c

should ideally know

1. the complete set of all available replicas R of a specific service type, and

2. the distance between c and each replica in R

in order to assign the correct replica to c.

Of course, due to the system's dynamics, the decentralization, and a variety of possible failures that may happen, a certain level of incorrectness must be tolerated. Keeping the location information held by the distributed Lookup Service instances as accurate as possible, even in the face of dynamics and failures, is the main goal of the Lookup System. To enable this, the system has some inherent mechanisms that enable self-healing and self-stabilization.

The key to these features is that we allow the overall system to degrade gracefully. Our definition of a correct system state under which the system operates acceptably well, includes a wide range of working conditions. We explicitly *allow inconsistencies and even errors* to occur in the Lookup System and devise a system that is able to deal with such situations and to repair them when they are critical.

The ASG Lookup Service has the following functions:

- **Registry of service types and replicas:** Whenever a replica is installed somewhere in the ASG, it registers at the Lookup Service. Similarly, a replica unregisters when it dissolves.

- **Maintenance of replica location information:** The ASG Lookup Service is specifically designed to keep the information about the current replica locations up-to-date even if they are migrating at runtime.

- **Discovery of services:** Clients may not know all service types that are available in an ASG. The Lookup Service offers a list of all service types to the user who may choose an appropriate one. For this purpose, an appropriate description should be provided for each type. This description could contain plain, human-readable text, syntactic information on how to invoke the service, and semantic information for automatically composing services. However, the concrete description technique is out of scope of this book.

- **Lookup of service replicas:** When a client has decided to use a specific service, it needs to access a replica of that service. Thus, after the discovery, the client queries the Lookup Service to find an *appropriate replica*. Thus, the Lookup Service implements the function $f_{CR}(t)$ defined by Equation (8.20) (on page 81). The appropriateness of a specific replica may depend on arbitrary runtime properties. One such property that is always implicitly used is the distance between the client and the replica. However, the Lookup Service is able to disseminate, collect, and store additional information about replicas. For example, the current load of replicas may also be used for selecting an appropriate one. The Lookup Service uses a fitness function that may combine several factors like distance and load to rank the available replicas and then it chooses the best service for the querying client. Note, however, that the discussion on possible additional ranking factors is out of scope here. We implicitly assume that replicas are ranked according to their distance to the client.

- **Downloading client application code:** Similar to Jini [159], the ASG
  Lookup Service allows clients to download client code for using a service. This
  code may be used by other software components at the user's device or by
  the user directly (e.g. a graphical user interface) to access the service. The
  mechanisms required for this kind of functionality are straight-forward and
  well-known. We will not discuss them any further in this book.

The rest of this chapter is structured as follows. First, we take a look at the foundations and related work in Section 9.1. Afterwards, we explain the overall architecture of the Lookup Service in Section 9.2 and explain how location information is
disseminated in an ASG network. Especially, the idea of partial consistency and the
self-healing ability will be discussed here. In Section 9.3, we will give a more formal
definition of what comprises a legal state of the Lookup System. We will see that
this definition is a very weak one, allowing for a broad range of working conditions
under which a correct mode of operation is preserved. Subsequently, we explain how
various classes of failures leading to incorrect states can be corrected automatically
by the Lookup System to restore a legal state. Experimental results, that confirm the
effectiveness and the efficiency of the Lookup System, will be presented in Section
9.4. Finally, we discuss several issues and possible shortcomings in Section 9.5.

9.1 Foundations and Related Work

Any service infrastructure that involves a certain degree of dynamics has to provide
some means for discovering and looking up services. Therefore, a wide variety of
different lookup architectures have been proposed and implemented by research and
industry. The most prominent industrial standards are Jini [159], UPnP [170], and
Salutation [168]. Jini was designed to support nomadic, Java-enabled environments
where mobile devices join an existing network and use services in an ad hoc manner.
A Jini lookup service is discovered using multicast. It may offer Java-based service
interfaces that are downloaded to a mobile device in order to interact with a given
service. Jini lookup services can form a hierarchy and requests may be passed up
this hierarchy for resolution. Universal Plug and Play (UPnP) is a framework defined at a much lower level than Jini. It offers IP address allocation and DNS name
assignment for mobile devices and builds, for example, on DHCP. UPnP's Simple
Service Discovery Protocol (SSDP) supports registration and discovery of devices.
This may involve dedicated directory services but does not rely on them. In Salutation, devices use a Salutation Manager (SLM) for the lookup process. SLMs may
exchange registration information and support clients by mediating data transport
that covers different transport protocols. A client queries a near-by SLM in a similar
way as is done in the ASG Lookup Service. However, none of these industry standards support service replication and mobility explicitly. The dynamics covered by
these approaches is related to *physical mobility* (device mobility) rather than *logical
mobility* (software mobility).

In mobile agent research, several lookup mechanisms have been devised that explicitly
support logical mobility [94, 150, 101]. They either use brute force mechanisms to
find a mobile agent, log current positions at a more or less centralized server, or
they set up forwarding chains to follow the route taken by agents [9]. However,

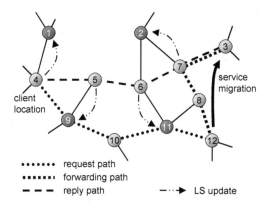

Figure 9.2: Reply-driven Lookup Service update.

maintaining replicated agents and mediating *adequate* replicas upon client requests is not an issue in this area.

9.2 Lookup Service Architecture

The ASG Lookup Service is decentralized. No single entity has control over the complete lookup system and the location information provided to clients. One instance of the distributed Lookup Service is running on each cluster head. Consequently, each node in the network either hosts an instance of the Lookup Service, or it has one running on one of its neighbor nodes. This is implied by the way in which the network is clustered (cf. Section 5.1.4 and, in particular, Figure 5.1). Thus, wherever a client connects to the ASG network, it can quickly discover services, lookup service replica, and download client-side service components. However, this also means that information about the positions of service replica needs to be disseminated across the Lookup Service instances in order for it to be available locally when needed. Since the ASG supports service replication and migration, this poses special problems not present in other lookup systems like Jini, UPnP, or Salutation.

9.2.1 Update Process Overview

Before we go into the details of the architecture and its elements, we give a high-level overview of the basic mechanisms employed. In the ASG, there is a fundamental trade-off between the network load caused by Lookup Service updates and the accuracy of the information provided by the Lookup Service. Keeping all Lookup Service instances up-to-date all the time would cause a large message overhead. Not doing so may cause clients to fail because they rely on outdated location information. To solve this problem, we employ a lazy, reply-driven update strategy that involves not only the Lookup Service instances themselves, but also the Proxy Agents and another set of components called *Lookup Snooper Agents* that are running on each node. These three distributed entities collaborate in the update process.

Figure 9.2 depicts the basic idea of the update scheme. We assume that, initially, a service replica r is running on node 12 and a requesting client c is connected to node 4. At that point, the Lookup Services at the cluster heads 1, 2, 9, and 11 have the correct location of r. This information gets outdated as r moves from node 12 to node 3. A reason for this migration could be a shift of request load that can be compensated by moving towards this direction. However, for the update protocol, this is not relevant. Immediately after the service migration, c still has the old service location information and continues sending its requests to node 12. The Proxy Agent on that node has been informed by r about its migration before r left. This Proxy forwards the requests to the new location of r (node 3). It stores meta information in the forwarded requests, that marks them as *forwarded* and contains the new location of r. r gets a forwarded request and generates a reply. The meta information from the request message is automatically copied into the reply. After that, r sends the reply back to c. As depicted in Figure 9.2, the reply message may take a different route than that traveled by the request. As the reply is routed through the network, the so-called *Lookup Snooper Agents* on that route inspect the message and extract its meta information. One Lookup Snooper Agent is running on each node. When such an agent detects a service reply message whose meta information marks it a belonging to a forwarded request, it sends a *service location update message* to its cluster head (depicted as arrows in Figure 9.2). This message is read by the cluster head's Lookup Service that, in turn, updates its location information base with the new location of r. Thus, triggered by the reply, all Lookup Services along the way, including the one used by the requesting client c on node 1, will eventually be updated. We assume that c regularly requests the current location of r at the Lookup Service. As a consequence, after some requests have been forwarded by the Proxy Agent on node 12, c finally gets the updated information and sends its requests directly to node 3. At that point, normal operation is restored and the Lookup Services at nodes 1, 2, 9, and 11 are up-to-date again.

9.2.2   Partial Consistency and Self-Healing Properties

Note how only those parts of the lookup infrastructure are updated that are close to the reply path. Lookup Services that are further away are not involved. Moreover, the update information is carried by reply messages. Only a small number of additional messages are necessary ("LS update" arrows in Figure 9.2, also called *snooping messages* hereafter). In this way, the network load caused by the update process is minimized, but at the same time, the *active parts* of the network are kept up-to-date. This is depicted in Figure 9.3. The request/reply path between two nodes and the update messages are shown using dashed lines and arrows. Lookup Service instances running on cluster heads outside the shaded region are not informed about the location change. They remain outdated until a request passes through their own cluster.

An active propagation phase precedes this process of continuous self-healing. This active propagation is triggered when a replica r is initially started. After its start, r registers with its local Lookup Service, that, in turn, propagates this new registration once to all other Lookup Services to establish this information throughout the system. This is necessary since a client needs at least the information about which replicas are running. This initial propagation uses a *cluster head broadcast* mechanism offered

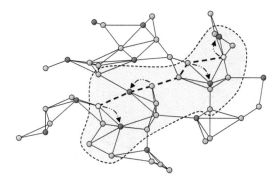

Figure 9.3: Example for the regional restriction of a single update.

by the routing system. A similar propagation is done to remove information from the system when a service replica dissolves.

Even in remote regions of the network, where no update arrives over extended periods of time, the outdated location information received during the initial registration of a replica is sufficient to find it. If a client request is issued from such a region, the forwarding mechanism directs it to the requested replica r. The client's local Lookup Service updates its table with the correct location received with the replica's reply. Since the prior information about r's location may have been very old, it may have moved further away in the meantime. Thus, upon the next query by the client, the Lookup Service may choose a different replica r' (of the same service type) that is assumed to be closer. The process of replica selection, request forwarding, and location updating in the Lookup Service may repeat itself a number of times as long as the selected replicas drop in the distance ranking and another replica appears at the top of the list. This mechanism may cause a number of replicas to drop in the distance-based ranking. However, it cannot cause an improvement in ranking for replicas that moved closer since the initial update. An example is depicted in Figure 9.4.

This configuration is the result of the following adaptations:

$$(8 \to \overset{r_2}{\cdots} \to 10)|(5 \to \overset{r_3}{\cdots} \to 3)|(10 \to \overset{r_4}{\cdots} \to 8)$$

The Lookup Service of client c at node 1 received its last update before these adaptations were issued by the replica placement system. Therefore, its replica table holds three outdated entries for r_2, r_3, and r_4. Only the entry for r_1 is still up-to-date. The table holds the replica ID (first column), the node it is located on (second column), and the distance to the replica (third column). At the bottom of Figure 9.4 the updates of the replica table of LS are shown that occur as c is first directed to r_3 and then to r_4. The respective replies cause an update and r_3 and r_4 are demoted to lower position in the table. Finally, r_1 reaches the top of the ranking, and since it is still 3 hops away, it is eventually used as the closest replica. Note that, in reality, r_2 is closer than r_1. But since it was never chosen, never received a request, and was never able to send a reply, its location has not been updated.

Thus, one Lookup Service may eventually choose a replica that is objectively not

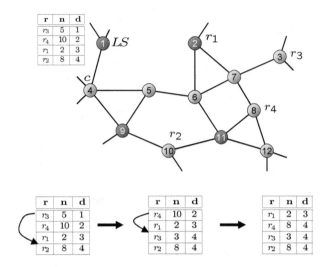

Figure 9.4: Incremental Lookup Service update.

the closest to its client even if we assume that the actual measurement of distances is correct. At first glance, this seems to violate our first feedback rule (cf. Section 8.4.1). However, if the request flow sent from the clients to the suboptimal replica r_1 is significant, then the replica placement algorithm will eventually push that replica closer to those clients. Therefore, the fact that it was appointed as the closest replica actually makes it the closest replica. If the request flow is not significant, then the suboptimal solution is tolerable. Note that such situations tend to be resolved by the general dynamics in the system. For example, replies issued for other clients in the same region are likely to correct the information in the outdated Lookup Service. Thus, such configurations in which clients work with replicas that are not closest to them may be active temporarily, but they are usually not permanent. Moreover, in high-load situations where such suboptimal configurations are not acceptable, the probability that they are resolved quickly is high since a high request/reply load implies that updates can be issued very quickly throughout the network. Vice versa, if such a configuration lasts for a long period of time, this is an indication that the overall system is not highly loaded and, thus, the suboptimal behavior is tolerable.

This lookup architecture is self-healing since the lazy updating process is active throughout the network at any time, and it is automatically triggered only if location changes occur. Thus, a divergence of location information is explicitly allowed and repaired as a *side effect* of the normal interaction between clients and services. The Lookup Services themselves are only passively involved in this process.

9.2.3   Request Forwarding by Proxy Agents

Even though the Proxy Agents are not merely dedicated to the lookup update process, they play an important role. At each node, the local Proxy Agent is responsible for relaying requests to services, analyzing request patterns, triggering migrations or

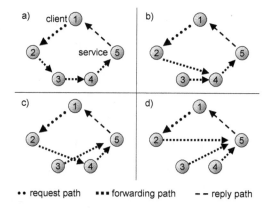

•• request path   ■■■ forwarding path   – – reply path

Figure 9.5: Establishing forwarding shortcuts.

replications, and forwarding requests to services that migrated away. The forwarding process may involve more than one Proxy if the service has gone through several migrations. If a replica r executed a series of migrations over the nodes $v_1, \ldots, v_k$, then the Proxy at node v_i only has the information that r has migrated to v_{i+1} (the replica's next location). When it forwards a request, the Proxy at that next location may also have to forward it because the service has already left for the next node v_{i+2}. Thus, a chain of forwards may occur. Note that forwarding loops can be avoided by removing any existing forward for a replica r if r arrives at a node it has visited previously.

A simple shortcut mechanism reduces the length of forwarding chains. This can save transmissions and reduce latency. Figure 9.5 depicts how shortcuts can be made in forwarding chains that eventually eliminate any intermediate Proxies between the one receiving the original request and the one currently hosting the service. This can be achieved by introducing one additional message type. If a Proxy receives a forwarded message from the previous Proxy in the chain, it sends a *redirect forward message* back to the sending Proxy to set that Proxy's next hop to its own next hop. For example, node 3 in Figure 9.5a sends a *redirect forward message* back to node 2 when it receives the forwarded request. The redirect contains the next forward hop of node 3 (which is node 4). Now, node 2 uses node 4 as its next hop and bypasses node 3 (Figure 9.5b). Next, node 4 redirects node 3 directly to node 5. Figure 9.5c shows the situation after the first request has been forwarded to the service's new location (node 5). When the second request is forwarded, node 4 redirects node 2 to use node 5 as its next hop. At that point, all forwards point directly to the service's new location and the chain is resolved (Figure 9.5d). This approach does not require any additional state in the forwarded messages. Moreover, it has the nice feature of reducing chains based on their usage: If a chain is not really used, no resources will be wasted to make it shorter. The more messages pass through it, the shorter it gets. An alternative would be to let the Proxy at the new service location send messages to all forwarding nodes and redirect them in one step. However, this requires the complete forwarding path to be put into the forwarded messages.

9.2.4   The Lookup Snooper Agent

A Lookup Snooper Agent (LSA) is running on each node and uses the snooping API provided by the middleware to inspect all messages that originate at or pass through the node. Its snooping filter matches all messages whose meta data marks them as *forwards* and as *service replies*. Every Proxy that forwards the respective request, puts the last known *service record*[1] of the requested service into the request's meta data. Thus, when the request eventually arrives at the service, it contains the correct service record. The request's meta data is simply copied into the respective reply message issued by the replica. This is done by the Proxy Agent as it receives the replica's reply and sends it to the client. Upon snooping a reply message, a LSA extracts the *service record* and sends it to its own cluster head where it is received by the local Lookup Service. The Lookup Service, in turn, replaces its outdated service record with the new one. To avoid multiple redundant snooping messages, an LSA uses two mechanisms:

1. It inspects the route taken by the reply message and discards it if it has already passed through one or more nodes in the same cluster. Since the first of these nodes has already sent the update to the Lookup Service, there is no need to resend it. If we assume that nodes 6 and 7 are both in the cluster of cluster head 2 in Figure 9.2, then node 6 does not send the update message to node 2 since it recognizes that node 7 must have already done so.

2. Each LSA keeps a limited history of service record uuids sent to the Lookup Service. If it finds a newly received record in this list, it does not resend it. Keep in mind that several requests may be forwarded before the lazy update has propagated and the client starts sending its requests to the correct address. Thus, without this history, a number of unnecessary retransmission would take place. For a network of 100 nodes, it turns out that a history of 10 records suffices to avoid unnecessary retransmissions almost completely.

9.2.5   The Lookup Service

The actual Lookup Service is rather simple. A client may query it in three different ways:

1. It may request information about a *specific replica* via its unique identifier;

2. it may request information about *all replicas of a specific service type*; or

3. it may request *a non-specific replica for a specific service type*.

In the latter case, the Lookup Service will choose the *most appropriate* replica and return its service record to the client.

---

[1]A service record is the data structure used by the Lookup Service to store all data pertaining to a registered service replica.

Service Records

When a service registers at a Lookup Service, a *service record* is created that holds all the information needed for accessing the service. A copy of this record is returned to a client as a result of a successful query. The record is also propagated within the network using the aforementioned mechanisms (initial broadcast and lazy reply-driven update). The information stored in a service record includes the following data:

- recordId: The unique ID of the record is needed to avoid duplicate updates with the same record. A new record with a new ID is created each time a replica migrates.

- type: The service type of the replica. This type description may include semantic information for a service matching algorithm.

- replicaId: The unique ID of the replica. Note that this is different from the ID of the record. The replica ID is assigned to the replica as it is created and never changes during the lifetime of the replica.

- replicaAddr: The node address of the replica's current location.

- routeToReplica The complete route between the Lookup Service storing the record and the replica's current location (replicaAddr). This route is taken from the message in which the Lookup Service instance received the service record.

- clientHops: The number of hops between a querying client and the service replica. This field is set when the Lookup Service creates a copy of the record for a querying client. clientHops is derived from routeToReplica and information about the local network topology as explained in the following section.

9.2.6 Estimating Distances

In order to assign the closest replica to a querying client, a specific Lookup Service (LS) instance must be able to estimate the distance between the querying client and each replica in its table. The Lookup Service knows the path over which it received the service record. However, this may not be of the same length as the path between the client and the replica.

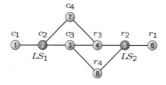

Figure 9.6: Example network for the distance estimation mechanism.

Figure 9.6 depicts a simple network that consists of two clusters: Nodes 1, 2, 3, and 7 with node 2 as their cluster head, and nodes 4, 5, 6, and 8 with node 5 as their

client	replica	distance
c_1	r_1	5
c_1	r_2	4
c_1	r_3	3
c_1	r_4	3
c_2	r_1	4
c_2	r_2	3
c_2	r_3	2
c_2	r_4	2
c_3	r_1	3
c_3	r_2	2
c_3	r_3	1
c_3	r_4	1
c_4	r_1	3
c_4	r_2	2
c_4	r_3	1
c_4	r_4	3

Table 9.1: Distance table.

cluster head. In the right cluster, there are 4 replicas of the same service type that are registered at Lookup Service LS_2. On the left side, there are 4 clients that send their queries to LS_1. LS_1 is faced with the task of estimating the distances between any pair (c_i, r_j) as accurately as possible such that each client is assigned the replica that is closest to it.

Let us assume that each replica has initially registered at LS_2. Thus, for each of them, the location has been broadcast by LS_2 to all remaining Lookup Services (only LS_1 in our case). Thus, LS_1 knows the paths $(5, 4, 3, 2)$ taken by each of these broadcast messages. Based on this information, LS_1 could estimate

$$\forall\, 1 \leq i, j \leq 4 : d(c_i, r_j) = 3. \tag{9.1}$$

However, as Table 9.1 shows, this is only accurate in 6 of the possible 16 combinations. In general, the distances are within a range between 1 and 5. Not being able to discriminate between a replica that is at distance 5 and one that is at distance 1 can make a big difference in networks that only have a diameter of about 10 hops (see Table 8.1 on page 84). Therefore, we need a more sophisticated mechanism that gives us a better estimation of the client-replica distance.

Obviously, the problem of inaccurate distance measurement is caused at both the replica and the client side. For both sides, we must take corrective actions. The basic mechanism used for this correction is based on limited knowledge of the local network topology. More specifically, we use information about the neighbors of the replica's node and the client's node in combination with the path taken by the message that was used to sent the record (denoted as m_r hereafter) to the receiving Lookup Service instance (LS_1 in our case).

A replica is required to provide the list of its immediate neighbors when it registers initially at some LS instance, this neighbor list is included in the registration propagation message that is broadcast to the remaining LS instances. A client, in turn, is required to provide its neighbor list upon each query. Based on the fundamental assumption that the routing mechanism used to transport m_r uses the shortest path, this is sufficient to correct the distance *in most cases*. There may be cases in which the correction does not work and, therefore, the correction mechanism that we introduce here is a heuristic. However, we will show that these cases are very rare.

Replica-Side Correction upon Initial Registration

We make the following definitions in preparation of the succeeding discussion:

- v_r is the node at which replica r is running;

- v_c is the node at which client c is running;

- v_S is the node at which the sending LS instance is running;

- v_R is the node at which the receiving LS instance is running;

- N_r is the neighbor set of v_r including v_r itself (note that $v_S \in N_r$);

- $\Pi(m_r)$ is the path taken by the message m_r (note that $\Pi(m_r)$ contains the sender v_S and the receiver v_R of m_r);

- $d(u, v)$ is the distance between the nodes u and v.

When m_r is received by v_R, we know the distance $d(v_R, v_S)$ between the two LS instances (in our example this is the distance between LS_1 and LS_2). But since this does not reflect the accurate distance in every case, we would first like to eliminate the replica-side inaccuracy and find a better estimation of $d(v_R, v_r)$. This is done by checking which neighbors of the replica r are on the path between v_S and v_R. Informally, if there is a neighbor of v_r (other than v_S) in the path, then this may represent a shortcut that decreases the distance $d(v_R, v_r)$.

Let v_n be the neighbor that is closest to v_R on the path $\Pi(m_r)$:

$$v_n \in N_r \cap \Pi(m_r) \quad \text{with} \quad \forall v_u \in N_r \cap \Pi(m_r) : d(v_R, v_n) \leq d(v_R, v_u) \qquad (9.2)$$

Note that $N_r \cap \Pi(m_r)$ is guaranteed to be non-empty since the clustered structure of the network enforces that v_r and v_S are neighbors ($v_S \in N_r$), and, due to our definitions, $v_S \in \Pi(m_r)$ also holds. For replica r_4 in Figure 9.6, v_n would be node 3 since it is the neighbor of r_4's node that is closest to LS_1.

Having found v_n, the corrected distance $d(v_R, v_r)$ becomes

$$d(v_R, v_r) = d(v_R, v_n) + 1 \qquad (9.3)$$

since a message from v_R to v_r would have to travel to v_n and then be relayed to v_n's neighbor, v_r. This holds for all the cases represented by replicas r_1 to r_4 in Figure 9.6 as long as the messages sent to v_r take the same general path that was used by m_r. As we will see later on, this may not always be the case.

Correspondingly, the LS instance that received the registration message m_r corrects the original path $\Pi(m_r) = \{v_R, \ldots, v_n, \ldots, v_S\}$ and stores $\Pi_r = \{v_R, \ldots, v_n, v_r\}$ in the `routeToReplica` field of the respective service record.

Client-Side Correction

At the client side, the same mechanism is used, based on the client's neighbor set N_c and the corrected route Π_r: The node $v_m \in N_c$ is chosen, such that v_m is closest to v_r in $\Pi_r = \{v_R, \ldots, v_m, \ldots, v_n, v_r\}$. The final corrected path from client c to replica r becomes $\Pi_{cr} = \{v_c, v_m, \ldots, v_n, v_r\}$, and the distance $d(v_c, v_r)$ is set to $d(v_m, v_r)+1$, correspondingly. When an LS instance receives a query from client c, this distance is calculated for all replicas that are registered at that LS instance, and the replica with the shortest distance is returned to c. If several replicas have the same shortest distance, then the LS instance is free in choosing any of these alternatives.

Correction upon Receiving Snooped Changes

When a replica changes its location, this change is propagated via the snooping mechanism, and not, as was done for initial registrations, with a broadcast among the LS instances. Thus, the message m_r by which the changed service record is transported is sent by the replica r itself and not by its LS instance, since such records are piggybacked by normal service reply messages. Therefore, the replica side of the path between client and replica does not need a correction in this case.

At the client side, the transmission of the Lookup Snooper Agent to the LS instance may add one hop (at most) to the path since the LSA sends snooped messages only to its own LS instance (same node or neighbor node). This can be easily corrected. When the receiving LS instance stores the new record, and a client sends a query, the same mechanism as before is used at the client side.

Accuracy of Estimation

There are cases, in which this simple mechanism fails to find the correct distance. These are the cases, in which a message routed from c to r takes a completely different path than the message m_r. Consider, for example, the ring topology that is depicted in Figure 9.7. There are two possible paths between the LS instances, both of the same length. LS_2 sends its registration message for replica r to LS_1 via the path on the right side. The correction heuristic eventually assumes that the actual distance between c and r is the length of $\Pi(m_r)$ incremented by two (corresponding to the dashed path), because r's only neighbor in $\Pi(m_r)$ is v_S (node 5) and c's only neighbor in $\Pi(m_r)$ is v_R (node 1). The final corrected path is $\Pi_{cr} = \{8, 1, 2, 3, 4, 5, 6\}$. The mechanism correctly assumes that a message sent over this path between c and r would need to travel one additional hop at each end. Compared to the resulting 6 hops, replica r' is closer to c (only 4 hops). However, the network routing mechanism would choose the much shorter path via node 7 to route requests from c to r. Thus, LS_1 falsely assumes that r' is the replica closest to c.

Note that Figure 9.7 actually depicts the worst case scenario, where the actual distance between c and r is overestimated by 4 hops. Increasing the length of $\Pi(m_r)$ by adding one or more nodes to the right-side path implies that m_r is sent over the left path which then becomes the shorter one. The same argument holds if we shorten the left-side path by removing nodes. Positioning either c or r on node 7 to increase the difference beyond 4 hops detaches it from its respective LS instance since node 7 is associated with a different cluster head (not depicted in the Figure). Thus, an equal

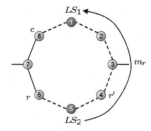

Figure 9.7: Pathological network leading to an incorrect distance estimation.

amount of nodes may be added on both sides to make both paths longer, but the worst case difference of 4 hops between the estimated and the actual path remains. This is also confirmed in our measurements (see Figure 9.8).

Figure 9.8 shows the result of running the distance correction mechanism over 20 different random network topologies with 50 nodes each. These experiments resulted in about 180000 unique client/replica interactions. For every client/replica interaction, we recorded the raw distance $d(v_S, v_R)$, the corrected distance $d(v_c, v_r)$, and the actual distance traveled by reply messages. The latter distance is the objective benchmark for our mechanism. Ideally, the distance estimated by the Lookup Service should be identical with this reply distance. Among all the recorded interactions, we eliminated duplicates. That is, when the same client c sent several requests to the same replica r and both were located at the same nodes (v_c and v_r), we only recorded the first of these interactions. More precisely, for each tuple (c, v_c, r, v_r) that occurred, we only recorded one interaction.

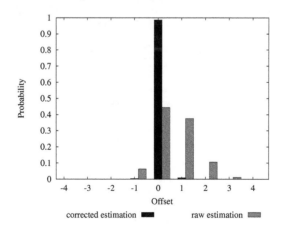

Figure 9.8: Distance estimation correctness compared.

Figure 9.8 depicts the probability distribution over the possible offsets from the actual distance for $d(v_S, v_R)$ (raw estimation) and $d(v_c, v_r)$ (corrected estimation). A negative offset means that the respective mechanisms underestimated the real distance; a positive offset indicates an overestimation. The results show that the raw distance tends to overestimate the real distance. It is in general rather inaccurate, yielding the right distance only in about 44% of all cases. The corrected estimation, on the other hand, yields the correct distance in 98.6% of all cases. In 0.94%, it overestimates the distance, and in the remaining 0.46% it underestimates it. Evidently, this fulfills our requirement for accurate distance measures to support the replica placement mechanism.

9.2.7 Maintaining other Dynamic Data

The ASG Lookup Service is designed to handle dynamic data (mainly service replica locations) efficiently and effectively. As a *by-product*, it is straightforward to update and maintain additional dynamically changing data and to provide it to clients. For example, we use this to disseminate the current load experienced by the service replicas throughout the ASG network. Each replica stores its load (e.g. number of requests processed during a certain time period) in the meta data of every n-th reply messages. The Lookup Snooper Agents listen for messages carrying load information and propagate it to their Lookup Services. This enables clients to choose services not only based on their distance, but also on their load. However, the dissemination of additional dynamic data using the message snooping mechanism has not been explored in great detail yet.

9.3 Self-Healing Properties

We argue that the described lookup system is self-healing. That is, it can compensate the inconsistencies caused by service mobility and possible failures and preserve a *legal state* without manual intervention. In order to show this, we first introduce our definition of a *legal state* with respect to the Lookup Service:

Definition 9.1 (Legal Lookup System States). *The state of the Lookup System is legal if and only if any client query*

1. *yields location information that eventually leads to the proper delivery of requests to an adequate service replica, or*

2. *results in a respective notification if no adequate service replica is present in the system.*

Any configuration that does not satisfy this definition is considered an *illegal state*. Note that this is a very weak definition. It does not state anything specific about the dissemination of location information. It neither requires any specific distribution of the information (e.g. that each LS instance needs to have all the available information), nor that clients are given up-to-date information. Instead, it takes a more abstract view in demanding that, based on the available lookup information, it must be possible for client requests to reach an appropriate replica, if such a replica exists. For the client, it is indeed irrelevant whether the result of its query is outdated. A stronger definition is not required. For the Lookup System, this weak definition does not enforce rigid and brittle mechanisms. Instead, it leaves room for flexible solutions.

The idea of *softening definitions* in software systems to avoid brittleness was first brought forward by Shaw [156]. In this approach, *absolute criteria for correctness* are replaced by *the fitness for the specific task*. A self-healing system constantly drives itself towards fitter states instead of detecting and explicitly correcting all possible errors based on rigid correctness criteria. The latter is generally a very tough task as there might not be sufficient knowledge about such errors. Such a self-healing, *soft* system may experience a degradation in fitness, but it is much less likely to break down completely.

In this sense, our definition of legal states is a soft one. It allows the system to degrade without breaking. For example, if a client acquires outdated location information from its current LS instance, this may lead to an increase in response time for the first few requests. But the system corrects this as a part of its normal operation through the snooping-based propagation of the replica's correct location. Thus, outdated information is not perceived as an error that causes a system failure, but rather as a temporary inconvenience that can be fixed to bring the system back into a desirable mode of operation. This *healing process* is pervasive throughout the entire system and through time. It never stops as long as there are outdated pieces of location information being used in the system.

Thus, in its *normal mode of operation*, the system is self-healing with respect to the lookup information. That is, as long as the only factor in the degradation of the system is the mobility of clients and services, the self-healing mechanism explained thus far is able to keep the system healthy. However, in a system like the ASG, there are also several *external influences* that may lead to erroneous states beyond those caused by mobility. In the remaining parts of this section, we will investigate possible disturbances and explain how the system autonomously returns to a legal state.

9.3.1 Topology Changes

The ASG topology changes if a new node is added or a node is removed or crashes. Note that the clustering and routing algorithms are able to compensate such events at the networking layer. The mechanisms used to achieve this are well-known and will not be explained. We simply assume that the routing infrastructure and the clustered structure are eventually restored. The question that we discuss here is, how does such a change effect the lookup information in the system and how can it recover from illegal states caused by these changes?

Adding Nodes

If a new node is added that has a cluster head within transmission range, it simply joins this cluster head. This has no effect on lookup information. If the new node cannot join any existing cluster head, it has to become a cluster head itself and starts its own Lookup Service L. To get valid lookup information, it queries the local routing table for the closest other cluster head until it finds one that has an operational Lookup Service L'. Then, L requests the entire service table of L' and uses it. Even if this service table is not up-to-date, this information is sufficient for the reply-driven update scheme to work properly. Thus, the system is in a legal state again. If any new information arrives (via a registration broadcast or a snooped location change) it is simply incorporated into the acquired service table.

Removing Nodes

We assume that there is a regular way of removing a node which gives the system the opportunity to prepare (e.g. migrate services to other nodes). A harder problem is occurring if a node crashes. If the crashed node v was a cluster head, then one of two situations may occur:

1. All the ordinary nodes, that were in v's cluster before, have other cluster heads as neighbors and can join these clusters. In this case, their addresses change. While the network routes will be fixed by the routing algorithm, the outdated addresses stored in Lookup Services must be fixed by the Lookup System. Therefore, the Lookup Service on each cluster head that integrates new nodes broadcasts the address changes to the other Lookup Services. In a sense, the address change of a node is the same as if the replicas on that node crash and new replicas are started shortly after that on a new node. In both cases (address change and crash), the respective replica is suddenly unreachable, especially by requests that are in transit to the replica. We will discuss the mechanism for dealing with replica crashes further down. Conversely, if the node is equipped with a new address, this is as if the node with the new address has already existed and now a replica is started on it.

2. At least one ordinary node u that was in v's cluster before has no other cluster head as a direct neighbor. In this case, u becomes a new cluster head itself. It starts its own Lookup Service and updates its empty service table in the same way explained above for newly added cluster heads.

If the crashed node was an ordinary node, the cluster structure is not damaged. Thus, no such repair processes have to be started. However, irrespective of whether the crashed node was a cluster head or an ordinary node, there are basically two problems that may arise for the Lookup System.

1. The node may have been part of a forwarding chain, which is now broken, or

2. the node may have hosted service replicas.

We will explain how to cope with both of these problems in the next two subsections.

9.3.2   Repairing Broken Forwarding Chains

A forwarding chain is broken if one Proxy in the chain does not have a valid next forwarding hop. Either this information is missing or the next forwarding hop is not reachable (has crashed). In addition to missing next hops, loops may occur in the chain if a service fails to remove old forwarding pointers. Missing forwarding pointers, loops, and crashed nodes can be detected by the last valid Proxy in the chain. Upon receiving a client request that requires forwarding, this Proxy sends a notification about the error back to the client that sent the request. This client, in turn, notifies its Lookup Service L about the problem. Note that a broken forwarding chain means that at least one service replica is not reachable using the information provided by L. Depending on the nature of the service, this may violate our definition (9.1) of a legal state, if no other replica exist or if other replicas are not adequate. Therefore, L tries to fix the problem. It removes its invalid lookup entry for the unreachable service and broadcasts a *reset* message containing the replica's uuid to all other Lookup Services. Any Lookup Service that receives this message and does not know the whereabouts of the replica in question also removes its entry for it. Only the Lookup Service that has the replica in its cluster reacts by propagating the correct information to all other LS instances. Thus, the service's location is updated throughout the ASG. Note that the remaining forwarding pointers of the broken chain do not present a problem. Since all Lookup Services in the system have the correct location after the repair, none of these pointers will be used again. Moreover, if the service returns to one of these nodes, it will remove the old pointer anyway if it has not already been garbage collected.

In the *reset* protocol described above, race conditions may occur. Consider three cluster head nodes v_1, v_2, and v_3. v_1 issues the *reset* message for replica r. This message is received by v_2 which knows about the replica and sends a broadcast. Now, assume that, due to some network issues, the broadcast message sent by v_2 reaches v_3 before the *reset* message. Without any additional mechanism, v_3 would react to the *reset* by removing the information received via the broadcast and by waiting for a new broadcast that should follow the *reset* message. Thus, due to the inversion of the two messages, v_3 has lost its information about r. Obviously, the broadcast message is causally depending on the *reset* message. Therefore, Lamport's logical clocks [97] would suffice to resolve this issue. In our case, v_2 includes the UUID of the *reset* message in its broadcast. Therefore, any node receiving this broadcast before the *reset* message recognizes that the *reset* message is still to come and may delay the processing of the new registration contained in the broadcast message until the *reset* message has been received.

9.3.3   Dealing with Crashed Replicas

If only the replica crashes due to a software error and its local Proxy remains operational, then the Proxy can unregister the service properly. If, however, a service vanishes, for example, due to a node crash, different measures have to take effect. To purge the system from location information pertaining to replicas that have crashed, each service has to send a periodic *registration refresh* message to its local Lookup Service. If a Lookup Service does not receive this message for an extended period of time, it assumes that the service has crashed and was unable to unregister properly. It reacts by broadcasting a *reset* message (see Section 9.3.2) to its fellow Lookup Services. This will remove the information about the replica completely from the Lookup System if it has really crashed. However, if it resides in a different location (failed to unregister properly before leaving), the correct location information will eventually be propagated as a reaction to the *reset* message. If a replica is unable to send its *registration refresh* message (e.g. due to high load) and the Lookup Service accidentally assumes a crash, then the service will eventually be able to send messages again. This results in a new system-wide registration, as if the replica has just been installed.

9.3.4 Avoiding False Negative Query Results

If, for some reason, a Lookup Service failed to gather the information about a new service type being introduced in the system, it would falsely answers client queries negatively, stating that nothing is known about any replica of that type. This would clearly violate our definition of legal states. Thus, before a Lookup Service returns a negative query result, it starts an incremental search to verify its correctness. It queries the routing table to find all existing cluster heads and their hop distances from its own node. Then it starts sending queries for the service type in question, gradually increasing the radius of its requests. The assumption here is that in most cases a near-by Lookup Service will have the desired information. If, for example, the service registration propagation failed at its source for some reason, this protocol will traverse the entire network. In this case, a normal cluster head broadcast would be much more efficient. However, the issuing Lookup Service instance is unable to recognize this. Note that in both cases, malicious clients may use this feature to run denial of service attacks by repeatedly querying for unknown services to overload the network. Resolving these problems will be subject to future research.

9.4 Quantitative Evaluation

In this section, we will evaluate our self-organizing Lookup Service with respect to two aspects:

1. Which level of *lookup information correctness* is achieved throughout an ASG network?

2. Which overhead is produced in terms of update traffic among the LS instances?

As a benchmark, we use an alternative Lookup Service implementation that uses broadcast messages for sending all location updates. That is, not only the initial occurrence and the removal of a replica is broadcast to all LS instances, but also each location change of an existing service replica.

9.4.1 The Correctness Measure

The first portion of our evaluation is based on the notion of *lookup information correctness*. As we stated, the lazy reply-driven protocol trades correctness for efficiency by updating only those regions through which service replies pass. To quantify this trade-off, we need to define what we mean by "correctness" in this context.

Each LS instance stores an entry for each replica that is active in the ASG network. Some of these entries may be outdated while others hold the correct current location of the replica. The lookup correctness measure (L) is simply given as the ratio of the number of correct entries to the number of exiting entries throughout the entire system:

$$L = \frac{L_c}{L_a} \tag{9.4}$$

L_c is the number of correct service entries in all LS instances and L_a is the number of all service entries (correct and incorrect) in all LS instances. In a straight-forward way, we define $L(t)$ as the lookup correctness at time index t and $\overline{L}$ as the average lookup correctness measured over the whole simulation time T. If $L(t) = 1$, then all entries in all LS instances hold the correct location of their respective replicas at time t.

9.4.2 Correctness for Increasing Number of Clients

First, we investigate how the reply-driven update protocol performs compared to the simple broadcast protocol in terms of lookup correctness if we increase the number of clients in the system. The reply-driven protocol uses the replies generated for client requests to propagate location changes throughout the ASG network. Thus, the update process is depending on the amount of client requests flowing through the network. Intuitively, one would expect that an increase in the number of clients in the system (leading to an increase of requests and, consequently, also of replies) would increase the correctness. After all, more reply messages over the same period of time imply more chances of propagating a location change.

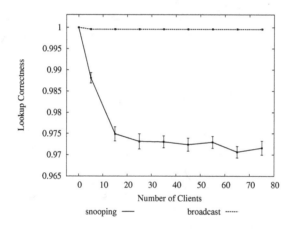

Figure 9.9: Average lookup correctness $\overline{L}$ for increasing number of clients.

Figure 9.9 shows that our intuition is not quite correct. The problem is that more clients create more dynamics and a greater stimulus for replica adaptations. The graph exhibits a rapid initial decrease in correctness due to the fact that the number of location changes increases vastly as we raise the number of clients from 0 to 15. As the number of clients increases beyond that point, the number location changes per time unit decreases and is countered by the increase in reply messages available for the update process. As a result, the correctness converges to a value of around $L = 0.97$. At the same time, the broadcast protocol remains unimpressed of the growing number of clients. Since each single location change is broadcast, the correctness stays nearly at 1. The actual value is around $L = 0.99957$. It is not quite 1 since it takes some time to propagate the changes, and during that time, a slight incorrectness in measured which decreases $\overline{L}$. Note that the loss in correctness for values beyond 20 clients is between 2.6% and 2.9%. Thus, the degradation in correctness is only small compared to the broadcast protocol.

9.4.3   Update Message Overhead

As we have seen, our lazy reply-driven protocol performs almost as well as the broadcast protocol. The big difference between the two lies in the message overhead that they produce. While the broadcast protocol achieves its extremely high correctness by flooding every bit of information that changes, our lazy protocol only sends updates when necessary.

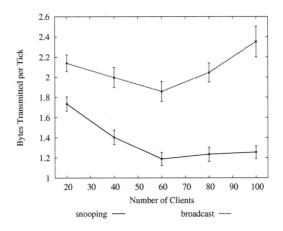

Figure 9.10: Message overhead produced by Lookup Service updates.

Figure 9.10 depicts the message overhead that is caused by both protocols. There is a large gap between the overhead produced by our protocol and that of the broadcast protocol. Moreover, this gap increases linearly from 19% at the beginning to 46.6% at the end. The scalability of our protocol is remarkably good while the broadcast protocol produces a steep linear increase for larger numbers of clients. The fact that both overhead graphs have a minimum can be explained by the numbers of adaptations that are executed by the replica placement system.

Figure 9.11 shows the number of migrations, replications, and dissolves issued on average per adaptation interval for the different numbers of clients. For low numbers of clients, there are more replications. This is due to the fact that clients are sparsely distributed in the network and, thus, the probability that requests arrive from outside the replication radius ρ is comparably high (cf. Section 8.5.3). The number of replications decreases as more clients start to be distributed more evenly throughout the network. For more than 60 clients, the number of migrations starts to increase and dominates the adaptations. Since adaptations represent the sole cause for updates, the number of messages required for these updates complies to the combined number of adaptations in the system.

The experimental results clearly show that our protocol achieves almost the same correctness as the broadcast protocol but causes much less update traffic.

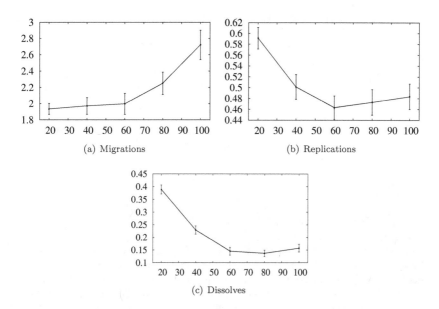

Figure 9.11: Adaptations per interval for increasing number of clients.

9.5 Discussion

While the proposed Lookup System in its current form achieves the desired goals
in terms of adaptability, effectiveness, and efficiency, it also has some drawbacks
and limitations. In this section, we shall briefly discuss some of the advantages and
disadvantages not presented thus far.

Services Replies

The general concept of the ASG Lookup System only works for services that generate replies. This does not present a general problem as any service can send a
reply even if it was only for the sake of keeping the Lookup System up-to-date.
Such *non-functional replies* could be produced and consumed by the Proxy Agents
transparently.

Snooping Overhead

Message snooping and the general concept of implementing routing and transport
mechanisms at the middleware layer may introduce additional overhead. We still
need to quantify this overhead. However, resolving the strictly layered structures of
classical distributed systems is necessary when it comes to achieving self-organization
at the higher layers. Thus, this problem is of a more general nature and not solely a
consequence of our approach.

Overhead through Forwarding Chains

The lazy update scheme, trades off efficiency of updating with the increased latency of initial updates passing through long forwarding chains. However, if a system is heavily used, forwarding chains rarely get longer than one or two hops. Thus, a longer route only has a minimal effect. On the other hand, if the system is lightly loaded (few clients), then forwarding chains may get longer since updates happen more infrequently. However, in these situations the additional networking resources needed are also available since few requests have to be transported through the system. This presents a nice feature as the network adapts to the request load, minimizing forwarding chains automatically as the load increases.

Security

Self-organizing software systems in general require new paradigms for achieving security, privacy, and integrity. Security is, in most cases, associated with explicit manual configuration and control. This is in stark contrast with the idea of letting a software system structure and control itself autonomously. The nature of adequate security paradigms is currently an open issue and a tough problem. Therefore, we consciously avoided this topic in the design of our system thus far. It seems obvious that some self-repair mechanisms, like sending a *reset* message when a query for an unknown service type is received, open the gates for denial of service attacks. Such problems will have to be resolved before platforms like the ASG become commercially exploitable.

Chapter 10

Data Consistency

Contents

Many useful services, that are conceivable in the ASG environment, are stateful. They maintain a mutable state that is updated and read simultaneously by multiple clients that use different replicas. The nature of the content and the update policies are application-dependent and may be diverse. However, for every stateful replicated service, there is a need to keep the state of its replicas consistent. For a reservation service, for example, it may not be acceptable if two or more clients successfully issue the same reservation without being notified about the collision. However, the dynamics and the degree of uncertainty in the ASG make it difficult to apply *pessimistic* mechanisms for enforcing consistency. A *pessimistic consistency protocol* attempts to *prevent* inconsistencies. The definition of the term *inconsistency* varies between the different pessimistic models. However, all of them recognize an inconsistency as something that is intolerable and must be avoided under all circumstances. The techniques applied to achieve this are often quite restrictive. The access to replicas may be blocked as long as a client is in the process of updating a service's state. This is undesirable in the ASG, especially because the set of replicas may change over time due to new replications and removals. Thus, no single replica may ever have a complete picture of the current overall configuration. As a consequence, a consistency model for the ASG environment must be able to handle incomplete information.

Similar problems were already encountered and successfully handled, for example, in the distributed operating system LOCUS [175], the distributed file system Coda [152], and the weakly connected replicated storage system Bayou [165, 166, 128]. All of these systems build on a so-called *weak consistency model* that enables a form of *optimistic replication*.

In this chapter, we build on the principles and mechanisms introduced in the aforementioned projects to design a consistency protocol for replicated ASG services. After a review of the concept of optimistic replication and related work in Section 10.1, we take a closer look at the requirements for a consistency protocol in the ASG environment in Section 10.2. The basic ASG consistency protocol is presented in Section 10.3, and an extended version that limits the divergence among the replicas' individual data stores is presented and discussed in Sections 10.5 and 10.6. Our quantitative evaluation in Section 10.7 will show which levels of consistency can be realized by the extended protocol and how this level can be fine-tuned for different applications using two parameters.

10.1 Foundations and Related Work

10.1.1 Optimistic vs. Pessimistic Data Replication

In systems with a fixed set of replicas, a reliable communication medium and minimal dynamics, classical methods for data replication may be used that take a pessimistic approach. "Pessimistic" means that the replication system assumes that concurrent updates on the data will most certainly lead to conflicts and inconsistencies that are critical. Thus, some form of *locking* must be applied in order to prevent inconsistent data. An update needs to be established on all replicas before the next update may be performed or even before the next client is allowed to read data. The result is a system that gives clients the illusion of using a single, highly available copy of the data that never runs into an inconsistent state. The basic assumption behind this approach is that communication is direct and fast and that the replication system has a complete view on the present set of replicas. But what if these conditions are not met by a given system?

In an environment with mobile devices that connect and disconnect spontaneously via volatile wireless networking technologies, pessimistic consistency models have severe drawbacks. The number of replicas (positioned on the mobile devices) is unknown and may change dynamically. There may be no single point in time at which all relevant replicas may be able to communicate with each other. Therefore, there is no way to test whether global consistency is achieved, and locking data is bound to bring the complete system to a halt in terms of data access. On the other hand, the requirements put up by applications may not necessarily imply the need for a pessimistic model. Some applications produce conflicts relatively rarely, or the conflicts that do happen are not critical. A classical example, that was also the motivation for systems like Coda, are files in a Unix file system. Measurements have shown that *write sharing* (i.e. two or more users writing the same file) happens only infrequently [125]. Thus, occasional conflicts may be tolerable if the availability of the data can be improved by relaxing the consistency model.

This has led to the invention of *weak consistency models* and *optimistic replication* mechanisms [148][1]. Optimistic replication systems allow concurrent write and read access to shared data without necessarily enforcing a priori synchronization. They assume that problems (conflicts and inconsistencies) will occur only rarely. Updates are usually propagated in the background and if conflicts occur, they will be fixed *after* they happen. Similar principles of manual conflict resolution can be found in popular version management systems like CVS [29]. The CVS is able to detect conflicts that arise if two developers change the same file concurrently. If these changes are compatible, CVS can merge them automatically. If they pertain to the same lines of code, however, the developer who commits first establishes his changes in the repository. If the second developer tries to commit his changes, he is notified by the system about the conflict. The commit fails, and he is required to merge the different versions manually. Note that, in practice, this problem should happen only rarely. A properly managed software project divides responsibilities between developers in a way that partitions the code and avoids concurrent work on the same files. This is a good example for an application that defines semantics on a higher level that lead to a negligible amount of conflicts. Therefore, the availability of the code in the repository can be maximized by removing any restrictions on concurrent updates.

Optimistic replication algorithms offer several advantages over pessimistic ones. Most notably, they improve the availability of data by avoiding locking mechanisms. Local updates are applied tentatively without checking for conflicts. This provides quick feedback for the user and allows them to be much more autonomous because the strong coupling between replicas is removed. Optimistic algorithms are flexible with respect to the network dynamics since they can tolerate disconnections and changing topologies. Finally, they may scale to much larger systems because of the reduction in synchronization between the different network sites.

However, these advantages come at a cost. There is an inherent trade-off between availability and consistency [38]. By opting for availability, optimistic algorithms accept that replicas diverge over time and that conflicts may occur. Thus, they are only useful for applications that can tolerate such a behavior. Fortunately, this set includes many real-world applications that enforce data partitioning and access arbitration by their very nature (like CVS).

10.1.2   Bayou – Weakly Consistent Replication

Bayou [165, 166, 128] is a database system that was specifically designed for weakly connected mobile networks. To enable access to shared data, each user has a Bayou server that replicates the data locally on his mobile host. The data is stored in a

---

[1]The survey by Yasushi Saito and Marc Shapiro [148] offers an excellent overview of pessimistic and optimistic consistency models and compares the two.

so-called *data store*. The user can read and write data without being blocked, even if his device is not connected to any other database server. Thus, mobile users can work stand-alone. Whenever two mobile database servers meet, they can run a reconciliation protocol to mutually update their data stores. Through successive, pair-wise reconciliation processes, updates propagate through the whole set of replicas. This protocol is called *anti-entropy* and builds on the theory of epidemics [39]. Through this *epidemic algorithm*, every update is eventually established on all participating servers, assuming that the servers *meet* regularly. This model is called *eventual consistency*.

An important feature of Bayou is that it does not assume any network infrastructure at all. As long as there are temporary connections between pairs of servers, the system runs fine. Also note that for two specific servers to synchronize, there is no need for them to ever meet "in person". Updates may propagate via a chain of encounters from one server to the other. Of course, the time needed to establish an update in the whole system is depending on the frequency of encounters between servers.

Write Logs

Bayou servers do not exchange the state of their data stores when reconciliating. Instead, each server stores the write operations (also simply called *Writes* hereafter) submitted by the local client(s) in a *write log*. The current data store of a server is the result of applying all Writes in the order in which they appear in the write log. This order is defined by logical timestamps that are assigned to Writes as they are submitted by clients (also called *accept timestamps*). Each Write is uniquely identified by its timestamp, and a write operation with a smaller timestamp is positioned before a Write with a higher timestamp. When two servers meet, they synchronize their write logs by exchanging operations if necessary. Via this reconciliation process, new write operations may be received that have to be *inserted* between two existing Writes in the log. Thus, the order of the write operations in a write log may change. To reconstruct the data store, the operations are *rolled back* to the point at which the first new Write has to be inserted into the log. Then the new Writes are merged into the existing log, and subsequently, the operations in the resulting log are executed again (rolled forward) from the end point of the roll-back to the last (most recent) Write in the log. Thus, by rolling back, the effects of the operations can be undone and by rolling forward, they are redone.

The timestamps assigned to Writes are based on Lamport's logical clocks [97]. To make each timestamp globally unique, the ID of the server that first accepted the Write (received it from a client) and assigned the timestamp, is appended. Thus, a timestamp has the form $< logical\ clock, server\ ID >$. The server ID is used to order Writes with equal timestamps. This defines a total order on all Writes in the system and enables all servers to agree on a global order in which to execute them. Note that Lamport's concept of logical clocks guarantees a causal ordering among the write operations submitted at different replicas. The following rules are applied for adjusting the servers' clocks:

1. Each server increments its logical clock if a new Write is submitted locally by a client.

2. If a server receives a set of write operations (also called *write set*) from another server, it takes the highest timestamp present in this write set, increments it by 1, and uses this value as its new logical clock.

Thus, receiving a Write from a local client and receiving a write set from another server are perceived as events in terms of Lamport's logical clocks.

Conflict Resolution

Conflicts may occur during the reconciliation process. For example, in a room reservation system, a server may have a reservation for a specific room at a certain time. This reservation is represented by the Write w_2. During the next reconciliation, it receives a second reservation w_1 for the same room at the same time with an earlier timestamp (subscripts denote timestamps). After merging its write log with the new Writes, the operation w_2 that was previously executed without any problem, collides with the results produced by w_1 that was executed before w_2 during the roll-forward. In Bayou, an operation may specify a *dependency check* and a *merge procedure*. The dependency check is run to detect conflicts. If it fails, the merge procedure is run to resolve the conflict. In the reservation scenario, the dependency check tests if the room is free at the specified time. If it fails, a useful merge procedure may try to reserve an adjacent time slot or another room with similar resources. If this also fails, the operation cannot be executed and is logged in an *error log*. The client that submitted w_2 can be notified later if possible. Bayou does not specify how this notification is delivered because this is depending on the application. A dependency check can read any data item from the data store to check for arbitrary dependencies. Thus, it is not only possible to detect direct conflicts but also to test arbitrary constraints for the execution of a Write. Note that w_2 leads to a conflict only after it has been accepted and successfully executed for the first time. This is the nature of so-called *tentative operations*. These operations may be rolled-back at any time, and they may also eventually fail. However, being an optimistic replication system, Bayou assumes that they will succeed. The concept of write commitment, explained below, ensures that, eventually, a dependable decision will be made as to whether a Write fails or succeeds.

Two important features ensure that Bayou servers achieve eventual consistency. The first one is the globally consistent ordering of write operations that is enabled through the timestamps. Thus two Writes will always be executed in the same order on all servers. The second feature is the deterministic execution of dependency checks and merge procedures. Bayou ensures that these procedures eventually produce the same results on all servers. That is, when executed on equivalent data stores, the same dependency check and merge procedures will produce the same results.

Write Commitment

With the mechanisms descried above, the write logs grow monotonically over time since there is no way to decide whether a Write is still needed. A server may have to roll back to the very start of the log if an *old* Write is received. To enable efficient write log management, Bayou *stabilizes* write operations. We also say that Writes are *committed*. A committed Write will never be rolled back again. Its effects on the data store are permanent. As a consequence, committed Writes can be removed from the write logs. Thus, the size of a write log can be kept at an acceptable level. Bayou does not define any algorithm for truncating write logs. Arbitrary strategies may be applied. This also means that explicit precautions have to be taken to cure the problems that occur if an aggressive truncation strategy removes committed Writes that may be needed in a later reconciliation process. Bayou cannot prevent this from happening due to the weakly connected nature of the servers. Thus, Bayou servers may also exchange the full state of their data stores if some Writes are missing that are necessary for the roll-back and roll-forward style of reconciliation.

Of course, some mechanism is needed that decides which Writes to commit. This mechanism has to ensure that a global ordering among Writes is preserved. Note that this is not necessarily the same order in which the tentative Writes appear. However, the global order induced by the Lamport time on the tentative Writes implies a causal order [97]. This causal order must be preserved even if some Writes that are not causally dependent on each other may be reordered by the commit scheme. Each Write that is committed is assigned a monotonically increasing *Commit Sequence Number* (CSN). The CSN is unique and defines a total order among all committed Writes. Uncommitted (tentative) Writes have a CSN of infinity. In the write log of a Bayou server, the committed Writes are ordered before any tentative Writes. Conceptually, the CSN extends the timestamp of a Write such that it becomes $< CSN,\ logical\ clock,\ server\ ID >$. The order among Writes is established with the CSN being the most significant factor. For tentative Writes (equal CSNs), the logical clock is used, and the server ID is used to break ties among Writes with an equal accept timestamp (logical clock).

Bayou does not assume any particular *commit scheme*. Any mechanism that ensures the conditions given above can be used. However, the implementation presented in several publications on Bayou [166, 128] assumes that a *primary server* is responsible for assigning CSNs and, thus, for committing Writes. The primary commits a Write as soon as it receives it. Then, it propagates the information about which Writes have been committed to other servers during the pair-wise reconciliation sessions. This commit scheme preserves the causal ordering among the committed Writes. This becomes intuitively clear if we assume that there are two Writes w_1 and w_2 with $w_1 \rightarrow w_2$ (w_1 "happens before" w_2). $w_1 \rightarrow w_2$ implies that the server S that assigned timestamp 2 to w_2 must have w_1 in its log. Either S received w_1 from a local client or from another server during a reconciliation process. Otherwise, the two Writes cannot have a causal relationship. The anti-entropy protocol that is used for pair-wise reconciliation and that will be explained below, guarantees that w_1 is always transmitted by S before w_2. Thus, any server that has w_2 must also have w_1 in its log, and the two operations have been inserted into the write log in the correct order. Therefore, the primary always receives Writes in the correct causal order, and committing them as they are received cannot corrupt this order.

The Anti-Entropy Protocol

Bayou's anti-entropy protocol (see Figure 10.1) uses a version vector $S.V$ at every server S. $S.V(X)$ holds the largest timestamp of any Write known to S that was originally accepted by server X. In its basic version, the protocol is very simple. The sender S gets the version vector $R.V$ from the receiver R and sends all Writes from its own write log to R that are unknown to R. S does so by comparing the timestamps of the Writes in its log with R's version vector. An important feature of this protocol is its incremental nature: It sends Writes in the logged order. Thus, it can tolerate interrupted transmissions since it is able to continue at the point where the protocol was interrupted.

```
     procedure ANTIENTROPY (S, R)
 2   begin
       Get R.V from receiving server R
       // Now send all the Writes unknown to R
       w = first Write in S.write_log
       while (w)
 7       if R.V(w.server_id) < w.accept_timestamp then
           // w is new for R
           SEND(write(w), R)
         endif
         w = next Write in S.write_log
12     endwhile
     end
```

Figure 10.1: Bayou's basic anti-entropy algorithm executed at the sending server S (adapted from [129]).

Figure 10.2 depicts a slightly more complicated version of this protocol that supports write commitment. Here, $S.CSN$ is the highest commit sequence number known to server S. Since CSNs define a total order, this single number represents the committed portion of S's write log in a concise way. If the receiver R has a CSN smaller than that of the sender S, then S has committed Writes that are completely unknown to R, or R has the write operations in its write log but no knowledge about the fact that they where committed. In the first case, S sends the complete operation to R. In the second case, S only send a notification that the Write has been committed and R uses the data associated with this notification to establish the commitment locally. After the committed portions of the write logs have been synchronized in this way, the tentative part of S's write log is transmitted to R in the same way as in the basic protocol.

10.2 Data Replication in the ASG Environment

In order to derive a useful data replication system for the ASG, we need to analyze the general properties of ASG services first. We do not restrict the nature of the services applicable in the ASG at this point. Instead, we try to find the best replication algorithm, based on the general nature of an ASG service and on the constraints defined by the ASG model.

The dynamic service distribution applied in the ASG results in a system that undergoes frequent fundamental reconfigurations. New replicas are created; existing ones may cease to exist. Thus, the number of replicas and their identity changes over time (cf. Chapter 8). In addition to these dynamics, the Lookup Service can detect crashes, but this may not be possible immediately after the crash happened due to the usage of heartbeats and timeouts. Thus, every replica may only have

```
     procedure ANTIENTROPY (S, R)
  2  begin
         Get R.V and R.CSN from receiving server R
         // first send all the committed Writes unknown
         // to R
         if R.CSN < S.CSN then
  7          w = first committed Write unknown to R
             while (w)
                 if w.accept_timestamp ≤ R.V(w.server_id) then
                     // R has the Write, but does not know
                     // it is committed
 12                  SEND(
                         commitNotification(
                             w.CSN,
                             w.accept_timestamp,
                             w.server_id), R)
 17                  else
                         SEND(write(w), R)
                     endif
                     w = next committed Write in S.write_log
             endwhile
 22      endif
         // now send all the tentative Writes
         w = first tentative Write in S.write_log
         while (w)
             if R.V(w.server_id) < w.accept_timestamp then
 27              // w is new for R
                 SEND(write(w), R);
             endif
             w = next Write in S.write_log
         endwhile
 32  end
```

Figure 10.2: Bayou's anti-entropy algorithm with support for committed Writes, executed at the sending server S (adapted from [129]).

incomplete and partially outdated information on the number, identity, and location of its fellow replicas. It may only be able to obtain an *educated guess* about the current group of fellow replicas using its nearby Lookup Service. Hereafter, we will call this information the replica's *view*.

Due to these reasons, we propose a data replication and consistency system that follows the same principles introduced in the Bayou system: Data is replicated in an optimistic way, and an epidemic protocol is used to achieve consistency among the relevant replicas of a service. However, we will exploit the slightly different nature of the ASG (compared to the Bayou environment) to introduce a protocol that may reconcile a larger group of replicas in a single process. Furthermore, our protocol tries to avoid costly state transfers to save network bandwidth.

10.3 Group Anti-Entropy Protocol (GAP)

The group anti-entropy protocol assumes that each replica knows a subset of all replicas that currently exist. Thus, it has knowledge about the replica group, albeit, this knowledge may be incomplete. This incompleteness is caused by the dynamics of the system. If a new replica is spawned or an old one is removed, the notification about this event may not reach all fellow replicas immediately and at the same time. Perhaps, it may even fail to reach some replicas completely. The GAP deals with this circumstance by running independent reconciliation processes among groups of replicas. Each replica has a *view* of the current replica group. If a replica chooses to reconcile (how this is done will be explained later) then it does so with all of the replicas in its current view. Like the original anti-entropy protocol, the GAP achieves eventual consistency by exploiting the epidemic nature of successive reconciliation processes among several subsets of replicas. A write operation may propagate via several reconciliation processes to finally spread among all replicas.

Each replica r_i holds a *version vector* $r_i.v$ that contains an entry for every known fellow replica r_j. This entry contains the timestamp of the most recent Write operation originating from r_j that is known to r_i. An example of a version vector for a replica r_1 in an overall group of four replicas could be

$$r_1.v = (5.1, 5.2, 7.3, 11.4). \tag{10.1}$$

The GAP is started by one replica. This replica is said to be *active*. All remaining replicas in its view are *passive*. First, the active replica requests all passive replicas to send their current version vectors. For demonstration purposes, let us assume that r_1 is active, that it has three other replicas (r_2, r_3, and r_4) in its view, and that the version vectors are the following:

$$\begin{aligned}
r_1.v &= (\underline{5.1}, \ 5.2, \ 7.3, 11.4\,) \\
r_2.v &= (\,3.1, \underline{11.2}, 10.3, 15.4\,) \\
r_3.v &= (\,3.1, \ 8.2, \underline{17.3}, 15.4\,) \\
r_4.v &= (\,3.1, \ 8.2, 10.3, \underline{15.4}\,)
\end{aligned} \tag{10.2}$$

Collecting the version vectors is the first phase of the protocol. After collecting all vectors, the active replica r_1 tries to retrieve all Writes that it does not already have from the replicas in its view. It tries to minimize the number of messages needed to reconcile by comparing the vectors and by calculating the best order in which to synchronize with the replicas in its view. To do this, r_1 applies a greedy strategy by selecting the passive replica that promises to produce the best update progress. Note that, unlike Bayou, the ASG does not synchronize its logical clocks with the system clock in any way. The reason for this is that unsynchronized clocks allow an educated guess about the number of events that happened between two timestamps since a logical clock is only advanced if some event occurs. Thus, based on the timestamps in the version vectors, r_i can calculate a *preference value* for every replica r_k in its view. This value is an indication of how much progress r_i could make by reconciliating with r_k. To calculate the preference value, we first compare the version vector of the active replica r_i with the version vectors of the other replicas in r_i's view. We do this component-wise and calculate the distance $d_{ik}(j)$ between the version vectors of replicas r_i and r_k for every vector component j. The result is the distance vector d_{ik} of r_i with respect to r_k:

$$d_{ik}(j) = \begin{cases} r_k.v(j) - r_i.v(j) & : \quad r_k.v(j) \text{ and } r_i.v(j) \text{ exist} \\ r_k.v(j) & : \quad r_k.v(j) \text{ exists and } r_i.v(j) \text{ does not exist} \\ 0 & : \quad r_k.v(j) \text{ does not exist and } r_i.v(j) \text{ exists} \end{cases} \quad (10.3)$$

If a component j exists in both vectors, then both replicas have operations originating from r_j. In this case, we simple subtract the two timestamps. If component j only exists in $r_k.v$, then r_i has never received any operation originating from r_j. Thus, the distance between the two timestamps is equal to the timestamp of $r_k.v(j)$. Finally, if component j only exists in $r_i.v$, then r_k does not provide any operations originating from r_j, and r_i would not gain anything from reconciliating with r_k, concerning operations from r_j.

The difference between two timestamps is defined as the difference of their logical clock components. The replica ID parts of the timestamps are ignored. Note that $d_{ik}(j)$ is negative if r_i's version for replica j is more recent than that of r_k. We define the preference value $p_{ik}(j)$ of r_i for r_k concerning component j to be 0 if $d_{ik}(j)$ is negative. The ratio behind this is that r_i will not profit from a reconciliation with r_k in terms of replica r_j since r_i's most recent write operation is newer. The definition of the preference vector p_{ik} is as follows:

$$p_{ik}(j) = \begin{cases} d_{ik}(j) & : \quad d_{ik}(j) > 0 \\ 0 & : \quad d_{ik}(j) \leq 0 \end{cases} \quad (10.4)$$

For every passive replica r_k, r_i sums up all preference value components and gets the total preference $pref_{ik}$ that r_i has for reconciliating with r_k:

$$pref_{ik} = \sum_j p_{ik}(j) \quad (10.5)$$

Finally, we select the replica r_l for which $\forall k : pref_{il} \geq pref_{ik}$ holds. That is, we select the replica with the highest accumulated preference because a reconciliation with this replica has the highest potential benefit. In other words, after a reconciliation of r_i with r_l, r_i will be *more up-to-date* than with any of the other replica in its view. For the reconciliation, r_i sends its current version vector to r_l and r_l sends all write operations that are missing on r_i.

After the reconciliation, r_i updates its version vector to reflect the newly received operations and repeats the procedure until $\forall k : pref_{ik} = 0$. That is, r_i has every write operation existing on the replicas in its view. Now, r_i merges these operations into its data store (roll-back, merge, and roll-forward).

In the final phase of the protocol, r_i sends all write operations missing on the other replicas in its view to the respective replicas who in turn merge them with their data stores. Now, all replicas in the group are perfectly synchronized with each other.

For the setup in our example, the replicas' initial version vectors are the following:

$$
\begin{aligned}
r_1.v &= (\ \underline{5.1}, \quad 5.2, \quad 7.3, 11.4\ ) \\
r_2.v &= (\ 3.1, \underline{11.2}, 10.3, 15.4\ ) \\
r_3.v &= (\ 3.1, \quad 8.2, \underline{17.3}, 15.4\ ) \\
r_4.v &= (\ 3.1, \quad 8.2, 10.3, \underline{15.4}\ )
\end{aligned}
\tag{10.6}
$$

Calculating the difference vector d_{1k} and the preference vector p_{1k} for every k results in:

$$
\begin{aligned}
p_{12} &= (\ 0, 6, \quad 3, 4\ ) \\
p_{13} &= (\ 0, 3, 10, 4\ ) \\
p_{14} &= (\ 0, 3, \quad 3, 4\ )
\end{aligned}
\tag{10.7}
$$

Since r_1 always has the most recent operations originating from itself, the first component of each preference vector is 0. If r_1 would reconcile with r_2, it could potentially receive 6 $(11 - 5)$ new operations submitted at r_2, 3 operations submitted at r_3, and 4 submitted at r_4. Note that it is not guaranteed that r_1 makes this progress in terms of the number of new operations. This is due to the way in which the logical clocks are incremented: A replica does not only increment its clock if a new operation is submitted, but it also increments it when it communicates with other replicas (cf. Section 10.1.2).

In our example, the preference values are the following:

$$
\begin{aligned}
pref_{12} &= 13 \\
pref_{13} &= 17 \\
pref_{14} &= 10
\end{aligned}
\tag{10.8}
$$

Thus, r_1 choses r_3 first and requests an update. Note that r_3's version vector completely covers that of r_4: For every component, r_3 provides at least the operations held by r_4. Thus, after updating its write log with the operations received from r_3, there is no need for r_1 to request an update from r_4 anymore.

After the update from r_3, the situation is as follows:

$$
\begin{aligned}
r_1.v &= (\ \underline{5.1}, \quad 8.2, 17.3, 15.4\ ) \\
r_2.v &= (\ 3.1, \underline{11.2}, 10.3, 15.4\ ) \\
r_3.v &= (\ 3.1, \quad 8.2, \underline{17.3}, 15.4\ ) \\
r_4.v &= (\ 3.1, \quad 8.2, 10.3, \underline{15.4}\ )
\end{aligned}
\tag{10.9}
$$

$$
\begin{aligned}
p_{12} &= (\ 0, 3, 0, 0\ ) \\
p_{13} &= (\ 0, 0, 0, 0\ ) \\
p_{14} &= (\ 0, 0, 0, 0\ )
\end{aligned}
\tag{10.10}
$$

$$
\begin{aligned}
pref_{12} &= 3 \\
pref_{13} &= 0 \\
pref_{14} &= 0
\end{aligned}
\tag{10.11}
$$

Now, r_2 is the only replica with a preference value greater than 0. r_2 potentially still holds 3 operations (submitted locally at r_2) that r_1 has not seen. After receiving an update from r_2, r_1 is consistent with the union of all replicas in its view. At this point, r_1 calculates the differences between its own log and that of the other replicas and updates each of them accordingly. Afterwards, all replicas hold the same set of operations. Thus, they are all pair-wise consistent with each other.

We assume that no Write is inserted into the write log during this reconciliation process. Before any replica enters the process, it takes a snapshot (a copy) of its log and executes the reconciliation process on this copy. We call this the *reconciliation copy*. All Writes that are submitted to a replica during the process are applied to the original log (which we call the *working copy*), not to the reconciliation copy. When the reconciliation process is complete, each replica merges the working copy and the reconciliation copy into one log. Conceptually, there is no difference between merging the local log with an update log received from a fellow replica and merging the reconciliation copy with the working copy. After merging the two logs, the resulting log is applied to the data store.

10.4 Committed Writes and Log Truncation

Like Bayou, the ASG consistency protocol employs the principle of *stable Writes* to be able to truncate the write logs of individual replicas. For this purpose, one replica (called the *primary*) is responsible for committing Writes when it receives them. We adopt this mechanism from Bayou since the development of a distributed scheme for committing Writes presents a major problem in the ASG context. We chose not to tackle this problem here and leave it to future work. The election of a primary will be discussed later. A committed Write cannot be rolled back. It remains stable and, therefore, the write operation is no longer needed since its effects have been permanently applied to the data store. A replica may decide to remove any stable write operations from its write log. In the original anti-entropy protocol, this creates the problem that the sender may have removed committed writes that the receiver has not seen yet. The receiver may have been isolated for a long time. Thus, there is no way to reconcile by exchanging write operations since some of them are missing. In Bayou, the solution for this problem is a complete transfer of the data store's state up to the first omitted Write. Before the state transfer, the state is rolled back to this position. In the ASG, we try to avoid this situation. The avoidance of state transfers is important because, complete state transfers can be very costly. This in turn has a negative influence on the overall cost of replication. The more expensive a replication becomes, the less likely any replication will be made since the costs may outweigh the benefits. Thus, by optimizing the running costs of any replication, we enable more replications in general which can be exploited to render the overall system more responsive and robust.

Before we give a detailed discussion of the mechanism employed to avoid complete state transfers, we define some new notations.

Definition 10.1 (Commit Sequence Numbers). CSN_i^j denotes the CSN of replica r_j as it is currently perceived by replica r_i. Note that this value can be outdated due to the fact that r_i may not have had contact with r_j for some time. Thus, $CSN_i^j \leq CSN_j$. CSN_i denotes the actual current CSN of r_i. This is equivalent to CSN_i^i. CSN_i^{min} is the minimal value of all CSNs currently perceived by r_i: $CSN_i^{min} = min_{1 \le j \le n} \left(CSN_i^j \right)$. CSN^{min} is the actual, current, minimal value over all CSNs. CSN_i^{max} and CSN^{max} are defined analogously. To denote the value of any of these parameters at some time index t, we write $CSN_i^j(t)$, $CSN_i(t)$, $CSN_i^{min}(t)$ etc. respectively. OSN_i denotes the Omit Sequence Number of replica r_i. The OSN is only known to the replica itself and indicates the CSN of the most recently omitted write operation.

Let $\{r_1, \ldots, r_n\}$ be the group of replicas that take part in the reconciliation. Let S be the set of the commit sequence numbers of those Writes that are sufficient in order to do a reconciliation without state transfer:

$$S = \left\{ s \mid CSN^{max} \ge s > CSN^{min} \right\} \tag{10.12}$$

To avoid state transfers during a reconciliation among the replicas $\{r_1, \ldots, r_n\}$, we need to ensure the following property:

$$\forall s \in S : \exists i \in \{1, \ldots, n\} : CSN_i \ge s > OSN_i \tag{10.13}$$

In other words, for every required write operation (all CSNs $s \in S$), there has to be some replica in the group that still holds the write operation. We call this property the *Bounded Divergence Property*. Figure 10.3 depicts an example of a reconciliation group of 4 replicas that fulfills this requirement. However, if r_4 was not present in the group, then the write operation with the commit sequence number 7 would not be present on any of the remaining 3 replicas. r_1 and r_3 have not yet received this Write and r_2 already removed it to save space. Thus, assuming that r_2 is the active replica, r_2 would have to transfer its state at least up to the result of the execution of write number 7 to both r_1 and r_3.

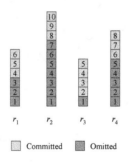

Figure 10.3: Group of four replicas with different write log states.

10.5 Bounded Divergence

In the following, we describe an extended version of the GAP that exploits the relaxed conditions in the ASG to avoid state transfers completely. We call this protocol the *Bounded Divergence Group Anti-Entropy Protocol* (BD-GAP). We introduce an additional timestamp vector which is called the *CSN vector*. Each replica r_i maintains such a vector that holds the values CSN_i^j as defined in Definition 10.1. Whenever i and j take part in the same reconciliation process, they mutually exchange their CSN vectors after all the write logs in the group have been synchronized. That is, if r_i takes part in a reconciliation with a total of n replicas, then r_i receives all $n-1$ CSN vectors of the other participants. After having received all of them, r_i updates its own CSN vector as follows:

$$CSN_i^j := max_{1 \leq k \leq n} \left(CSN_k^j \right) \tag{10.14}$$

Thus, CSN_i^j now holds the highest CSN for replica r_j that was perceived by any of the participants in the current reconciliation process. This represents the best guess of r_j's current CSN. Note that r_j may not be participating in the current reconciliation. Therefore, this guess may be based on a CSN received by one of the participants in an earlier reconciliation. If r_j is currently participating, then CSN_i^j is up-to-date on all replicas in the current reconciliation group.

The goal is to limit the divergence of the write logs such that state transfers do not happen. The basic idea to achieve this is to set a limit to the write operations that a replica may omit in a way that avoids "gaps" in the combined list of committed writes seen during a reconciliation. The term "gap" denotes a violation of property (10.13). Removing r_4 in Figure 10.3 would create a gap at position number 7. To avoid this, we introduce a simple rule for the removal (omission) of Writes from the write log:

Definition 10.2 (Omission Rule). *r_i must never omit a committed Write that has a CSN higher than $CSN_i^{min} = min_{1 \leq j \leq n} \left(CSN_i^j \right)$.*

This means, we take the smallest known CSN among all known replicas (not only the participating ones!) and set it as the *omit limit*. Thus, we only omit Writes that have been received by all known replicas. If permanent partitions are avoided by means that are outside the scope of this discussion, then this algorithm is also guaranteed not to let logs grow indefinitely. A replica r_k whose low CSN keeps other replicas from omitting Writes from their log will eventually take part in another reconciliation, either actively or passively since it is in somebody else's view. Thus, its CSN will be updated as it receives new committed Writes, and its updated CSN will propagate to the other participants of the reconciliation. These, in turn, will propagate it further. After a finite number of reconciliations, all replicas will hold the updated CSN of r_k which is higher than the previous one. Therefore, they can remove all Writes up to the new CSN^{min} which is higher than the previous one set by r_k. In the following, we prove that the Bounded Divergence Property holds if the Omission Rule is obeyed and that write logs cannot grow indefinitely if partitions are only temporary. In preparation of these proofs, we state some necessary claims.

Claim 10.1. *All replicas of a given service stem from a single, initial replica either directly or indirectly.*

Claim 10.1 holds for any distribution algorithm that starts with one initial service instance which is then replicated over one or more generations. This holds for the replica distribution algorithms presented in Chapter 8.

Claim 10.2. *The CSN of a replica never decreases:*

$$\forall t_0, t_1 | t_0 < t_1 : CSN_i(t_0) \leq CSN_i(t_1). \tag{10.15}$$

Claim 10.2 simply follows from the definition of write stabilization: A stabilized (or committed) write is established permanently in the replica's data store and will never be rolled-back.

Claim 10.3. *A replication always produces a spawned replica r_s with a CSN equal to the CSN of the parent replica r_p: $CSN_s = CSN_p$*

Claim 10.3 holds since all the state of the parent replica is simply duplicated in a replication. The fact that r_p spawned (produced a new replica) r_s directly is denoted as $r_p \succ r_s$ (cf. Section 8.4.2). To denote that r_s was spawned directly or indirectly (through a series of one or more replications: $r_p \succ r_1 \succ \ldots \succ r_k \succ r_s$) by r_p, we write $r_p \overset{*}{\succ} r_s$. The negations of these predicates are $r_p \not\succ r_s$ and $r_p \overset{*}{\not\succ} r_s$, respectively. Now we can state and proof the first Theorem.

Theorem 10.1. *For schemes with a single primary replica that has the exclusive right to commit Writes, the Omission Rule guarantees that the* Bounded Divergence Property *(10.13) holds even if partitions occur.*

Proof. Without loss of generality, we assume that a group g (see Figure 10.5) has reconciled at time t_1. At t_2 a partition occurs that divides g into g_1 and g_2. In any such partition, only the members of one group will be able to access the single primary replica. In Figure 10.5, r_2 in group g_1 is the primary. Thus, no Writes will be committed in group g_2 for the duration of the partition. All replicas in g_1 have received and stored the values $CSN_j(t_1)$ for all $r_j \in g_2$ during the reconciliation at time t_1. Since they cannot contact any replica in g_2 after t_2, CSN_i^j will remain at the value set at $t_1 \; \forall r_i \in g_1 \wedge r_j \in g_2 \; (CSN_i^j(t_1) = 6$ in Figure 10.5). This also keeps the CSN_i^{min} value of all replicas $r_i \in g_1$ at $CSN_i^{min}(t_1)$ and no write operations above that CSN can be removed in group g_1. The replicas $r_j \in g_2$, in turn, cannot commit any Writes due to the partition from the primary. Thus, their CSN values will stay at $CSN^{min}(t_1)$. Therefore, if g_1 and g_2 join again, there will be no gap in the list of available write operations and a state transfer will not be necessary.

g may only be a subset of all the replicas in the overall system. Thus, we still need to show that no replica r_o outside g can have a CSN smaller than the CSN^{min} agreed upon by the members of g. If this were the case, a later reconciliation between any subset of g and r_o could require a state transfer because the *Bounded Divergence Property* would be violated.

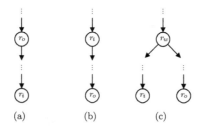

Figure 10.4: Possible cases for the sequence of replications.

Let r_o be a replica outside g. Due to Claim 10.1, for each replica $r_i \in g$, one of the following cases may occur:

1. $r_o \overset{*}{\succ} r_i$: There is a linear sequence of replications by which r_o produces r_i (cf. Figure 10.4(a)). In this case, r_i has an element CSN_i^o for r_o in its CSN vector that represents the most recent known value of r_o's CSN. This element was handed from one replica to the next during the chain of replications from r_o to r_i. Thus, the definition of CSN_i^{min} ensures that within the group g, $CSN_i^{min} \leq CSN_i^o$. Due to Claims 10.2 and 10.3, the current value of r_o's CSN (CSN_o) must be greater or equal to CSN_i^o. Thus, $CSN_i^{min} \leq CSN_i^o \leq CSN_o$. Therefore, r_o cannot have a CSN smaller than CSN_i^{min}.

2. $r_i \overset{*}{\succ} r_o$: There is a linear sequence of replications by which r_i produces r_o (cf. Figure 10.4(b)). Let us assume that there exists some replica r_k with $r_i \succ r_k$ and $r_k \overset{*}{\succ} r_o$. While spawning r_k, r_i stores an element CSN_i^k in its CSN vector. Due to Claims 10.2 and 10.3, the series of replications involved in $r_k \overset{*}{\succ} r_o$ cannot produce any intermediary replica with a CSN smaller than CSN_i^k. Thus, $CSN_i^{min} \leq CSN_i^k \leq CSN_k \leq CSN_o$ holds. The first inequation holds because r_i contributes CSN_i^k to the calculation of CSN_i^{min}. The second inequation holds because of Claim 10.2: CSN_k is the current value of r_k's CSN, CSN_i^k was stored by r_i when r_k was created (in the past), and CSNs never decrease. The last inequation is true due to Claims 10.2 and 10.3. If there is no intermediate replica in the replication sequence between r_i and r_o, then $CSN_i^{min} \leq CSN_i^o \leq CSN_o$ holds analogously.

3. $\exists r_w : r_w \overset{*}{\succ} r_i \wedge r_w \overset{*}{\succ} r_o \wedge r_i \overset{*}{\not\succ} r_o \wedge r_o \overset{*}{\not\succ} r_i$: There is a replica r_w at which the replication sequence branches such that r_w is an ancestor of both r_i and r_o, but r_i and r_o are not created in a direct sequence (cf. Figure 10.4(c)). We assume that r_o and r_i are directly spawned by r_w. The following proof also holds for cases in which there are intermediate replicas in the replication sequence between r_w and r_o and r_i respectively, due to Claims 10.2 and 10.3. Let t_a be the time at which $r_w \succ r_i$, and let t_b be the time at which $r_w \succ r_o$. We need to prove the Theorem for the following two sub-cases:

   (a) $t_a > t_b$: This means that r_o is replicated before r_i. Thus, $CSN_w^o(t_a) = CSN_o(t_b)$, which becomes an element of r_i's CSN vector as it is created by r_w, limits CSN_i^{min}: $CSN_i^{min}(t_a) \leq CSN_w^o(t_a) \leq CSN_o(t_b)$. Due to Claim 10.2 and the fact that $t_a > t_b$, $CSN_o(t_b) \leq CSN_o(t_a)$ must hold. Therefore, $CSN_i^{min}(t_a) \leq CSN_o(t_a)$ holds. As long as CSN_i^o is not updated with a more recent value of r_o's CSN, $CSN_i^{min}(t_c) \leq CSN_o(t_c)$ holds for any time $t_c > t_a$ since CSN_o cannot decrease. If such an update happens, then the new value cannot be higher than the current value of CSN_o and, thus, $CSN_i^{min}(t_c) \leq CSN_o(t_c)$ still holds for any time $t_c > t_a$.

   (b) $t_a \leq t_b$: In this case, r_i is created before or in parallel with r_o. This means that r_i may not have direct knowledge of CSN_o when r_o is created. However, since r_w contributes $CSN_w(t_a)$ to r_i's CSN vector at creation time t_a, $CSN_i^{min} \leq CSN_w(t_a)$ holds until r_i gains knowledge of a later value of CSN_w. Furthermore, $CSN_w(t_a) \leq CSN_w(t_b)$ due to Claim 10.2, and $CSN_w(t_b) \leq CSN_o(t_b)$ holds since r_o simply inherits the

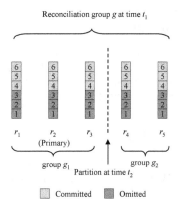

Figure 10.5: A partitioned reconciliation group.

CSN of r_w. Thus, when r_o is created at t_b, $CSN_i^{min}(t_b) \leq CSN_w(t_a) \leq CSN_w(t_b) \leq CSN_o(t_b)$ holds. $CSN_i^{min}(t_c) \leq CSN_o(t_c)$ can only be violated for any $t_c > t_b$, if $CSN_i^{min}(t_c)$ increases beyond $CSN_o(t_c)$. However, since $CSN_w(t_a)$ is in r_i's CSN vector, $CSN_i^{min} \leq CSN_o$ continues to hold until r_i gains knowledge of a more recent value of CSN_w. This may happen directly through an encounter with r_w or indirectly via some other replica that has met r_w after time t_b. In both cases, r_i does not only receive a new (possibly higher) value of CSN_w, but also a past value of CSN_o. Since r_w has stored CSN_o in its CSN vector at replication time t_b, any new value of CSN_w after time t_b is accompanied by a value of $CSN_o(t_d)$ with $t_b \leq t_d \leq t_c$. This value must be less or equal to the current value $CSN_o(t_c)$ due to Claim 10.2. Thus, $CSN_i^{min}(t_c) \leq CSN_o(t_d) \leq CSN_o(t_c)$.

$\square$

Note that in this proof we do not assume that partitions are temporary. They may also be permanent and still the *Bounded Divergence Property* holds. However, in this case, the write logs of some replicas may grow indefinitely large. We will cope with this problem in Theorem 10.2.

Theorem 10.2. *If partitions are only temporary, the* Bounded Divergence GAP *does not let write logs grow indefinitely.*

The basic idea of the proof is the following: We assume that a replica exists that can never remove any Write from its write log and show that this can only happen if permanent partitions occur. This is the reverse implication of Theorem 10.2.

Proof. We assume that a replica r_i exists that can never remove any write operation from its write log due to the Omission Rule. This must be a result of r_i's CSN^{min} value never being increased. For CSN^{min} to remain at the same value, r_i's CSN vector must be invariant in at least one position. That is, one replica r_k must exist whose element CSN_i^k in r_i's vector never increases. This can be directly concluded from the Omission Rule. We assume that new write operations are constantly being submitted somewhere in the system. Otherwise, indefinite growth could never occur. If r_i's value for r_k's CSN never increases, then either r_k never receives any new committed write, or it is unable to propagate its new CSN to r_i. In the first case, r_k must be permanently separated from the primary replica. In the latter case, r_i must be permanently separated from r_k. Thus, in both cases, a permanent partition must exist.   □

10.5.1   Replica Removal

Until now, we have ignored the fact that replicas may also disappear. The disappearance of a replica may have two reasons:

1. A replica chooses to dissolve because some predicate defined by the distribution algorithm is fulfilled (e.g. the replica is idle for too long), or

2. a replica simply crashes without any prior notice.

If a replica r_d dissolves, it is required to reconcile with at least one other replica before it actually removes itself. This ensures that the *Bounded Divergence Property* still holds since no committed Write is lost. Thus, a dissolving replica cannot create a gap. However, other replicas may still have an element for r_d in their CSN vector. Since r_d is no longer active, the remaining elements CSN_i^d in the CSN vectors of the other replicas will never increase which causes CSN^{min} to remain invariant and prevents write operations from being removed from any write log. A simple approach to avoid this is to let r_d set its CSN to ∞ before its final reconciliation. The other replicas participating in this reconciliation will store ∞ as their new value for r_d's CSN and eventually propagate it to the rest of the replicas. However, this means that CSN vectors will get bigger over time and no element will ever be removed. Since there is no boundary on the time needed to propagate the removal of a replica ($CSN_d = \infty$) throughout the whole system, we cannot simply remove an element that equals ∞. It may be *re-imported* by some replica that still holds an old value $< \infty$ which would keep replicas from properly purging their write logs.

The growth of the CSN vectors seems acceptable, since replication and removal do not happen with a high frequency. When the distribution algorithm has adapted to the currently perceived usage patterns, replications should not occur any longer until the next notable change in usage patterns.

If a replica crashes, it will not be able to reconcile with any other replicas. This may possibly cause the loss of tentative Writes that were not yet sent to other replicas. It may also cause the loss of committed Writes if the crashed replica happened to be the primary and some committed Writes have not yet been transmitted to other replica. The recovery of a lost primary will be discussed later. Here, we have to investigate the possible effects in terms of data consistency. An interesting feature of the Bounded Divergence GAP is that a crashed replica can never cause a violation of the Bounded Divergence Property. Hence, it is uncritical in terms of the requirement for state transfers. This follows directly from Theorem 10.1 since a crash is equivalent to a permanent partition between the crashed replica and the rest of the replicas.

However, in order to ensure that this does not cause indefinite write log growth, we still need to propagate the information about the disappearance of the replica in order to set the corresponding entry in the CSN vectors to ∞. To do this, we exploit the ability of the Lookup Services to detect replica crashes (cf. Section 9.3.3).

10.6 The Bounded Divergence GAP

Figure 10.6 depicts the state diagram of the BD-GAP. A replica may be in one of three major states. If it is not currently involved in any reconciliation process, it is "Ready". An active reconciliation may be "triggered" either if a certain number of Writes have been submitted locally by clients or if a timeout occurs[2]. If this happens, the replica goes to "Active Reconciliation" mode in order to start a new reconciliation process actively. If a vv_request message is received, the replica goes to "Passive Reconciliation" to engage with the sender passively. The interactions between active and passive replicas are also shown in detail in the sequence diagram in Figure 10.7.

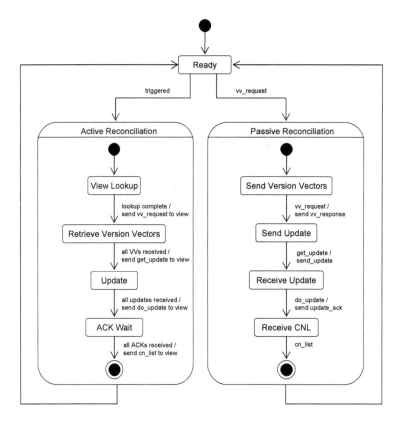

Figure 10.6: Simplified state diagram of the BD-GAP.

---

[2]Details about the triggering mechanism are given below, in Section 10.6.2.

The protocol has four major stages:

1. Initially, an active replica has to find out what its current view (set of known replicas of the same service type) is. It does so by querying the Lookup Service.

2. After having received its view, an active replica starts the protocol by requesting the version vectors of all fellow replicas in its view. This is done when entering the state "Retrieve Version Vectors". When all version vectors have been received, the active replica calculates the order in which it will request updates from the different passive replicas (cf. Section 10.3), and it calculates the version vectors characterizing these update requests accordingly. Then it sends out the requests for these updates and goes to state "Update".

3. Having received all requested updates, the active replica merges them into one update log. Using the version vectors of the passive replicas, it calculates an individual update log for each of them. It sends out these updates (do_update messages) and goes to state "ACK Wait". Each do_update message also contains the current CSN (commit sequence number) of the active replica. If the active replica is the primary, it commits the newly received Writes and sends the new CSN in this step. If it is a passive replica, it extracts the highest CSN from the merged update log and its own log and used it as its new CSN. Each passive replica needs the CSN to compile a *commit notification list* for the active side. The CNL contains notifications assigning commit sequence numbers to Write IDs. A passive replica may have a committed Write of which an uncommitted version is also present in the active replica's log. In this case, it does not send the complete Write but only a notification that the Write has been committed together with the respective CSN. This is called a *commit notification*. A whole list of commit notifications may be compiled by the passive replica and sent to the active side in the next step.

4. Each passive replica sends an acknowledgment message (update_ack) containing its own CSN and its commit notification list. Note that if one of the passive replicas is the primary, then this replica commits the update received from the active replica. Thus, its CSN is higher than that send by the active replica in the previous stage of the protocol. The active replica applies the commit notifications to its log and updates the sender's CSN in its own CSN vector. After having received all update acknowledgments, the active replica compiles a CNL for each passive replica and sends it together with its complete CSN vector in a cn_list message. At this point, the active replica is up-to-date. After receiving the cn_list message, each passive replica applies the CNL and merges the CSN vector into its own vector. Now, the passive replicas are up-to-date, too, and the reconciliation process has finished. Active and passive replicas go back to the "Ready" state.

Figures 10.6 and 10.7 are simplified. They do not depict the details of resolving conflicts in the protocol. This aspect is orthogonal to the normal protocol functions and will be discussed in Section 10.6.3.

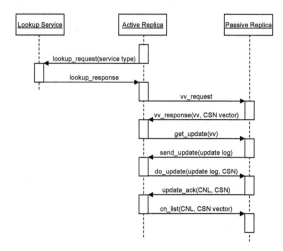

Figure 10.7: Simplified sequence diagram of the BD-GAP.

10.6.1 Selecting the Primary

The initial replica of a specific service type that is installed in an ASG automatically becomes the primary. Having a single primary copy is a simple solution to the problem of committing Writes. However, it also creates well-known problems. The primary is a central point of failure. The consequences of a primary failure are twofold: First of all, all updates submitted to the primary replica by clients are lost. However, this is true for every replica. Thus, in terms of lost updates, loosing the primary is no different from loosing any replica. The second and more severe consequence is the lack of Write commitments which lets Write logs grow monotonically on all remaining replicas. We assume that the primary's Proxy will not crash. This means that the Proxy Agent can detect that the primary replica is not operational anymore and restart it. Based on a saved snapshot of its write log, the primary may resume.

The primary may crash at any stage of the BD-GAP protocol without causing irreparable inconsistencies. The following situations may occur if the primary crashes while being involved in a reconciliation process:

- **Replicas' write logs may not be updated.** This does not represent an unusual situation for the system. Updates will be made when the next reconciliation is executed. Since a replica only modifies its write log when it has correctly received a valid update, write logs cannot be corrupted by a primary crash. Either the primary sends a correct update or it does not send an update at all. Situations in which only some of the replicas in the reconciliation group are updated are not a problem either.

- **Writes received by the primary before its crash may not be committed.** Committing the Writes can be done after the primary has resumed without causing any damage.

- **Commit notification lists may not be transmitted to passive replicas.**
  This will be fixed when the next reconciliation is executed. Until then, these
  Writes remain tentative.

- **Commit sequence numbers may not be updated.** A crash may cause the
  CSN vector of one or more replicas to keep its previous value. However, as long
  as it does not decrease, this is no problem. Until the next reconciliation, committed Writes may remain in the write log which causes unnecessary memory
  consumption. But this will be corrected in the next reconciliation process.

Usually, central components in distributed systems pose the danger of forming bottlenecks. In the ASG, the primary does not receive more or less messages than any
other replica. Neither does it have any central position in directing or relaying message flows or executing control actions. The only difference between the primary and
a normal replica is that the primary may commit the Writes it receives. Thus, the
primary replica is no bottleneck.

10.6.2   Triggering Reconciliations

Each replica decides locally when to actively start a new reconciliation process. This
decision is taken

1. if the number of Writes received from clients since the last reconciliation process exceeds the threshold value W_{rec} (this value is called the *reconcile write
   threshold*), or

2. if the time that has passed since the last reconciliation process exceeds the
   reconcile timeout value T_{rec}, and at least one Write has been received locally
   in the last T_{rec} time units.

These two predicates are called *reconciliation rules*. The first rule sets a limit to the
level of inconsistency that may occur within a group of replicas. If N is the number
of replica in the group, then they may at most reach the inconsistency level equal
to having $N \cdot W_{rec}$ different Writes in the group. This upper limit is reached if all
replicas in the group receive an equal amount of W_{rec} Writes in the time period
T_{rec}. However, in most cases, it is more likely that they experience slightly different
load conditions. Thus, a new reconciliation process will be started by one replica
that reaches the limit first while other replicas may have less Writes. The term
level of inconsistency is very hard to quantify because it largely depends on the
application and the type of operations submitted. However, we assume that each
Write contributes more or less to this level.

The second rule ensures that even if it takes very long for a replica to reach the write
threshold, reconciliation processes will take place in regular intervals. Of course, this
only happens if there is at least one Write that has not yet been reconciled with the
fellow replicas. If this rule was not applied, there could be slowly developing but
long-lasting periods of growing inconsistency.

10.6.3   Resolving Reconciliation Conflicts

To keep the reconciliation protocol as simple as possible, we decided that each replica may only be involved in one reconciliation process at a time. Therefore, conflicts may result from the fact that each replica may decide on its own when to start an active reconciliation process. However, we deal with this fact in an optimistic fashion, too: When a replica decides to actively start a new reconciliation process, it does *not* check whether the fellow replicas in its current view are already involved in another process. Instead, it ignores this possibility and simply starts the process, assuming that in most cases it will succeed in doing so. If, however, one of its fellows has already started an active process, there is a conflict resolution mechanism that decides which replica may proceed and which one must abort its attempt.

10.6.4   Resolution Mechanism

The basic rule applied by the conflict resolution mechanism is: *The replica with the lowest ID wins.* A replica A that has started an active process may abort it if another active replica B with a lower ID sends a request. This may happen until A has entered the "Retrieve Updates" state (see. Figure 10.6) and has requested updates from its passive fellow replicas. Thus, until it has sent the first get_update message (see. Figure 10.7), an active replica may assume a passive role engaging with another active replica. After having entered the state "Update", A will not abort its active reconciliation process, and it will decline the request of B. An active replica that receives an abort message (in this case B), reacts by removing the sender from its view and continues with those passive replicas that accepted its request. A passive replica may abort any ongoing reconciliation process as long as it has not entered the state "Send Update" and has not yet sent an update to its current active replica. Therefore, a passive replica may accept incoming requests from replicas with a lower ID until that point. If a replica that is not currently involved in any reconciliation process, receives two or more requests from active replicas at the same time, then it accepts the request of the replica with the lowest ID and aborts the rest.

The sequence diagram (Figure 10.7) and the state diagram (Figure 10.6) show a simplified version of the reconciliation protocol. Conflict resolution adds some complexity to the individual protocol states because each replica must detect conflicts, resolve them by sending abort messages, and react to incoming abort messages. Figure 10.8 depicts this mechanism in greater detail. It shows how the state "Retrieve Version Vectors" works internally. Note that in this view, the sending of vv_request messages is a part of this state, while in the simplified diagram, it belongs to the state "View Lookup".

The bold elements in this chart deal with the problem of conflicts while the remaining elements represent the normal protocol behavior. There are two *Abort* states, one "Early Abort" and one "Late Abort". The Early Abort state handles requests that come in immediately before requests are sent out. If such a request arrives, no further action is necessary. The replica (called A hereafter) simply goes into passive mode entering the state "Send Version Vectors". However, if requests have already been sent out, an abort situation must be handled by sending out abort messages to all replicas that are not aware of the fact that a new replica B has assumed the active role. Thus, A sends abort messages to all replicas that are not in B's view. The

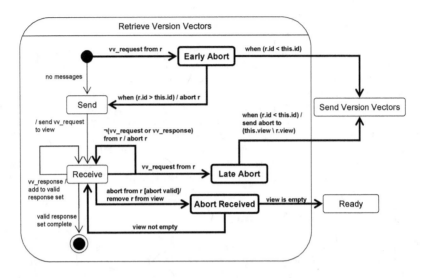

Figure 10.8: Conflict resolution mechanism.

replicas in B's view will automatically detect the change and accept B as the new active replica. The remaining replicas in A's view must be informed. After having sent out the abort messages, A switches to passive mode engaging with the new active replica B. If A receives any messages other than vv_request or vv_response, it sends an abort message to the sender indicating that it is not ready for whatever the sender planned. Finally, if A receives an abort message itself, it removes the sender from its view and carries on as long as there are still replicas left in its view. From now on, the sender does not participate in the reconciliation process any longer. If the last remaining replica in A's view aborts, A cancels the process and switches to the state "Ready".

10.6.5   Deadlocks, Lifelocks, and Fairness

The reconciliation protocol avoids deadlocks as well as lifelocks. Both of these situations may occur if two (or more) replicas start an active process at the same time and each of them has the other replica(s) in its view. If both replicas send their vv_request and wait for the vv_response to arrive from the other side, the result is a deadlock. If, on the other hand, both replicas choose to abort the process, no reconciliation takes place at all. If both sides repeat their request after the same timeout, the same situation occurs repeatedly without any progress which results in a lifelock. Deadlocks are avoided because in the phase of the protocol in which the roles are not ultimately decided yet, both sides may abort. This removes the *circular wait* condition necessary to enter a deadlock state [34]. The fact that, based on the replicas' IDs, both sides know who is the legitimate active replica, enables them to prevent lifelocks: The winning replica will not abort while the loser does abort. This means that one of the replicas will execute a reconciliation process. Moreover, after having received all send_update message from the passive replicas, the winning active replica can be sure that none of the passive replicas will abort the process. The protocol can also guarantee *fairness*. In our scenario, we define the protocol to be fair if no replica is kept for ever from reconciliating with its fellow replicas.

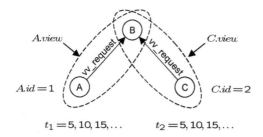

Figure 10.9: Unfair state: C is kept from reconciliating with B.

Consider the situation depicted in Figure 10.9: A and C have B in their views but they do not see each other. We assume that both A and C trigger an active reconciliation at the same time. Both do so because they run into the reconcile timeout T_{rec}. If the volume of submitted Writes never reaches a level at which the write threshold is exceeded, then A and C will continue to send vv_request messages to B at the same points time (t_1 and t_2). Each time B picks A as its active replica and declines C's request because A has the lower ID. Therefore, C never gets to reconcile, and the overall inconsistency grows. We avoid this situation by adjusting T_{rec} whenever a conflict is detected in a reconciliation process that was triggered by a timeout. A random value in the range of 5 to 10% of the current value of T_{rec} is added to T_{rec} on each aborted active reconciliation that was triggered by the timeout. Thus, eventually, C's request will succeed when it arrives at a point in time at which B is not engaged with A.

10.7 Quantitative Evaluation

The quantitative results from our experiments are twofold:

1. They give an indication of the best working point with respect to the two tunable parameters introduced above: the *reconcile write threshold* W_{rec} and the *reconcile timeout* T_{rec}.

2. They show how the system's overall consistency develops as we increase the *write ratio* w. This value is defined by the application our system is subjected to it. The write ratio has profound influence on the operation of the consistency protocol.

We start our evaluation by introducing the consistency measure on which our results are based.

10.7.1   The Consistency Measure

To produce a benchmark scenario that is easy to implement and reasonably quick to simulate, we modeled the data stores of the replicas as bit strings of ℓ bits each ($\ell = 100$ in the following). Each write operation produced by a client c toggles one of the bits of the data store associated with the replica used by c. When a client produces a write operation (with probability w), it chooses a position between 0 and $\ell - 1$ (according to a uniform distribution) and produces a bit string with a 1 at that position and 0s at the remaining $\ell - 1$ positions. When such a write operation is received by a replica, the bit string from the operation and the current bit string in the replica's data store are combined using the XOR operation to produce the replica's new bit string. The XOR toggles the respective bit in the data store and the reverse operation is another XOR between the new data store bit string and the original bit string from the operation. This reverse operation is needed to roll back operations. More formally, if B_c is the bit string provided by the client and B_r is the current bit string held by the data store of the replica that receives c's request, then the new bit string of the replica is $B_r' = B_r \oplus B_c$ and the reverse operation is $B_r = B_r' \oplus B_c$.

This artificial application (setting bits in a bit string) enables us to come up with a simple measure for the consistency among an arbitrary number of replicas. For this purpose, we introduce a global data store represented by the bit string B_G. This data store is the result of all operations from all clients being executed in the correct order on a single bit string. In reality, this string does not exist, but in the simulation, we can easily construct it by executing each Write on the single bit string B_G in addition to the execution on the real locally existing bit string B_r. Let $|B|$ denote the number of 1-bits in the bit string B. Our consistency measure κ is defined as follows:

$$\kappa = 1 - \frac{\sum_{r \in R} |B_r \oplus B_G|}{|R| \cdot \ell} \tag{10.16}$$

The numerator in the second term is the number of differences between B_G and all the bit strings B_r found in the set of existing replicas R. The denominator is the number of bits existing in all data stores. The fraction measures the inconsistency found in the system. To find the consistency, we subtract it from 1. κ is 1 if all replicas hold identical bit strings, and it is 0 if each B_r is the negation of B_G. One can easily verify that, if the individual bit strings are independent, the expected value of κ is 0.5. This is true since the probability for a pair of random bits being different is 0.5 and we normalize the sum of differences by the number of bits. Thus, if κ is close to 0.5, this indicates that no correlation exists among the data stores. In this case, they are obviously completely independent. From a reasonable consistency protocol, we would expect values much high than 0.5.

We denote the time-dependent consistency function as $\kappa(t)$. $\kappa(t)$ is simply computed from the bit strings and the value of $|R|$ at time t. The average consistency $\overline{\kappa}$ for a complete simulation run is defined as follows:

$$\overline{\kappa} = \frac{\sum_{t \in [0, T-1]} \kappa(t)}{T} \tag{10.17}$$

10.7.2 Experimental Results

Figure 10.10 shows the basic behavior of the BD-GAP consistency protocol. The graph depicts the consistency measure κ for a single simulation run over a small time window. At the start ($t < 10000$), we have a single replica and, therefore, $\kappa = 1$. As soon as there is a second replica (created at $t = 10000$), the consistency decreases since each of the replicas receives Writes from its clients and incorporates them into its data store. At $t = 11000$, the consistency protocol is executed and complete consistency is restored ($\kappa(11000) = 1$). Between the reconciliation processes, the consistency drops each time. If no further reconciliations would occur, $\kappa(t)$ would eventually converge to 0.5. Note that the average value of κ, in this case, is only around 0.8 even though complete consistency is restored each time.

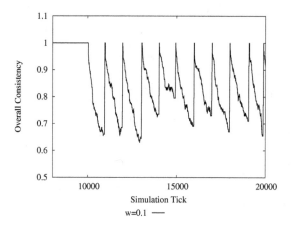

Figure 10.10: Overall consistency κ plotted against simulation time for $w = 0.1$.

Average Consistency for Increasing Write Ratio

In Figure 10.11, the average consistency $\overline{\kappa}$ is depicted for increasing write ratio w. As expected, an increasing write ratio reduces the consistency. However, it decreases only by about 10% from the maximal value at $w = 0.1$ to the minimal value at $w = 0.4$. Moreover, after an initial steep drop, the consistency stabelizes around a value of about 0.715. This behavior is the result of the combination of the *reconcile write threshold* W_{rec} and the *reconcile timeout* T_{rec}. Initially, (approximately for $w < 0.3$) the number of Writes received by a replica on average is not high enough to trigger the write threshold rule. Reconciliations are always triggered by the timeout rule. Therefore, an increasing write ratio causes more inconsistency in this phase as the time intervals between consecutive reconciliations are approximately equal. However, as w is increased beyond a certain value, the intervals start getting shorter as the write threshold rule takes over: After a certain number of Writes is received, a replica starts a reconciliation process, and for large w this point is reached before the timeout expires. One can easily see that doing a reconciliation after a prescribed number of Writes have modified the data store limits the inconsistency experienced throughout the whole system. This keeps the system at a constant consistency level.

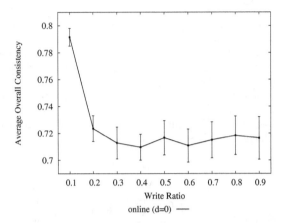

Figure 10.11: Average overall consistency $\bar{\kappa}$ plotted against the write ratio w.

As we will see in the subsequent experiments, lowering W_{rec} raises the level to which the consistency converges for large values of w. The price is, of course, an increase in the overhead caused by reconciliation messages. Note that if we would remove the timeout rule completely, the system would always experience a constant consistency level of about $\bar{\kappa} = 0.715$ for $w = 0.1$. The timeout enforces that a considerably higher consistency level can be achieved for low write ratios that are common for many applications [83].

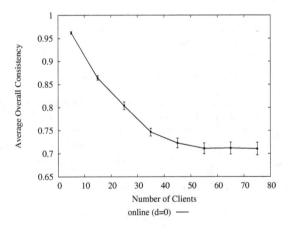

Figure 10.12: Average overall consistency $\bar{\kappa}$ for increasing number of clients.

Figure 10.12 shows how $\bar{\kappa}$ develops as the number of clients in the system increases. In this experiment, the write ratio was kept constant at a value of 0.1. The same general behavior as for a growing write ratio can also be observed here: $\bar{\kappa}$ drops until it converges to a value of about 0.71. The reason is that a growing number of clients produce a growing number of write operations. Therefore, the timeout rule fires in the initial stages (for a low number of clients), and the write threshold takes over for a higher number of clients.

Investigation of Parameter Settings

As we have seen, the write threshold W_{rec} and the timeout T_{rec} interact with each other to achieve a good performance for commonly observed working conditions and to limit the consistency degradation as the volume of write operations increases (higher write ratio or higher number of clients).

T_{rec} sets a hard limit to the time period that is necessary for a newly received Write to propagate in the system: When a replica receives a Write, then its fellow replicas have to wait at most T_{rec} time units until they receive this Write. This holds, irrespective of the rate at which Writes are produced in the system. This fixed timeout introduces a certain guarantee about how up-to-date data items are.

However, the fact that T_{rec} is fixed also implies that if the rate at which Writes are produced in the system increases, then the consistency decreases. Let us denote this rate as ω. ω is the number of Writes produced throughout the system over a specific period of time Δt (ω is also called the *system write rate*):

$$\omega = \frac{\Delta |W|}{\Delta t} \tag{10.18}$$

Let us denote $|W|_{rec}$ as the number of Writes that are produced throughout the system over the course of T_{rec} time units. With Equation (10.18), we get

$$|W|_{rec} = \omega \cdot T_{rec}. \tag{10.19}$$

Thus, if ω increases, then $|W|_{rec}$ increases. If no other mechanism than the timeout T_{rec} is used to trigger reconciliations, then the consistency measure κ is solely depending on $|W|_{rec}$. If ω is very high, then κ quickly converges to 0.5. Thus, a large number of Writes is allowed to take effect on the data stores to a point where there is merely any correlation between them.

This total disappearance of consistency is avoided by introducing W_{rec}. With W_{rec}, there is not only a limit on the time period for which a new Write is withheld from the fellow replicas but also on the number of Writes received by a replica between two reconciliations and, thus, on κ.

In fact, W_{rec} functions as an additional *variable timeout* that is *adaptive to the system's overall write rate* ω. If we transform Equation (10.18) and set $\Delta |W| = W_{rec}$, we get

$$\Delta t = \frac{W_{rec}}{\omega}. \tag{10.20}$$

Δt is the time it takes for W_{rec} Writes to be produced at a system write rate of ω. If we include the write threshold rule for triggering reconciliations and ω increases to a point where $\omega \geq \frac{W_{rec}}{T_{rec}}$, then $\Delta t \leq T_{rec}$ and reconciliations are triggered after the time Δt. Our reconciliation rule that is a combination of reconcile timeout and write threshold can be rewritten as follows: A reconciliation is triggered after $\min(T_{rec}, \frac{W_{rec}}{\omega})$ time units.

Figure 10.13 illustrates the relation between T_{rec}, W_{rec}, ω, and Δt graphically. Figure 10.13(c) shows how the adaptive timeout Δt reacts to different settings of W_{rec} and dynamic changes in ω. Figures 10.13(a) and 10.13(b) show how Δt decreases with a growing ω, until $\Delta t < T_{rec}$ and $|W|_{rec}$ stays constant as ω continues to increase.

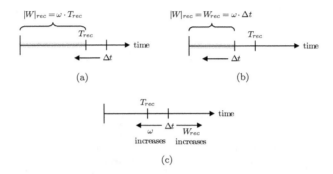

Figure 10.13: Illustration of the combined reconciliation rule.

Figure 10.14 sketches how the quality of the reconciliation process can explicitly be modeled using the tunable parameters T_{rec} and W_{rec}. Changes in these two parameters effect the position of what we call the *working point*. W_{rec} defines to which general level of consistency the system converges for high values of the system write rate ω. If we increase W_{rec}, more Writes are allowed to alter the data stores, and this level approaches the system's theoretical lower consistency bound. Changes in T_{rec}, on the other hand, effect the system write rate at which the convergence sets in. If T_{rec} is increased to very large values, then Δt will always be the relevant timeout and the system will allow W_{rec} Writes before a reconciliation is triggered, irrespective of ω. In this case, the working point would be shifted to the extreme left of the coordinate system in the Figure, and $\overline{\kappa}$ would be constant at the level defined by W_{rec} for all values of ω. If, on the other hand, T_{rec} would be decreased to very small values, then the level of consistency would only drop very slowly with ω since reconciliation would take place very often. Eventually, for extremely high values of ω, Δt would fall below T_{rec}, and $\overline{\kappa}$ would drop to the level defined by W_{rec}.

In order to apply this model, one needs to find the application-dependent consistency measure κ and a relation between κ and W_{rec}. Then, we can define a tolerable level of consistency κ_{min} and set W_{rec} such that $\kappa \geq \kappa_{min}$ for any system write rate ω. Decreasing T_{rec} establishes a higher consistency level for higher values of ω and a shorter time interval before new Writes are propagated, but it also increases the reconciliation overhead.

10.8   Discussion

In this chapter, we have presented an optimistic consistency model for ASG services. This model is derived from the well-known Bayou system and introduces some new features and relaxations that are based on the specific nature of the ASG. We propose the bounded divergence mechanism that helps avoiding costly state transfers between

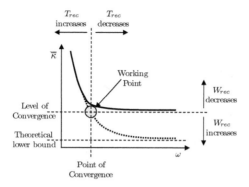

Figure 10.14: Working point of the reconciliation process.

replicas. The optimistic model introduces a great relaxation over pessimistic models that require global synchronization and locking mechanisms. This enables service replicas to exploit their autonomy in order to adapt in the best possible way. The system can deal with the fact that the number of existing replicas may be unknown and dynamic. It may also compensate temporary network partitions. Finally, we introduced a model for fine-tuning the level of consistency produced by the system via two simple parameters. This mechanism allows the adjustment of the reconciliation process to the specific requirements of an application.

However, the model also has its drawbacks. A technical insufficiency is represented by the fact that we rely on a primary replica scheme for committing Writes. We have already discussed the possible consequences in Section 10.6.1. Future work should investigate whether other, more robust schemes may also be used without violating the bounded divergence principle.

A second issue is the conflict resolution at the client side. Assuming an optimistic point of view, we say that conflicts do not occur very often following the lines of Bayou, Coda, and other related projects. We do not care about how conflicts are presented to the user and how he may resolve them. It should be noted that in the bulk of publications about the Bayou system, the authors opted to do the same. Thus, this is an open issue that requires some attention in the future.

Altogether, the question arises, as to which class of applications may be realized using the proposed consistency protocol. In an immediate and intuitive answer, we would rule out any applications that involve critical tasks. For example, financial transaction that may fail and remain in an inconsistent state without immediate notice and roll-back are certainly outside the scope of applications we target with our system. In general, applications should be analyzed closely to find their vulnerability to inconsistencies and their probability to produce such inconsistencies. This analysis is highly application-dependent, and we consider it to be out of scope of this book.

It could also be worthwhile investigating the applicability of more strict and more pessimistic models. Maybe there are tolerable models that do not hinder the ASG system too much in its ability to adapt and that could allow for more critical applications. This would be a problem worth investigating in greater detail.

Chapter 11

Architectural Implications

Contents

In the preceding chapters, we have presented solutions to three major problems associated with the self-organization of Ambient Services. These mechanisms were implicitly built on some assumptions about a middleware that were presented in Section 7. Now that we have given a detailed insight into the algorithms that are necessary to render an ASG self-organizing, we can derive the requirements for the underlying middleware platform more precisely.

In this chapter, we will explain the basic features of such a middleware in more detail. Subsequently, we give an overview of the platform that we have designed in order to support the operation of an ASG. In this discussion, we will only concentrate on the core features of such a middleware.

11.1 Middleware Platform Requirements

There are three essential requirements that follow from the preceding presentation of our algorithms and protocols:

1. Service replicas must be able to relocate themselves autonomously and in a decentralized fashion. Thus, the components used to implement such objects must be mobile. As was already motivated in Section 7.1, we chose the mobile agent paradigm for this purpose.

2. Decoupled asynchronous communication is needed to cope with the dynamics present in the ASG environment. Since the most important entities in the ASG (client and replicas) are mobile, we need the ability to decouple the interactions between these entities. Request and reply messages must be buffered and redirected if necessary, and other entities must be able to process such messages on behalf of the original recipient. Furthermore, the style of communication present in an ASG is best matched by an event-based system. Replicas and infrastructure elements must be able to react to situations that occur spontaneously. Especially the core mechanisms proposed for self-organizational processes (message snooping, Proxy Agents etc.) must react to events that are not directly targeted at them. They must be able to intercept messages, derive information from them and alter them to enforce a specific form of organization.

3. The third core requirement is closely related to the preceding one: A cross-layer view must be established for higher-level components since low-level information about the communication in the system is a key ingredient of the self-organization processes advocated in this book. For example, the replica placement system needs information about the path of client messages, and the Lookup Service needs meta information that are encapsulated in reply messages in order to organize according to the usage patterns inherent to the system. The best means for implementing such mechanisms is event-based communication.

11.2   Middleware Architecture

From the requirements stated above and from the features explained in Chapter 7, we now derive a basic middleware architecture. This architecture was implemented in the simulation environment that we used to validate our concepts and to collect the experimental data presented above. Apart from this implementation, we have also realized these and some other features in a real middleware called MESHMdl [69].

Figure 11.1 depicts the basic communication architecture of the ASG middleware system. The collection of entities found in an ASG system can be divided into two parts:

1. At the service provisioning side, the replicas of value-added services and the clients are located. Both emit events (send messages) and consume events (receive messages) via the ASG infrastructure.

2. At the Serviceware side, a heterogeneous collection of agents is responsible for providing the necessary support for the service provisioning such that clients and replicas may abstract from these issues and concentrate on their task.

The core architecture is based on a micro-kernel approach. That is, the core only provides minimal functionality, and extended functions are added as agents. The core functions are threefold:

- The *event system* is responsible for realizing a basic event-based communication service.

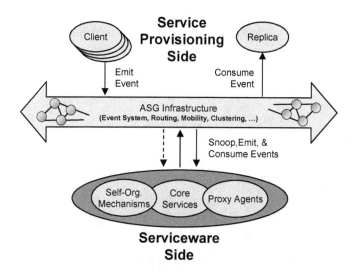

Figure 11.1: ASG communication architecture.

- The *agent runtime environment* provides basic support for managing agents (starting, stopping, migrating, cloning etc.).

- The clustering module (not depicted) runs the algorithm for managing the network's clustered structure (cf. Section 5.1.4).

We will not go into the details of the agent runtime since this is not really important for the issues discussed in this book. We also leave out details about the clustering mechanism. The information given in Section 5.1.4 is sufficient, and the technical realization is straight forward. In the next section, we will discuss the event system in more detail as it takes a central role in the implementation of the self-organization processes.

11.3   The Event System

Figure 11.1 shows the basic communication primitives. The means for interaction are events which can be emitted, consumed, and snooped. All three of these actions are based on the tuple space paradigm (cf. Section 7.2). One of the main tasks of the ASG infrastructure, which is depicted in the center of the Figure, is to transport events. The architecture of the event transport and delivery system is depicted in Figure 11.2.

It is based on the so-called *Event Space* which serves as a communication medium. An Event Space provides the basic function of associative, anonymous, and asynchronous communication that is well-known from the tuple space paradigm (cf. Section 7.2). An event is put into the space and can be collected by any entity in the system based on its content. For this associative selection of events from the Event Space,

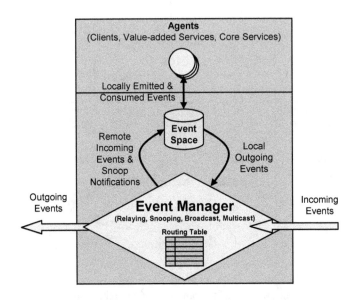

Figure 11.2: ASG event system.

an *event template* is provided that contains a partial specification of the desired events' content. Thus, the Event Space stores all events that are relevant to the local system, and clients and replicas, as well as the components belonging to the Serviceware, access these events using a small number of primitives for writing and associative reading of event objects.

The second component of the event system is the *Event Manager*. It allows for a multi-hop event-based communication using a standard routing mechanism and by providing means for sending *broadcast events* (targeted at all nodes in the system) and *cluster head broadcast events* (targeted only at the cluster head nodes, see Section 5.1.4). Furthermore, the Event Manager is responsible for implementing the message snooping mechanism that was introduced in Section 7.3 and employed in the lazy reply-driven update scheme of the ASG Lookup Service. Agents may register as *snoopers* providing an event template to specify which events they are interested in. While the basic notification service provided by the Event Space only works for events that are put into the event space, the snooping mechanism also covers all events that only transit through the node. Such events never occur in the local space as they are not targeted to any local agents.

The event flow inside a single event system consists of the events that are coming into the system (right side of Figure 11.2) and events that go out of the system (left side of Figure 11.2). Figure 11.3 depicts how this flow is composed.

A large portion of all events simply flows through the system and is routed to the respective next hop Service Cubes using the routing table. A fraction of the incoming events is destined for the local node and, thus, put into the local Event Space to make them accessible for local agents. Before this happens, these events are snooped. Remember that in general the communication is decoupled. This means that any

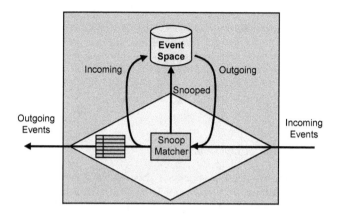

Figure 11.3: Flow composition in the ASG event system.

agent that is interested in snooping some event may not be present of scanning the space at the time at which the desired event comes in. Thus, even though the incoming events are put into the space, they are still snooped and an extra *snoop notification* event is produced for snooping agents. The outgoing events are snooped too, as they are normally not made accessible through the local space. Finally, the events in transit are also snooped. Thus, each event flows through the Snoop Matcher. Those events that are targeted for remote Service Cubes are then routed to the next hop.

11.3.1 The Style of Communication

It is important to note that the provision of an anonymous and asynchronous associative communication medium does not enforce this kind of communication paradigm. Any application may choose to communicate non-anonymously, in a synchronous fashion and with an explicit addressing scheme. This can be easily accomplished by designing the contents of application events accordingly. It is possible to provide appropriate interfaces in the middleware to relieve the programmer from the burden of doing this. The event system offers the flexibility of choosing whatever communication scheme appears to be most appropriate for the respective application.

11.3.2 Event Workflows

A feature that is very important for the self-organizational processes investigated here are *event workflows*. In a simple, direct interaction between a sender and a receiver, the sender s emits an event e_1 and the receiver r reads e_1 from the space using a template t_1. If, however, it is necessary to do some intermediary processing of the event between the sender and the receiver, then it is quite easy to implement it using the event system. Let us assume that the original event e_1 shall be processed through a chain of $k-1$ intermediary agents $a_1, \ldots, a_{k-1}$. Then, a_1 should consume e_1, process it, and emit event e_2. e_2 is consumed by a_2, and a_2 emits e_3, and so on. The last intermediate agent a_{k-1} consumes e_{k-1} and emits e_k which is destined at the receiver r. To enable this workflow, r needs to be aware of the intermediate processing. Instead of consuming e_1 directly, it consumes e_k if it appears in the space. For the sender, this is transparent. An analogous workflow may be constructed that is transparent for the receiver by enforcing the sender to emit an event e_1' instead of e_1. Note that even if r knows about the existence of an intermediate event workflow, it is not required to know the details (e.g. how many intermediary agents exist). The intermediary workflow can be dynamic and new agents may join in if necessary.

11.3.3 The Structure of Events

To enable the communication mechanisms discussed in the preceding sections, an event must have a certain set of attributes. We will take a brief look at these attributes and explain each of them:

- id: A universally unique identifier for the event.

- inReplyTo: If the event has been emitted in response to another event, the other event's ID can be stored in this field. This is important, for example, to associate a replica's response with the right request in the client.

- references: This is a list of IDs of events that the event refers to. If a workflow exists between the sender and the receiver, is can be helpful to identify it using the IDs of intermediate events.

- senderAddress: The network address of the sender's node. This is only set if the event is destined for a remote node to enable the receiver to identify the source node and send replies.

- receiverAddress: The network address of the receiver's node. This is used for routing.

- nextHop: The network address of the next hop in the event's route through the network. This is set on each node that relays the event on its way to its destination.

- route: The complete route of the event is recorded in this field. This is needed, for example, in the Event Flow Tree placement algorithm (cf. Section 8.6).

- sourceRoute: If the event shall be explicitly routed via a specific route, then this route can be set in this field.

- metaData: A table in which arbitrary information may be stored under a name. Meta data may be put into an event at any time during its life cycle, either by the sender itself or by an intermediate entity. This principle is exploited by the Lookup Service to propagate location information in the network.

- payload: The contents of the event. Internally, this content consists of fields that may be addressed associatively according to the tuple space model.

- Maintenance information for the Event Space: This includes for example a timeout after which the event can be garbage-collected if it has not been consumed.

11.4 The Function of Proxy Agents

The Proxy Agent has an important role in the ASG Serviceware. It is implemented using the event workflow mechanism. A service replica never receives a request directly from the client, and it never sends a reply directly to the client. All requests are pre-processed by the Proxy Agent at the replica's Service Cube, and all replies are post-processed. This is necessary to decouple the clients from the mobile replicas and to enable replica adaptations.

A replica does not need to take care of the details involved with its migrations. The Proxy simply tells it when and in which way it shall adapt and handles the rest. The Proxy Agent takes over the following tasks for the replicas:

- It registers and unregisters the replica at the Lookup Service,

- it buffers requests as long as the replica is involved in a migration,

- it forwards the buffered requests as soon as the replica is operational again,

- it collects statistics about the message flows that are used in adaptation decisions (cf. Section 8.5.1), and

- it triggers the adaptation algorithm and informs the replica about the decision.

This frees the replica completely from the burden of dealing with issues other than how to provide its service. Moreover, any adaptation strategies are encapsulated in the Proxy. Thus, if the adaptation algorithm shall be changed, the value-added services do not need to be changed.

A replica only communicates with its local Proxy. The Proxy intercepts client requests, creates local request events from them, and sends these to the respective replica. The replica's replies are picked up by the Proxy, associated with the information about their origin and send out to the network and to the client. All of this is achieved using the simple event workflow mechanism explained above.

11.5 Discussion

The Serviceware that we sketched above implements all core features needed for self-organization processes in the ASG: It enables application and service mobility, it provides decoupled communication to deal with the dynamics, and it offers access to important information about the lower-level communication patterns. It offers a limited set of intuitively understandable concepts and simplifies the development of ASG applications greatly. However, the system also has its drawbacks which we shall discuss briefly in the following.

The first shortcoming is the lack of appropriate security measures. The tuple tpace paradigm makes it rather hard to render communication secure since the content of tuples has to be accessed for addressing them. This becomes very hard, if we encrypt the contents. Different concepts have been proposed to make space-based communication secure [63, 174]. However, discussing this issue in greater detail is out of scope, here.

The second security-related concern that may be brought forwards is related to the snooping mechanism. If anyone may intercept an entry in transit, then this opens a hole for spying the contents of a communication process. This problem can be countered by restricting the view of the snooping agent to the meta data only. That is, not the entire event is passed to that agent but only to meta data section. We assume that the meta data is not used to transport any confidential information. It is a place where publicly accessibly control information may be stored.

Another issue related to the message snooping mechanism is performance. The additional filtering of all events may introduce performance losses and slow down the transport of events through the network. Currently, we cannot really counter this objection. This problem should be investigated more closely to come up with a snooping mechanism that is as efficient as possible.

Finally, the space-based communication paradigm is well-suited for request/reply communication, where individual messages are sent. However, it is inappropriate for streaming media. One can imagine that providing audio and video streams may be an important service in an ASG. Such streams must be transported by some other protocol that does not rely on tuple spaces. The events as we advocate them here may then be used to control this stream, and another, much more efficient communication protocol may be used for the actual stream transport.

Part IV

Conclusions

Chapter 12

Summary

In this book, we have set out to get a better understanding of the problems involved with creating Ambient Intelligence. More specifically, we laid the foundations for an AmI Serviceware platform that may be used in diverse scenarios to provide Wireless Ambient Services to enable users to interact with their immediate environment. The core requirement for this platform was that it is independent from manual interventions and administration while still being able to cope with diverse dynamic changes in the environment.

Our analysis of the current state-of-the-art in the area of AmI platforms has shown that past and current research projects have almost exclusively concentrated on the micro-level of the interaction between users and services. Thus far, the focus was on the design of middleware architectures that are able to support individual users in their interaction with an AmI environment. Especially, the internal structuring of services and applications and the on-the-fly composition of services that fulfill specific user demands are addressed by the research community. Adaptivity is mostly viewed as something that happens inside a service and that is concerned with the way in which software components are composed.

Complementary to these valuable approaches, we proposed to take a more global view at the macro-level interactions in such a system. Instead of focusing on the internal structures of applications and services, we address the *external structures* that are necessary for supporting users in the best possible way. In our approach, we view users not individually but rather at the group level as the source of collective stimuli that help us in structuring an overall system of service replicas accordingly.

The contributions of this book and of the work that led to its completion are the following

1. We have proposed a basic model for a multi-purpose AmI infrastructure. This model is called *Ad hoc Service Grid* and comprises a hardware platform, a network model, a usage model, and a variety of possible business models that may be realized.

2. We have defined and solved three algorithmic problems that comprise core challenges in the realization of the proposed AmI platform: *Self-organizing replica placement, self-organizing service lookup,* and *optimistic data consistency.* The

solution to these problems enables the creation of a basic platform that may provide services to users while not requiring intensive manual administration.

3. From the requirements defined by our solutions to the three afore-mentioned algorithmic problems, we derived the basic architecture of an appropriate middleware and Serviceware platform. An implementation of this platform and the algorithms in a simulation environment showed that the approach is viable and that the concepts are valid.

4. Based on extensive studies of self-organizing systems and our own experiences in implementing them, we have proposed a detailed general model for self-organizing software systems and a classification methodology that enables an objective evaluation of diverse systems. This model was also used to evaluate our own solutions.

Service Replication and Distribution

The ASG is a dynamically changing environment that provides resources for the execution of services. Service Cubes may be removed, on purpose to scale the network or due to failures. They may also be added to expand the system as a reaction to a growing user demand. Two problems occur in this scenario:

1. Manual administration is not feasible due to the dynamics and the massive distribution of the system, and

2. placing services in suboptimal locations inside the ASG network can severely degrade the performance of the system.

As a consequence, a self-organizing mechanism is required that replicates and places service replicas in a way that is appropriate for the current usage patterns and without external intervention. In Chapter 8, we have introduced distributed algorithms that achieve this without any direct communication among replicas. Based on simple rules, we designed a system that is able to adapt the overall replica placement to the perceived message flows in the system. These message flows represent the usage patterns displayed by clients. By exploiting a basic feedback mechanism, the system creates a cost-efficient stable configuration very quickly and adapts this configuration when the usage patterns change. We have introduced a detailed cost model and evaluated the system by comparing it with three other algorithms. Our results show that the replica placement system performs well under diverse conditions.

Service Discovery and Lookup

The basic concept of dynamic service replication and placement creates a second problem: How can dynamic replicas be found in the ASG? The issues we faced in our attempt to solve this problem were the following:

- The Lookup Service must be distributed over the network in order to avoid central points of failure and bottlenecks. Regarding the distributed and dynamic nature of the ASG, this is a very fundamental premise. The distribution of the Lookup Service implies that a special protocol is required to update the information about the changing locations of replicas throughout the system.

- The overhead caused by the update protocol must be minimal since wireless network bandwidth is considered the most critical resource in the ASG.

- As a consequence of the above requirements, the overall system must be able to deal with temporary inconsistencies in the information provided by the Lookup Service.

A simple approach that uses flooding to update location information in the distributed Lookup Service instances achieves the basic task. However, such an update protocol produces an intolerable overhead. The solution presented in Chapter 9 is based on a lazy, reply-driven approach: The location information pertaining to a replica becomes outdated in most Lookup Service instances when the replica migrates, but it still remains valid. This is achieved by creating forwarding chains such that requests do eventually reach their destination replica, even if it has moved. The forwarding process introduces a slight degradation in performance but the basic functionality is preserved. To counter this degradation, we realized a lazy update protocol that propagates changed location information along the path taken by service replies on their way to the client. Update information is piggybacked by normal service reply messages and a message snooping mechanism is used throughout the ASG network to detect such information and to transport it to the near-by Lookup Service instances. This mechanism refreshes the location information only in those regions in which it is really used and avoids updates in regions that do not need it. As a consequence, the update protocol has a very low overhead.

Data Consistency

A second, very fundamental problem that is caused by having dynamic groups of service replicas populate the ASG network is the preservation of data consistency in stateful services. The following issues arise in this scenario:

- There is no global view on the system, and no central entity keeps track of the number or the state of the existing replicas.

- We would like to be able to realize stateful services that enable clients to read and write information on a single replica. The effects of write operations should then propagate to all other replicas of the service.

- Strict consistency models are not an option in the ASG. Mechanisms that lock data items and execute global, atomic synchronization processes would remove the advantages of the ASG concept (decentralization, robustness, flexibility, etc.).

In Chapter 10, we propose a optimistic consistency protocol that achieves *eventual consistency* among all replicas of a single service under specific conditions. We used the general concept found in the Bayou database system for mobile computers and adapted it to fit the somewhat relaxed conditions present in the ASG. The result is a consistency protocol that avoids costly full state transfers while keeping write logs at an acceptable size as long as network partitions are only temporary. We showed how the consistency characteristics provided to different services may be fine-tuned using only two simple parameters.

Chapter 13

Conclusions

The conclusions drawn from our work fall into two different categories. The first category of conclusions is technical in nature and deals with the immediate achievements and contributions presented in this book. The second category consists of lessons learned. The development of self-organizing software systems is a major task for the next few years. Up to now, the approaches in this area are not guided by any common design principle. They are mostly a matter of trial and error and the results claimed by researchers are hard to verify. Therefore, we take a few steps back and review our results as well as the way towards their realization in order to derive some higher-level principles that may serve as a guideline.

Validity of the Ad hoc Service Grid Model

We have shown how a dedicated hardware and software infrastructure can be applied to the problem of providing Ambient Intelligence. The way towards the realization of the AmI visions may take several steps via more conventional technical phases. The next stages may be based on existing WLAN hotspots and mobile phone networks. However, we think that a dedicated hardware platform equipped with a self-organizing software platform is necessary in order to enable local autonomous provisioning of facility-specific Ambient Services. If a large number of local providers decide to offer such services, then any centralized infrastructure (e.g. set up by major telecommunications companies) will be insufficient. The bandwidth requirements as well as the volumes of data that need to be stored will experience a vast growth. Therefore, an infrastructure for supporting such services must be scalable. Furthermore, the services that we envision are local by nature. Thus, it would not make sense to centralize them. Finally, a local decentralized infrastructure like the ASG offers maximal autonomy to the local providers.

For these reasons, we think that the ASG is a fitting model for the visions and technical constraints set by AmI. However, the problem of administration must be solved to enable this sort of model. In our work, we have shown that the set of core problems existing in the ASG can be solved in a self-organizing way. Our simulation results show that the overall system is able to adapt to diverse dynamic changes and still provide an acceptable level of functionality.

Usage-driven Adaptation

A *usage-driven approach* has proven to be adequate for realizing adaptivity in such a system. While the current research focuses mostly on adapting applications internally to individual users, the stimuli produced by the overall group of users may be applied to adapt the system on a global scale. This is clearly shown by our work. Both approaches complement each other, and both are required.

The Role of Transparency

The classical approach to introduce transparency in order to simplify the development and the maintenance of software systems appears to be problematic in environments like the one advocated here. As we have seen, there is an inherent need for cross-layer information exchange that exposes details of underlying layers that would rather be hidden from the classical point of view. Both the replica placement system and the Lookup Service need information pertaining to the messages flows in the system. We were able to provide this information since we have designed a new architecture from scratch. It remains unclear how well-known and proven concepts from classical network communication (like TCP) can be integrated into a paradigm like the ASG.

Transparency may also be a problem when applied vertically, at the boundaries between different subsystems of an AmI infrastructure. If multiple self-organizing systems interact, the result is not necessarily a higher-level self-organizing system. In fact, the opposite may be the case, and the overall system may *self-disorganize* as a result of the interactions. We have sketched a simple example for such a system in [74]. If the subsystems are developed in isolation and work transparently, they may counteract each other. The different solutions presented in this book were designed, realized, and tested in a single development process. The effects observable in the interaction of two or more subsystems that use some kind of feedback process may be subtle; they may depend on internal details within these systems. We think that this issue of transparency and the isolated design could be a major problem not only in the design of self-organizing AmI system, but for any complex self-organizing software system.

The Right Middleware Abstraction

An important conclusion in terms of basic middleware abstractions is that the components of an AmI system should communicate via events. The whole vision of AmI is based on the principle of *reactiveness*. Environments should react appropriately to a user's actions, and the system's structure must adapt in reaction to the patterns observed in the environment. Events offer a fitting abstraction for the implementation of reactive software systems. Moreover, they can be used to decouple components, which renders the overall system much more robust. An associative, anonymous form of addressing components and accessing data generated by others is also helpful in environments that are as open as those envisioned in AmI.

Laziness Sometimes Pays Off

In engineering disciplines (and elsewhere in life), there is often the desire to be proactive: If we can prepare for what could happen, it will be easier to cope with it, once it is happening. Intuitively, this seems to be reasonable. However, if a system is subject to highly dynamic unforeseen changes, such a proactive approach may be counterproductive. Being proactive has something to do with predicting the future and building structures in advance. In a system like the ASG, this creates two problems:

1. "Prediction is very difficult, especially if it's about the future" (Nils Bohr). To predict a future state of some process, one needs an accurate model of this process. For a complex process, such as collective user behavior, models are hard to derive and inaccurate by nature. Thus, the predictions may not hold.

2. In addition to the loss of proactiveness in case of a false prediction, an allegedly proactive system may have build some structures (e.g. routing tables) that are useless due to the false prediction. Thus, resources have been spent to build these structures and maybe even more resources have to be spent to revert them and to create appropriate structures to replace them. This does not only waste resources but also precious time.

Therefore, we advocate systems that can *react quickly* (instead of acting proactively) and *degrade gracefully*. It is important that both properties are combined, since reactive system need time to react, and during this time, the system must still function properly, albeit, maybe in a suboptimal fashion.

This philosophy is inherent to all three solutions presented in this book:

- The replica placement system constantly tries to find better locations for replicas in reaction to changes in usage patterns. A degradation (suboptimal placement) may reduce the quality of service temporarily, but the system stays operational and counters this degradation eventually.

- The Lookup Service fixes inconsistencies only when they become problems. Forwarding chains may consume more time and bandwidth, but they shorten themselves as they are used to gradually restore the best possible mode of operation.

- The consistency protocol allows data stores to diverge temporarily but it limits this divergence and constantly restores consistency to achieve an overall level of consistency that is configurable.

Being Optimistic

The assumptions behind the development of self-organizing AmI systems should be fundamentally optimistic. There is a class of systems that inherently build on the pessimistic assumption that things will go wrong and, if we do not avoid this by all means, this could result in catastrophic consequences. An example for this class of applications is a banking system: A major financial transaction must by no means go wrong. Such applications should not be part of an AmI system.

This restricts the class of services that could be offered via an ASG to those that have a low probability of something going wrong and that can deal with faults and inconsistencies (graceful degradation). Overly pessimistic assumptions require strict procedures that are usually rather obstructive when it comes to concepts like flexibility, dynamics, and decentralization. Pessimistic consistency models, for example, usually require some form of global lock on data items that are being written. This would either not be possible in an ASG, or it would change the properties of the ASG completely and remove much of its attractiveness.

Keep it Simple

Building systems *as simple as possible but no simpler* is a fundamental task of all engineering disciplines. This is especially true for artificial self-organizing systems that shall adapt their structure to react to diverse environmental conditions. Especially if such a system possesses some internal feedback mechanism, its behavior gets very complex rather quickly. What is even worse, is that this complex behavior is not necessarily close to the desired one. Interestingly, it took the author quite a while to understand what exactly is happening in the proposed systems on a larger scale and how the different possible ways of tuning this behavior actually work. Getting a deep understanding of the mechanisms that are really at work when the systems are running was more of an empirical nature than a straight-forward deductive process. This complex task of understanding and fine-tuning a self-organizing system is greatly simplified when the possible ways of tuning the system are limited. If a system is designed with too many tunable parameters and too many degrees of freedom, it gets out of hand very quickly. Moreover, a system that is complicated usually introduces a large quantity of possible failures. This reduces robustness considerably. Therefore, it is very important to start the development process with the simplest system. After having understood the processes that make it work, one may increase the system's complexity gradually to improve its power.

Generalization of the Results

In this book, we studied several self-organization mechanisms with respect to a particular application scenario. The ASG presents a concrete framework to which concrete mechanisms can be fit. However, the question arises as to whether the protocols, algorithms, and mechanisms laid our in this work are also applicable in general, and under which constraints and modifications this would be the case.

Generalized Replica Placement

The replica placement algorithms could also be applied in the placement systems presented in Section 8.1. A self-organizing placement mechanism that is based on feedback rules may be an alternative wherever the burden of controlling such a placement gets too high. However, this presents an important trade-off: Control is delegated to the placement system and taken out of the hands of the administrative staff. The system has to be controlled at a different level, using the tunable parameters (cf.

Section 8.7.2). The task of selecting different combinations of parameters to create quantitatively and qualitatively different global behaviors should be investigated in greater detail to enable such a higher-level control. Additionally, the interworking of the feedback rules (cf. Section 8.4.1) and the constraining factors that provide a stabilizing negative feedback effect (replication cost, replication radius etc.) must be fine-tuned to the particular application scenario. Finally, the problem of scalability must be investigated carefully in large-scale application domains. As we discussed in Section 8.7.4, scalability can be a weak point of our approach as it was not specifically designed for such scenarios. If these issues are carefully studied, an application of our basic placement mechanism in the area of Content Distribution Networks like Akamai could be beneficial.

Generalized Lookup Service

The combination of the lazy updating mechanism and the relaxed correctness requirements employed by the ASG Lookup Service may also be applied in more general settings. The problem of locating mobile objects, that is relevant, for example, in the domain of mobile agent systems, can be solved by this approach. The hardest problem in this respect is certainly the transition from rigorous correctness requirements found in most systems today to softer requirements (cf. Section 9.3). Reply-driven information propagation is a rather general approach that may be employed wherever the requirements for the up-to-dateness of information in a certain network region is coupled to the request/reply activity in this region. The nature of the information that is propagated via this mechanism is not restricted to object locations. As we sketched in Section 9.2.7, it may also be used, for example, to spread load information in a certain application context.

Generalized BD-GAP

The Bounded Divergence Group Anti-entropy Protocol discussed in Section 10.6 is the most ASG-specific mechanism introduced in this book. It exploits the relaxed conditions found in the ASG concerning the ability of replicas to connect to each other. In contrast to Bayou, the ASG model assumes that replicas are able to establish a connection to each other in most cases. Situations in which replicas are not aware of the existence of certain fellow replicas or in which temporary network partitions occur are within the normal working conditions of the ASG consistency protocol. However, the extremely loosely coupled nature of a plain Bayou environment would cause the write logs to grow considerably. Thus, the protocol may not be easily applied to the plain Bayou system. However, in replication systems that enjoy similar relaxed conditions as the ASG and that can benefit from an optimistic consistency model, the BD-GAP can be applied.

Generalized Self-Organization

As far as the application of the *self-organization mechanisms* formulated in this book is concerned, it is hard to generalize them in order to get a concept that is more specific and more tangible than the well-known universal principle of interacting positive and negative feedback processes. An approach that can be of help in practice is to think in terms of forces that drive the system to adopt a certain structure. We have discussed the analogy of our cost model to physical forces in Section 8.2.1. Our basic feedback rules (cf. Section 8.4.1), that govern the behavior of replicas, are simply a tool that implements these forces: The rules drive the system into a stable state in which all forces are at an equilibrium with respect to the current environmental stimuli (client usage patterns). Thus, a valid general process by which self-organization can be introduced in a software system could be sketched as follows:

1. Define what a good stable state (or structure) is in the context of the system. This is in line with the definition of the system's structure in a valid classification (cf. Section 4.6). The definition of a good state usually depends on some cost function that is to be minimized. Under such a cost function, any structure, that produces minimal cost, is good.

2. Define what comprises the external stimuli that apply *non-specific pressure* to the system from the outside. This is essentially the system's environment and its interaction with this environment.

3. Find the forces that apply to the system (or its components) and that drive it to adopt a good stable structure. These forces are usually directly associated with the cost function formulated under bullet 1.

4. Find a feedback mechanism, involving the environment and the system's components, that implements these forces. In the positive feedback process, the system's components as well as the environment try to minimize the cost. In most cases, there exists some negative feedback element that slows down and limits the exponential build-up involved with positive feedback. Usually, some resource that is necessary for the build-up is depleted by this very process. This negative feedback element must be identified and integrated into the feedback rules if it is not already implicit.

This *general recipe* for implementing self-organization is still rather fuzzy, and a great deal of intuition and experimenting has to be invested to generate a working solution for a specific problem from it. However, it represents a good generalization of our approach.

Chapter 14

Outlook

Although we cover a considerable range of different problems and concepts in this book, our work only represents the first step towards the realization of an ASG. Since we exploited the possibility to simulate our concepts, we enjoyed the freedom to stay at a rather abstract conceptual level. Even on this level, there is still a number of major challenges we have not tackled. However, our work lays the foundations for more practical models. In this section, we will discuss the immediate next steps that may follow the completion of our work.

Federated Ad hoc Service Grids

The ASG model that we introduced in Chapter 5 assumes that an ASG is an isolated entity running on its own at some location. The services that we used as examples were provided and used by local parties such that the whole ASG was self-contained. However, in a more realistic scenario, an ASG should have a connection to the Internet. The technical realization of this up-link is no real challenge. One or more Service Cubes may simply have a second network interface that connects them to the Internet. This extension can be used to enhance the local services offers with external services. For example, users may simply be enabled to access their private email. Special *proxy services* may be distributed in the ASG to realize this concept. These *external* proxies may replicate and migrate in the same way as the normal ASG services do.

This represents a straight-forward and simple extension of the model into the Internet world that we have today. However, it also enables individual ASGs to *federate*. If two ASGs have an Internet gateway, they may connect to each other and share information. This could be exploited to offer continuous support for individual users: When a user leaves one ASG and enters a new one, he may access the same context he was in at the first ASG. This could be used to carry over personalization data from one facility to another. This concept and its implications should be investigated in greater detail.

Personalization

One of the great benefits that AmI is envisioned to provide is the personalization of services. A profile shall be maintained for each user that enables a long-term customization of services. Such a personalization poses some questions that have not been addressed in this book. The personalization service is a core platform service similar to the Lookup Service. Many value-added services may benefit from accessing it. How would a user profile be structured? Which kind of data would be stored in such a multi-purpose profile? What are the issues involved with sharing such profiles in a federated ASG?

Security and Privacy

Personalization and the sharing of user profiles also pose questions concerning the security and privacy of such sensitive information. These two problems have not been addressed in our work thus far. Rendering the ASG secure is a very challenging task. Many of the concepts introduced here seem to be counter-productive in terms of security concerns. The interesting questions are:

- How much security is needed in an ASG?

- How much of the functionality of the ASG model must be sacrificed in order to introduce an acceptable level of security?

- How does the openness of the event system and the anonymous, associative addressing scheme effect the chances of introducing security measures?

- Which further limitations does the resulting security concept imply on the possible class of services that may be provided in an ASG?

Client-Side Support

Our focus has clearly been on the service side. We tried to find mechanisms to make services adaptive and self-organizing. However, the client side also deserves some attention. For example, the handover of a moving client device between different Services Cubes may be an issue. What happens if a client has a long-running session with a service? Service replies must be forwarded to moving clients in a similar fashion as client requests are forwarded to service replicas. Thus, some sort of proxy is also required for clients. Such questions have deliberately been ignored to keep the complexity of our task manageable. However, it is necessary to investigate them in the future.

More Sophisticated Dynamics Models

As we have discussed in Section 8.3.3, the models for the dynamics in usage patterns are rather artificial. We chose to use these artificial models since there is no real basis for the introduction of models that match the behavior of real users in a real ASG. However, as long as we do not have such a model, any simulative study must be questioned. The development of a realistic model of the behavior of groups of users would be a significant advance in the refinement of the solutions we proposed.

Another aspect that has only been touched here is the dynamics of the network topology (cf. Section 9.3). We have not altered the ASG network as such over the course of a simulation run. Nodes that crash, newly added nodes, and nodes that are purposefully removed will introduce additional problems that must be countered by appropriate self-organization and adaptation mechanisms.

Transition to a More Realistic Network Model

The unit disk network model was introduced as the basis of our simulations in Section 5.2. This is a very simple model that cannot capture the characteristics of a real wireless network. The next step in this respect would be to transfer the simulation to a simulator like *ns-2* that is able to create realistic wireless channel characteristics for different networking technologies. Do our models hold in such an environment? How do they have to be adapted to preserve their validity?

Implementing Selected Applications

Since our simulative studies required a large number of experiments to create the quantitative results presented. The evaluation of realistic services was prohibitive. A single simulation run was required to run as fast as possible. Thus, we had to make a compromise by implementing a rather artificial application (cf. Section 10.7.1). In the next step, real applications should be implemented on top of our system to get a better understanding of the class of applications that the ASG model is applicable to in general. A small set of different applications with different properties concerning the size of replicas, the write rate (cf. Section 8.8.3), and their consistency requirements (cf. Section 10.7.2) should suffice. The experience gained through these applications can be used to further refine the different mechanisms involved with replica placement, service lookup, and data consistency.

Appendix

Appendix A

List of Symbols

Symbol	Description	Reference[1]	
$\mathcal{A}$	general symbol for any replica distribution algorithm	98	(8.4.2)
a_{cn}	a client allocation (assignment of clients in K to nodes in N)	77	(8.2.1)
a_{rn}	a replica allocation (assignment of replicas in R to nodes in N)	77	(8.2.1)
$\mathcal{A}_v$	the instance of the algorithm $\mathcal{A}$ running on node v	98	(8.4.2)
$\mathcal{A}_v(r, t)$	the adaptation that results from the execution of algorithm $\mathcal{A}$ on node v for replica r at time t	98	(8.4.2)
$\mathfrak{C}$	a subsystem that acts as a central controller	39	(4.4)
$\mathcal{C}$	the system configuration ($\mathcal{C} = (G, a_{cn}, a_{rn})$)	81	(8.2.2)
$\overline{C}$	the average overall cost over a time interval $[0, T]$	81	(8.1)
$C(t)$	overall time-dependent cost function	79	(8.2.1)
c_i	commonly used to denote the i-th client (c is used for a single client)	90	(8.4.1)
C_M	migration cost function	78	(8.3)
$C_m(t)$	time-dependent migration cost function	78	(8.4)
C_Q	request cost function	78	(8.2)
$C_q(t)$	time-dependent request cost function	79	(8.2.1)
C_{qr}	the combined request and replication cost minimized by the replica distribution algorithms	98	(8.5)
C_R	replication cost function	77	(8.1)
$C_r(t)$	time-dependent replication cost function	79	(8.2.1)

---

[1]Page and Section

231

δ	tunable parameter of the oscillating dynamics model	89	(8.3.3)
D	network diameter (length of the longest shortest path between any pair of nodes in a network G)	84	(8.3.1)
$\mathfrak{D}$	a description of a system	44	(4.7)
$d(u, v)$	the distance (number of network hops) in the shortest path between nodes u and w in the network graph G	80	(8.2.2)
$d_{CR}(c, r, t)$	the distance (number of network hops on the shortest path) between client c and replica r at time t	80	(8.17)
$d_{Rep}(r, t)$	the replication distance (sum of distances between replica r and each of its fellow-replicas)	116	(8.54)
η	the *stability threshold* (used to test whether the conditions triggering a replica migration hold stably)	100	(8.5.1)
E	an event flow tree (EFT)	110	(8.6.1)
$\mathcal{E}$	the event flow tree algorithm for replica distribution (see also: $\mathcal{A}$, $\mathcal{A}_v$, and $\mathcal{A}_v(r, t)$)	98	(8.4.2)
$\mathcal{F}(u)$	the *flow measure* of node u in an event flow tree	111	(8.45)
f_A	the replica selection function (assigns a set of *appropriate* replicas to each client)	80	(8.2.2)
f_C	the time-dependent client allocation function (generates a client allocation a_{cn} by assigning each client in K to a node in N)	79	(8.7)
f_{CR}	the client-replica allocation function (selects a specific replica for each client)	80	(8.2.2)
$\mathcal{F}_e(u)$	the *emitted flow measure* of node u in an event flow tree (individual contribution of node u to $\mathcal{F}(u)$)	112	(8.48)
f_M	the time-dependent migration function (generates a replica allocation a_{rn} by assigning each replica in R to a node in N)	80	(8.2.2)
f_Q	the time-dependent client request function (generates a request distribution $q(t)$)	79	(8.9)
f_R	the time-dependent replication function (generates a series of replica sets as the result of replication and dissolve operations)	80	(8.11)
γ	index of a concrete input function from the possible input functions of an adaptive system	38	(4.3)
Γ	set of indices of input functions that an adaptive system is subjected to	39	(4.3)

G	the network graph of a given ASG ($G = (N, L)$)	76	(8.2)
$\mathcal{G}$	the generalized replica distribution algorithm	114	(8.6.3)
K	the set of clients in a given ASG	76	(8.2)
κ	the application-dependent consistency measure	198	(10.7.1)
$\overline{\kappa}$	the average consistency in the time interval $[0, T]$	198	(10.17)
L	the edges (links) in a network graph G	76	(8.2)
$\overline{L}$	the average *lookup information correctness* in the time interval $[0, T]$	169	(9.4.1)
L_E	the set of edges in an event flow tree E	110	(8.6.1)
$L(t)$	the *lookup information correctness* throughout the entire ASG system at time t	168	(9.4)
m_c	the average size of a client message	115	(8.7.1)
N	the nodes in a network graph G	76	(8.2)
N_E	the set of nodes in an event flow tree E	110	(8.6.1)
N_v	the set of neighbor nodes of node v (note: $v \in N_v$)	99	(8.25)
ω	the *system write rate* (number of write operations produced throughout the system per time unit)	201	(10.7.2)
$\Pi(m)$	the path traveled trough the network by message m	109	(8.6.1)
$P(\gamma)$	performance function for an adaptive system	38	(4.3)
$q(t)$	the time-dependent request distribution (defines how many requests are sent from each node in N at time t)	79	(8.2.2)
ρ	the *replication radius* (used to trigger replications based on the length of request paths)	102	(8.5.3)
R	a set of replicas ($R(t)$ is the time-dependent set of replicas)	76	(8.2)
r_i	commonly used to denote the i-th replica (r is used for a single replica)	90	(8.4.1)
$r_i.v$	the version vector of replica r_i	181	(10.3)
σ	the average size of a replica's state measured given as a number average client messages	117	(8.7.1)
ς	the range of sight of the generalized replica distribution algorithm $\mathcal{G}$	114	(8.6.3)
S	the set of service types	76	(8.2)
s	a single service type	76	(8.2)

S	the simple algorithm for replica distribution (see also: $\mathcal{A}$, $\mathcal{A}_v$, and $\mathcal{A}_v(r,t)$)	98	(8.4.2)
$\mathfrak{S}$	general notation for a *system*	38	(4.3)
$\mathfrak{S}_\mathfrak{D}$	a system under a description $\mathfrak{D}$	44	(4.7)
$\{S_\gamma\}$	family of possible input functions for an adaptive system	38	(4.3)
SO	the class of self-organizing software systems (the complement of SO is $\overline{SO}$)	44	(4.7)
T	duration of a complete simulation run (measured in ticks)	81	(8.2.3)
T_a	the adaptation interval (adaptations are issued every T_a time units)	93	(8.4.2)
T_h	the time window of past data that is used to make adaptation decisions	93	(8.4.2)
T_{rec}	the reconcile timeout (number of time units after which a new reconciliation process is actively triggered if W_{rec} has not been exceeded before)	194	(10.6.2)
u, v, w	commonly used to denote nodes in a network graph	96	(8.4.2)
w	the application-dependent write ratio ($w = \frac{\#Writes}{\#Reads+\#Writes}$)	116	(8.7.1)
W	criterion of acceptability for the performance of an adaptive system	38	(4.3)
w_e	the application-dependent effective write rate	116	(8.7.1)
w_i	the i-the write operation	178	(10.1.2)
W_{rec}	the write threshold (number of write operations after which a new reconciliation process is actively triggered)	194	(10.6.2)

Appendix B

List of Abbreviations

Abbreviation	Description
ACI	Autonomic Computing Initiative
ACO	Ant Colony Optimization
AmI	Ambient Intelligence
ASG	Ad hoc Service Grid
CDN	Content Distribution Network
CH	Cluster Head
CNL	Commit Notification List
CORBA	Common Object Request Broker
CSN	Commit Sequence Number
CVS	Concurrent Versioning System
DMAC	Distributed Mobility-Adaptive Clustering
EFT	Event Flow Tree
LS	Lookup Service
LSA	Lookup Snooper Agent
MANET	Mobile Ad hoc Network
MAS	Multi-Agent System
OC	Organic Computing
OSPF	Open Shortest Path First
PDA	Personal Digital Assistant
QoS	Quality of Service
RFID	Radio Frequency ID
RPA	Replica Placement Algorithm
SO	Self-Organization
SOSS	Self-Organizing Software System
UUID	Universally Unique Identifier
VV	Version Vector
WMN	Wireless Mesh Network

Bibliography

[1] ADAMIC, L. The Small World Web. In *Proceedings of the European Conference on Digital Libraries* (1999).

[2] AHUJA, S., CARRIERO, N., AND GELERTNER, D. Linda and Friends. *IEEE Computer 19*, 8 (Aug. 1986), 26–34.

[3] AKYILDIZ, I. F., SU, W., SANKARASUBRAMANIAM, Y., AND CAYIRCI, E. Wireless Sensor Networks: A Survey. *Computer Networks 38*, 4 (2002), 393–422.

[4] AKYILDIZ, I. F., WANG, X., AND WANG, W. Wireless Mesh Networks: A Survey. *Computer Networks 47*, 4 (2005), 445–487.

[5] ALBERS, S., AND LEONARDI, S. On-line Algorithms. *ACM Computing Surveys 31*, 3es (1999), 4.

[6] ALBERT, R., AND BARABÁSI, A.-L. Statistical Mechanics of Complex Networks. *Reviews of Modern Physics 74*, 1 (Jan. 2002), 47–97.

[7] ANDERSON, C. Self-Organization in Relation to Several Similar Concepts: Are the Boundaries to Self-Organization Indistinct? *The Biological Bulletin 202*, 3 (June 2002), 247–255.

[8] ANDRZEJAK, A., GRAUPNER, S., KOTOV, V., AND TRINKS, H. Algorithms for Self-Organization and Adaptive Service Placement in Dynamic Distributed Systems. Technical Report HPL-2002-259, HP Laboratories Palo Alto, 2002.

[9] ARIDOR, Y., AND OSHIMA, M. Infrastructure for Mobile Agents: Requirements and Design. In *Proceedings of the 2nd International Workshop on Mobile Agents* (1998), K. Rothermel and F. Hohl, Eds., vol. 1477 of *Lecture Notes in Computer Science*, Springer-Verlag, pp. 38–49.

[10] ASHBY, R. Principles of the Self-Organizing Dynamic System. *Journal of General Psychology 37* (1947), 125–128.

[11] ASHBY, W. R. Principles of the Self-Organizing System. In *Principles of Self-Organization*, H. V. Foerster and J. G. W. Zopf, Eds. Pergamon, 1962, pp. 255–278.

[12] BABAOGLU, O., MELING, H., AND MONTRESOR, A. Anthill: A Framework for the Development of Agent-Based Peer-to-Peer Systems. In *Proceedings of the*

22nd International Conference on Distributed Computing Systems (ICDCS), Vienna, Austria (July 2002).

[13] BABLOYANTZ, A., Ed. *Self-organization, Emerging Properties, and Learning*, vol. B260 of *A. NATO ASI Series*. Plenum Press, New York, 1991.

[14] BAKER, M., AND BUYYA, R. Cluster Computing: The Commodity Super-computer. *Software – Practice & Experience 29*, 6 (1999), 551–576.

[15] BAL, H., DE LAAT, C., HARIDI, S., JEFFERY, K., LABARTA, J., LAFORENZA, D., MACCALLUM, P., MASS, J., MATYSKA, L., PRIOL, T., REINEFELD, A., REUTER, A., RIGUIDEL, M., SNELLING, D., AND VAN STEEN, M. Next Generation Grid(s), European Grid Research 2005-2010. Technical Report, Expert Group Report for the EU, 2003.

[16] BARABÁSI, A.-L., AND ALBERT, R. Emergence of Scaling in Random Networks. *Science 286* (Oct. 1999), 509–512.

[17] BASAGNI, S. Distributed Clustering for Ad Hoc Networks. In *Proceedings of the IEEE International Symposium on Parallel Architectures, Algorithms, and Networks (I-SPAN)* (June 1999), pp. 310–315.

[18] BECKER, C., SCHIELE, G., GUBBELS, H., AND ROTHERMEL, K. BASE – A Micro-Broker-Based Middleware for Pervasive Computing. In *Proceedings of the IEEE International Conference on Pervasive Computing and Communication (PerCom 2003)* (2003).

[19] BELLAVISTA, P., CORRADI, A., AND MONTI, S. Integrating Web Services and Mobile Agent Systems. In *Proceedings of the First International Workshop on Services and Infrastructures for the Ubiquitous and Mobile Internet (SIUMI'05)* (2005).

[20] BELLAVISTA, P., CORRADI, A., AND STEFANELLI, C. The Ubiquitous Provisioning of Internet Services to Portable Devices. *IEEE Pervasive Computing 1*, 3 (July – Sept. 2002), 81–87.

[21] BHATIA, R., AND KODIALAM, M. On Power Efficient Communication Over Multi-Hop Wireless Networks: Joint Routing, Scheduling and Power Control. In *Proceeding of IEEE INFOCOM* (2004).

[22] BOLLEN, J., AND HEYLIGHEN, F. Algorithms for the Self-organisation of Distributed, Multi-user Networks. In *Cybernetics and Systems'96: Proceedings of the Thirteenth European Meeting on Cybernetics and Systems Research* (Apr. 1996), R. Trappl, Ed., pp. 955–960.

[23] BONABEAU, E., AND THERAULAZ, G. Swarm Smarts. *Scientific American* (Mar. 2000), 72–79.

[24] BRYCE, C., PAWLAK, M., TOLLE, K., WERNER, P., AND ZICARI, R. Agent-Based Services for Information Portals. In *SAC '03: Proceedings of the 2003 ACM symposium on Applied computing* (New York, NY, USA, 2003), ACM Press, pp. 1191–1198.

[25] CABRI, G., FERRARI, L., LEONARDI, L., AND ZAMBONELLI, F. The LAICA project: supporting ambient intelligence via agents and ad-hoc middleware. In *Proceedings of the 14th IEEE International Workshops on Enabling Technologies: Infrastructure for Collaborative Enterprise* (June 2005), pp. 39–44.

[26] CAMAZINE, S., DENEUBOURG, J.-L., FRANKS, N. R., SNEYD, J., THERAULAZ, G., AND BONABEAU, E. *Self-Organization in Biological Systems.* Princeton University Press, 2001.

[27] CARO, G. D., DUCATELLE, F., AND GAMBARDELLA, L. M. AntHocNet: an Ant-Based Hybrid Routing Algorithm for Mobile Ad Hoc Networks. Technical Report No. IDSIA-25-04-2004, Dalle Molle Institute for Artifcial Intelligence, Galleria 2, 6928 Manno, Switzerland, Aug. 2004.

[28] CARRILLO, L., MARZO, J. L., VILÀ, P., AND MANTILLA, C. A. MAntS-Hoc: A Multi-Agent Ant-Based System for Routing in Mobile Ad Hoc Networks. In *Proceedings of Setè Congrés Català d'Intelligència Artificial (CCIA'2004)* (2004), pp. 285–292.

[29] CEDERQVIST, P. Version Management with CVS for cvs 1.12.10. https://www.cvshome.org/docs/manual/. (Nov. 1, 2006).

[30] CHANDRA, R., QIU, L., JAIN, K., AND MAHDIAN, M. Optimizing the Placement of Integration Points in Multihop Wireless Networks. In *Proceedings of the Twelfth IEEE International Conference on Network Protocols* (2004).

[31] CHARIKAR, M., GUHA, S., TARDOS, É., AND SHMOYS, D. B. A constant-factor approximation algorithm for the k-median problem. In *STOC '99: Proceedings of the thirty-first annual ACM symposium on Theory of computing* (New York, NY, USA, 1999), ACM Press, pp. 1–10.

[32] CHLAMTAC, I., CONTI, M., AND LIU, J. J.-N. Mobile Ad hoc Networking: Imperatives and Challenges. *Ad Hoc Networks 1*, 1 (2003), 13–64.

[33] CHOI, S., AND SHAVITT, Y. Placing Servers for Session-Oriented Services. Technical Report WUCS-2001-41, Department of Computer Science, Washington University, 2001.

[34] COFFMAN, E. G., ELPHICK, M., AND SHOSHANI, A. System Deadlocks. *ACM Computing Surveys 3*, 2 (1971), 67–78.

[35] COONEY, D., AND ROE, P. Mobile Agents Make for Flexible Web Services. In *Proceedings of the Ninth Australian World Wide Web Conference* (2003).

[36] COPPENS, J., WAUTERS, T., TURCK, F. D., DHOEDT, B., AND DEMEESTER, P. Evaluation of Replica Placement and Retrieval Algorithms in Self-Organizing CDNs. In *Proceeding of the IFIP/IEEE International Workshop on Self-Managed Systems & Services (SelfMan 2005)* (May 2005).

[37] CRONIN, E., JAMIN, S., JIN, C., KURC, A., RAZ, D., AND SHAVITT, Y. Constrained Mirror Placement on the Internet. *IEEE Journal on Selected Areas in Communications 20*, 7 (Sept. 2002), 1369–1382.

[38] DAVIDSON, S. B., GARCIA-MOLINA, H., AND SKEEN, D. Consistency in a
Partitioned Network: A Survey. *ACM Computing Surveys 17*, 3 (1985), 341–
370.

[39] DEMERS, A., GREENE, D., HAUSER, C., IRISH, W., LARSON, J., SHENKCR,
S., STURGIS, H., SWINEHART, D., AND TERRY, D. Epidemic Algorithms for
Replicated Database Maintenance. In *Proceedings of the Sixth Annual ACM
Symposium on Principles of Distributed Computing* (New York, NY, USA,
1987), ACM Press, pp. 1–12.

[40] DENEUBOURG, J., GOSS, S., FRANKS, N., SENDOVA-FRANKS, A., DETRAIN,
C., AND CHRÉTIEN., L. The Dynamics of Collective Sorting Robot-like Ants
and Ant-like Robots. In *Proceedings of the First International Conference on
Simulation of Adaptive Behavior: From Animals to Animats SAB90* (1990),
pp. 356–363.

[41] DI CARO, G., AND DORIGO, M. Ant Colonies for Adaptive Routing in Packet-
Switched Communications Networks. In *Proceedings of the 5th International
Conference on Parallel Problem Solving from Nature - PPSN V* (1998), A. E.
Eiben, T. Bäck, M. Schoenauer, and H.-P. Schwefel, Eds., vol. 1498 of *Lecture
Notes in Computer Science*, Springer-Verlag, pp. 673–682.

[42] DI CARO, G., AND DORIGO, M. AntNet: Distributed Stigmergetic Control
for Communications Networks. *Journal of Artificial Intelligence Research 9*
(1998), 317–365.

[43] DIAO, Y., ESKESEN, F., FRÖHLICH, S., HELLERSTEIN, J. L., SPAINHOWER,
L. F., AND SURENDRA, M. Generic Online Optimization of Multiple Configuration Parameters With Application to a Database Server. In *Proceedings of
the 14th IFIP/IEEE Workshop on Distributed Systems: Operations and Management (DSOM 2003)* (Oct. 2003).

[44] DIJKSTRA, E. W. Self-Stabilizing Systems in Spite of Distributed Control.
Communications of the ACM 17, 11 (1974), 643–644.

[45] DOLEV, S. *Self-Stabilization*. MIT Press, 2000.

[46] DORIGO, M., BONABEAU, E., AND THERAULAZ, G. Ant Algorithms and
Stigmergy. *Future Generation Computer Systems 16*, 9 (2000), 851–871.

[47] DORIGO, M., CARO, G. D., AND GAMBARDELLA, L. M. The Ant Colony
Optimization Meta-Heuristic. *Artificial Life 5*, 2 (1999), 137–172.

[48] DUCATEL, K., BOGDANOWICZ, M., SCAPOLO, F., LEIJTEN, J., AND
BURGELMAN, J.-C. Scenarios for Ambient Intelligence in 2010. Technical
Report, The IST Advisory Group (ISTAG), 2001.

[49] DUDENHOEFFER, D., AND JONES, M. A Formation Behavior for Large-Scale
Micro-Robot Force Deployment. In *Simulation Conference Proceedings, 2000.
Winter* (2000), vol. 1, pp. 972–982.

[50] FLAKE, G. W., LAWRENCE, S., GILES, C. L., AND COETZEE, F. Self-
Organization of the Web and Identification of Communities. *IEEE Computer
35*, 3 (2002), 66–71.

[51] FORREST, S., HOFMEYR, S. A., AND SOMAYAJI, A. Computer Immunology. *Communications of the ACM 40*, 10 (Oct. 1997), 88–96.

[52] FOSTER, I., AND KESSELMAN, C., Eds. *The Grid: Blueprint for a New Computing Infrastructure*. Morgan Kaufmann Publishers, San Fransisco, 1999.

[53] FUENTES, L., AND JIMÉNEZ, D. An Aspect-Oriented Ambient Intelligence Middleware Platform. In *Proceedings of the 3rd International Workshop on Middleware for Pervasive and Ad-hoc Computing (MPAC '05)* (New York, NY, USA, 2005), ACM Press, pp. 1–8.

[54] FUGGETTA, A., PICCO, G. P., AND VIGNA, G. Understanding Code Mobility. *IEEE Transactions on Software Engineering 24*, 5 (1998), 342–361.

[55] GARNER, W. R., AND MCGILL, W. J. The Relation between Information and Variance Analysis. *Psychometrika 21* (1956), 219–228.

[56] GEIHS, K., KHAN, M., RICHLE, R., SOLBERG, A., AND HALLSTEINSEN, S. Modeling of Component-based Adaptive Distributed Applications. In *Proceedings of the 21st ACM Symposium of Applied Computing 2006* (New York, NY, USA, 2006), ACM Press.

[57] GELERNTER, D. Generative Communication in Linda. *ACM Transactions on Programming Languages and Systems 7*, 1 (1985), 80–112.

[58] GEORGE, S., EVANS, D., AND DAVIDSON, L. A biologically Inspired Programming Model for Self-Healing Systems. In *Proceedings of the First ACM SIGSOFT Workshop on Self-Healing Systems (WOSS '02)* (Nov. 2002).

[59] GERSHENSON, C. A General Methodology for Designing Self-Organizing Systems. Technical Report 2005-05, ECCO, May 2005.

[60] GIORDANO, S. *Mobile Ad hoc Networks*. John Wiley & Sons, Inc., New York, NY, USA, 2002, pp. 325–346.

[61] GRASSÉ, P. P. La reconstruction du nid et les coordinations inter-individuelles chez *Bellicositermes natalensis* et *Cubitermes sp*. La théorie de la stigmergie: Essai d'interpretation des termites constructeurs. *Insectes Sociaux 6* (1959), 41–83.

[62] HAKEN, H. *Information and Self-Organization*. Springer-Verlag, Berlin, 1988.

[63] HANDOREAN, R., AND ROMAN, G.-C. Secure Sharing of Tuple Spaces in Ad Hoc Settings. *Electronic Notes in Theoretical Computer Science 85*, 3 (2003), 1–20.

[64] HAVERKORT, B. R. Model-Based Self-Configuration for Quality-of-Service. In *Proceedings of SELF-STAR: International Workshop on Self-* Properties in Complex Information Systems* (May 2004).

[65] HEISS, H.-U., AND DORMANNS, M. Partitioning and Mapping of Parallel Programs by Self-Organization. *Concurrency – Practice and Experience 8*, 9 (Nov. 1996), 685–706.

[66] HEISS, H.-U., AND SCHMITZ, M. Decentralized Dynamic Load Balancing: The Particles Approach. *Information Sciences 84*, 1–2 (May 1995), 115–128.

[67] HELLENSCHMIDT, M. Distributed Implementation of a Self-Organizing Appliance Middleware. In *Proceedings of sOc-EUSAI 2005 (Smart Objects Conference)* (2005), G. Bailly, Ed., pp. 201–206.

[68] HELLENSCHMIDT, M., AND KIRSTE, T. SodaPop: A Software Infrastructure Supporting Self-Organization in Intelligent Environments. In *Proceedings of the 2nd IEEE Conference on Industrial Informatics, INDIN 04* (June 2004).

[69] HERRMANN, K. MESHMdl – A Middleware for Self-Organization in Ad hoc Networks. In *Proceedings of the 1st International Workshop on Mobile Distributed Computing (MDC'03)* (May 2003).

[70] HERRMANN, K. Modeling the Sociological Aspects of Mobility in Ad hoc Networks. In *Proceedings of the 8th international workshop on Modeling analysis and simulation of wireless and mobile systems* (New York, NY, USA, Sept. 2003), ACM Press, pp. 128–129.

[71] HERRMANN, K. Ad hoc Service Grid – Self-Organizing Distribution of Ambient Services. Report PTB-IT-13 of the PTB (Physikalische Technische Bundesanstalt), 2004. ISBN 3-86509-509-7.

[72] HERRMANN, K., AND GEIHS, K. Integrating Mobile Agents and Neural Networks for Proactive Management. In *New Developments in Distributed Applications and Interoperable Systems, IFIP TC6 / WG6.1 Third International Working Conference on Distributed Applications and Interoperable Systems* (Dordrecht, Netherlends, 2001), Kluwer Academic Publishers, pp. 203–216.

[73] HERRMANN, K., GEIHS, K., AND MÜHL, G. Ad hoc Service Grid – A Self-Organizing Infrastructure for Mobile Commerce. In *Proceedings of the IFIP TC8 Working Conference on Mobile Information Systems (MOBIS 2004)* (Sept. 2004), IFIP – International Federation for Information Processing, Springer-Verlag.

[74] HERRMANN, K., MÜHL, G., AND GEIHS, K. Self-Management: The Solution to Complexity or Just Another Problem? *IEEE Distributed Systems Online 6*, 1 (Jan. 2005).

[75] HERRMANN, K., MÜHL, G., AND JAEGER, M. A. A Self-Organizing Lookup Service for Dynamic Ambient Services. In *25th International Conference on Distributed Computing Systems (ICDCS 2005)* (Piscataway, NJ, USA, June 2005), IEEE Computer Society Press, pp. 707–716.

[76] HERRMANN, K., WERNER, M., AND MÜHL, G. A Methodology for Classifying Self-Organizing Software Systems. In *International Conference on Self-Organization and Autonomous Systems in Computing and Communications (SOAS'2006)* (Sept. 2006).

[77] HEYLIGHEN, F. Self-Organization, Emergence and the Architecture of Complexity. In *Proceedings of the 1st European Conference on System Science, (AFCET, Paris)* (1989), pp. 23–32.

[78] HEYLIGHEN, F. Principia Cybernetica Web. http://pespmc1.vub.ac.be/ SELFORG.html, Jan. 1997. (Jan. 31, 2006).

[79] HEYLIGHEN, F., AND GERSHENSON, C. The Meaning of Self-organization in Computing. *IEEE Intelligent Systems 18*, 4 (July – Aug. 2003), 72–75.

[80] HOE, K. M., LAI, W. K., AND TAI, T. S. Homogeneous Ants for Web Document Similarity Modeling and Categorization. In *Proceedings of the Third International Workshop on Ant Algorithms (ANTS 2002)* (Sept. 2002).

[81] HOLLAND, O., AND MELHUISH, C. Stigmergy, Self-Organization, and Sorting in Collective Robotics. *Artificial Life 5*, 2 (1999), 173–202.

[82] HORN, P. AUTONOMIC COMPUTING: IBM's Perspective on the State of Information Technology. http://www.research.ibm.com/autonomic/ manifesto/autonomic_computing.pdf, Oct. 2001. (May 8, 2006).

[83] HSU, W. W., SMITH, A. J., AND YOUNG, H. C. I/O Reference Behavior of Production Database Workloads and the TPC Benchmarks–An Analysis at the Logical Level. *ACM Transactions on Database Systems 26*, 1 (Mar. 2001), 96–143.

[84] IBM. Autonomic Computing: IBM's Perspective on the State of Information Technology. http://www-1.ibm.com/industries/government/doc/ content/resource/thought/278606109.html (2006, February 4).

[85] ISHIKAWA, F., TAHARA, Y., YOSHIOKA, N., AND HONIDEN, S. A Framework for Synthesis of Web Services and Mobile Agents. *International Journal of Pervasive Computing and Communications (JPCC) 1*, 3 (Sept. 2005), 227–245.

[86] ISSARNY, V., SACCHETTI, D., TARTANOGLU, F., SAILHAN, F., CHIBOUT, R., LÉVY, N., AND TALAMONA, A. Developing Ambient Intelligence Systems: A Solution based on Web Services. *Automated Software Engineering 12*, 1 (2005), 101–137.

[87] JAIN, K., PADHYE, J., PADMANABHAN, V. N., AND QIU, L. Impact of Interference on Multi-Hop Wireless Network Performance. In *Proceedings of the 9th Annual International Conference on Mobile Computing and Networking (MobiCom'03)* (New York, NY, USA, 2003), ACM Press, pp. 66–80.

[88] JAIN, K., AND VAZIRANI, V. V. Approximation Algorithms for Metric Facility Location and k-Median Problems Using the Primal-Dual Schema and Lagrangian Relaxation. *J. ACM 48*, 2 (2001), 274–296.

[89] JIA, X., LI, D., HU, X., AND DU, D. Optimal Placement of Web Proxies for Replicated Web Servers in the Internet. *The Computer Journal 44*, 5 (2001), 329–339.

[90] JIA, X., LI, D., HU, X., AND DU, D. Placement of Read-Write Web Proxies in the Internet. In *Proceedings of the 21st International Conference on Distributed Computing Systems (ICDCS 2001)* (Apr. 2001), pp. 687–690.

[91] KANGASHARJU, J., ROBERTS, J., AND ROSS, K. W. Object Replication Strategies in Content Distribution Networks. *Computer Communications 25*, 4 (Mar. 2002), 367–383.

[92] KARLSSON, M., AND KARAMANOLIS, C. Choosing Replica Placement Heuristics for Wide-Area Systems. In *Proceedings of the International Conference on Distributed Computing Systems (ICDCS)* (Mar. 2004), pp. 350–359.

[93] KASSABALIDIS, I., M.A.EL-SHARKAWI, II, R., ARABSHAHI, P., AND A.A.GRAY. Swarm Intelligence for Routing in Communication Networks. In *Proceedings of the IEEE Globecom 2001* (Nov. 2001).

[94] KASTIDOU, G., PITOURA, E., AND SAMARAS, G. A Scalable Mobile Agent Location Mechanism. In *Proceedings of the 1st International Workshop on Mobile Distributed Computing (MDC'03)* (May 2003).

[95] KEPHART, J., AND CHESS, D. The Vision of Autonomic Computing. *IEEE Computer 36*, 1 (Jan. 2003), 41–50.

[96] KO, B.-J., AND RUBENSTEIN, D. Distributed Server Replication in Large Scale Networks. In *Proceedings of the 14th International Workshop on Network and Operating Systems Support for Digital Audio and Video* (New York, NY, USA, 2004), ACM Press, pp. 127–132.

[97] LAMPORT, L. Time, Clocks, and the Ordering of Events in a Distributed System. *Communications of the ACM 21*, 7 (1978), 558–565.

[98] LEE, B.-D., AND WEISSMAN, J. B. Dynamic Replica Management in the Service Grid. In *Proceedings of the 10th IEEE International Symposium on High Performance Distributed Computing (HPDC-10'01)* (Aug. 2001).

[99] LI, B., DENG, X., GOLIN, M. J., AND SOHRABY, K. On the Optimal Placement of Web Proxies in the Internet. In *HPN '98: Proceedings of the IFIP TC-6 Eighth International Conference on High Performance Networking* (Deventer, The Netherlands, 1998), Kluwer Academic Publishers, pp. 485–495.

[100] LI, K., AND SHEN, H. Optimal Placement of Web Proxies for Tree Networks. In *Proceedings of 2004 IEEE International Conference on e-Technology, e-Commerce and e-Service (EEE'04)* (2004), pp. 479–486.

[101] LI, T.-Y., AND LAM, K.-Y. An Optimal Location Update and Searching Algorithm for Tracking Mobile Agent. In *Proceedings of the first international joint conference on Autonomous agents and multiagent systems* (New York, NY, USA, 2002), ACM Press, pp. 639–646.

[102] LIM, A. Distributed Services for Information Dissemination in Self-Organizing Sensor Networks. *Journal of Franklin Institute 338*, 6 (Sept. 2001), 707–727.

[103] LIU, K., LUI, J., AND ZHANG, Z.-L. On Service Replication Strategy for Service Overlay Networks. In *Proceedings of the Network Operations and Management Symposium (NOMS 2004)* (Apr. 2004), pp. 643–656.

[104] LIU, K. Y., LUI, J. C., AND ZHANG, Z.-L. Distributed Algorithm for Service Replication in Service Overlay Network. In *Proceedings of the 3rd IEEE/IFIP TC-6 Networking Conference (Networking2004)* (2004).

[105] MAGGS, B., MATHESON, L., AND TARJAN, R. Models of Parallel Computation: A Survey and Synthesis. In *Proceedings of the Twenty-Eighth Hawaii International Conference on System Sciences* (Jan. 1995), vol. 2, pp. 61–70.

[106] MALEK, M., SALFNER, F., AND HOFFMANN, G. A. Self Rejuvenation – An Effective Way to High Availability. In *Proceedings of SELF-STAR: International Workshop on Self-* Properties in Complex Information Systems* (May 2004).

[107] MAMEI, M., AND ZAMBONELLI, F. Self-Organization in Multi Agent Systems: a Middleware Approach. In *Engineering Self-Organising Applications, First International Workshop, ESOA 2003. Melbourne, Victoria, July 15th, 2003. Workshop Notes* (July 2003), G. D. M. Serugendo, A. Karageorgos, O. F. Rana, and F. Zambonelli, Eds., pp. 1–10.

[108] MANIEZZO, V., GAMBARDELLA, L., AND LUIGI, F. D. *New Optimization Techniques in Engineering.* Springer-Verlag, Berlin Heidelberg, 2004, ch. Ant Colony Optimization, pp. 101–117.

[109] MANZANO, Y., AND YILMAZ, E. Surveying Formal and Practical Approaches for Optimal Placement of Replicas on the Web. Technical Report TR-020701, Department of Computer Science, Florida State University, Apr. 2002.

[110] MARTINOLI, A. Collective Complexity out of Individual Simplicity. Invited book review on "Swarm Intelligence: From Natural to Artificial Systems" by E. Bonabeau, M. Dorigo, and G. Theraulaz. *Artificial Life 7*, 3 (2001), 315–319.

[111] MICROSOFT COOPERATION. Dynamic Systems Initiative Overview White Paper. http://www.microsoft.com/windowsserversystem/dsi/dsiwp.mspx, Mar. 2004. (Feb. 4, 2006).

[112] MILNOR, J. On the Concept of Attractor. *Communications in Mathematical Physics 99*, 2 (1985), 177–195.

[113] MINAR, N., KRAMER, K. H., AND MAES, P. *Software Agents for Future Communication Systems.* Springer-Verlag, 1999, ch. Cooperating Mobile Agents for Dynamic Network Routing.

[114] MOY, J. OSPF Version 2. RFC 2328 (Standard), Apr. 1998.

[115] MÜLLER-SCHLOER, C. Organic Computing: On the Feasibility of Controlled Emergence. In *CODES+ISSS* (New York, NY, USA, 2004), A. Orailoglu, P. H. Chou, P. Eles, and A. Jantsch, Eds., ACM Press, pp. 2–5.

[116] MURPHY, A. L., PICCO, G. P., AND ROMAN, G.-C. Lime: A Middleware for Physical and Logical Mobility. In *Proceedings of the 21st International Conference on Distributed Computing Systems (ICDCS-21), Phoenix, AZ, USA* (Apr. 2001), pp. 524–533.

[117] NAGPAL, R., KONDACS, A., AND CHANG, C. Programming Methodology for Biologically-Inspired Self-Assembling Systems. In *Proceedings of the AAAI Spring Symposium on Computational Synthesis: From Basic Building Blocks to High-Level Functionality* (Mar. 2003).

[118] NAKANO, T., AND SUDA, T. Self-Organizing Network Services with Evolutionary Adaptation. *IEEE Transactions on Neural Networks 16*, 5 (Sept. 2005), 1269–1278.

[119] NICOLIS, G., AND PRIGOGINE, I. *Self-Organization in Non-Equilibrium Systems*. John Wiley & Sons, Inc., New York, NY, USA, 1977.

[120] NITTO, E. D., GHEZZI, C., SABBA, M., AND SELVINI, P. Using Agents in Performing Multi-site Queries. In *CIA '01: Proceedings of the 5th International Workshop on Cooperative Information Agents V* (London, UK, 2001), Springer-Verlag, pp. 100–105.

[121] NWANA, H. S. Software Agents: An Overview. *Knowledge Engineering Review 11*, 3 (Oct. / Nov. 1996), 205–244.

[122] O'HARE, G. M. P., O'GRADY, M. J., COLLIER, R. W., KEEGAN, S., O'KANE, D., TYNAN, R., AND MARSH, D. Ambient Intelligence Through Agile Agents. In *Ambient Intelligence for Scientific Discovery* (2004), Y. Cai, Ed., vol. 3345 of *Lecture Notes in Computer Science*, Springer-Verlag, pp. 286–310.

[123] OHTAKI, Y., WAKAMIYA, N., MURATA, M., AND IMASE, M. Scalable Ant-based Routing Algorithm for Ad-hoc Networks. In *Proceedings of the 3rd IASTED International Conference on Communications, Internet, and Information Technology (CIIT 2004)* (2004).

[124] OTTINO, J. M. Engineering Complex Systems. *Nature 427* (Jan. 2004), 399.

[125] OUSTERHOUT, J. K., COSTA, H. D., HARRISON, D., KUNZE, J. A., KUPFER, M., AND THOMPSON, J. G. A Trace-driven Analysis of the UNIX 4.2 BSD File System. *ACM SIGOPS Operating Systems Review 19*, 5 (1985), 15–24.

[126] PACZUSKI, M., AND BAK, P. Self-Organization of Complex Systems. In *Proceedings of 12th Chris Engelbrecht Summer School* (1999).

[127] PETERS, J. Integration of Mobile Agents and Web Services. In *Proceedings of the First European Young Researchers Workshop on Service Oriented Computing (YR-SOC 2005)* (2005), pp. 53–58.

[128] PETERSEN, K., SPREITZER, M. J., TERRY, D. B., THEIMER, M. M., AND DEMERS, A. J. Flexible Update Propagation for Weakly Consistent Replication. In *Proceedings of the Sixteenth ACM Symposium on Operating Systems Principles* (New York, NY, USA, 1997), ACM Press, pp. 288–301.

[129] PETERSEN, K., SPREITZER, M. J., TERRY, D. B., THEIMER, M. M., AND DEMERS, A. J. Flexible Update Propagation for Weakly Consistent Replication. In *Proceedings of the Sixteenth ACM Symposium on Operating Systems Principles* (New York, NY, USA, 1997), ACM Press, pp. 288–301.

[130] PICCO, G. P. Mobile Agents: An Introduction. *Journal of Microprocessors and Microsystems 25*, 2 (Apr. 2001), 65–74.

[131] PIERRE, G., VAN STEEN, M., AND TANENBAUM, A. S. Dynamically Selecting Optimal Distribution Strategies for Web Documents. *IEEE Transactions on Computers 51*, 6 (June 2002), 637–651.

[132] PINSDORF, U., PETERS, J., HOFFMANN, M., AND GUPTA, P. Context-Aware Services based on Secure Mobile Agents. In *10th International Conference on Software, Telecommunications & Computer Networks (SoftCOM 2002)* (Oct. 2002), N. Rozic and D. Begusic, Eds., Faculty of Electrical Engineering, Mechanical Engineering and Naval Architecture, pp. 366–370. ISBN 953-6114-52-6.

[133] POPPER, K. R. *The Logic of Scientific Discovery.* Harper and Row, 1959.

[134] PUDER, A., AND GEIHS, K. System Support for Knowledge-Based Trading in Open Service Markets. In *EW 7: Proceedings of the 7th Workshop on ACM SIGOPS European Workshop* (New York, NY, USA, 1996), ACM Press, pp. 289–296.

[135] PUDER, A., MARKWITZ, S., GUDERMANN, F., AND GEIHS, K. AI-based Trading in Open Distributed Environments. In *Proceedings of the 3rd International IFIP TC6 Conference on Open Distributed Processing (ICODP'95)* (1995).

[136] QIU, L., PADMANABHAN, N. V., AND VOELKER, M. G. On the Placement of Web Server Replicas. In *Proceedings of IEEE INFOCOM* (2001), pp. 12–22.

[137] RABINOVICH, M., AND AGGARWAL, A. RaDaR: A Scalable Architecture for a Global Web Hosting Service. In *Proceedings of the 8th International World Wide Web Conference* (May 1999).

[138] RABINOVICH, M., RABINOVICH, I., RAJARAMAN, R., AND AGGARWAL, A. A Dynamic Object Replication and Migration Protocol for an Internet Hosting Service. In *Proceedings of IEEE International Conference on Distributed Computing Systems* (May 1999).

[139] RADOSLAVOV, P., GOVINDAN, R., AND ESTRIN, D. Topology-Informed Internet Replica Placement. In *Proceedings of the Sixth International Workshop on Web Caching and Content Distribution* (June 2001).

[140] RAMOS, V., AND MERELO, J. J. Self-Organized Stigmergic Document Maps: Environment as a Mechanism for Context Learning. In *AEB'2002 – 1st Spanish Conference on Evolutionary and Bio-Inspired Algorithms* (Feb. 2002), pp. 284–293.

[141] REGMI, A., SANDOVAL, R., BYRNE, R., TANNER, H., AND ABDALLAH, C. Experimental Implementation of Flocking Algorithms in Wheeled Mobile Robots. In *Proceedings of the 2005 American Control Conference* (Piscataway, NJ, USA, 2005), IEEE Computer Society Press, pp. 4917–4922.

[142] REYNOLDS, C. W. Flocks, Herds, and Schools: A Distributed Behavioral Model. In *SIGGRAPH '87: Proceedings of the 14th Annual Conference on Computer Graphics and Interactive Techniques* (New York, NY, USA, 1987), ACM Press, pp. 25–34.

[143] RODRÍGUEZ, M., FAVELA, J., PRECIADO, A., AND VIZCAÍNO, A. An Agent Middleware for Supporting Ambient Intelligence for Healthcare. In *Second Workshop on Agents Applied in Health Care (ECAI 2004)* (Aug. 2004).

[144] RONALD, E. M. A., SIPPER, M., AND CAPCARRÈRE, M. S. Design, Observation, Surprise! A Test of Emergence. *Artificial Life 5*, 3 (1999), 225–239.

[145] ROSSIER, D., AND SCHEURER, R. An Ecosystem-Inspired Mobile Agent Middleware for Active Network Management. In *MATA'02: 4th International Workshop on Mobile Agents in Telecommunications Applications, Barcelona, Spain* (Oct. 2002), vol. 2521 of *Lecture Notes in Computer Science*, Springer-Verlag, pp. 73–82.

[146] ROUSE, W. B. Engineering Complex Systems: Implications for Research in Systems Engineering. *IEEE Transactions on Systems, Man, and Cybernetics – Part C: Applications and Reviews 33*, 2 (May 2003), 154–156.

[147] ROUSSEAU, F., OPRESCU, J., PAUN, L.-S., AND DUDA, A. Omnisphere: A Personal Communication Environment. In *Proceedings of the 36th Hawaii International Conference on System Sciences (HICSS-36 2003)* (2003).

[148] SAITO, Y., AND SHAPIRO, M. Optimistic Replication. *ACM Computing Surveys 37*, 1 (2005), 42–81.

[149] SAMARAS, G., KARENOS, K., CHRYSANTHIS, P., AND PITOURA, E. ViSMA: Extendible, Mobile-Agent Based Services for the Materialization and Maintenance of Personalized and Shareable Web Views. In *Proceedings of the 14th International Workshop on Database and Expert Systems Applications* (2003).

[150] SAMARAS, G., SPYROU, C., PITOURA, E., AND DIKAIAKOS, M. Tracker: A Universal Location Management System for Mobile Agents. In *Proceedings fo the European Wireless 2002 Conference* (Feb. 2002).

[151] SATOH, I. Mobile Agents for Ambient Intelligence. In *Proceedings of the First International Workshop on Massively Multi-Agent Systems (MMAS 2004)* (2004), T. Ishida, L. Gasser, and H. Nakashima, Eds., vol. 3446 of *Lecture Notes in Computer Science*, Springer-Verlag, pp. 187–201.

[152] SATYANARAYANAN, M. Coda: A Highly Available File System for a Distributed Workstation Environment. In *Proceedings of the Second IEEE Workshop on Workstation Operating Systems* (Sept. 1989).

[153] SCHMECK, H. Organic Computing – A New Vision for Distributed Embedded Systems. In *Proceedings of the Eighth IEEE International Symposium on Object-Oriented Real-Time Distributed Computing (ISORC 2005)* (May 2005), IEEE Computer Society Press, pp. 201–203.

[154] SCHOONDERWOERD, R., HOLLAND, O., AND BRUTEN., J. Ant-like Agents for Load Balancing in Telecommunications networks. In *Agents '97, Proceedings of the First International Conference on Autonomous Agents* (New York, NY, USA, 1997), ACM Press, pp. 209–216.

[155] SHANNON, C. E. A Mathematical Theory of Communication. *Bell System Technical Journal 27* (July and Oct. 1948), 379–423 and 623–656.

[156] SHAW, M. Self-Healing: Softening Precision to Avoid Brittleness. In *Proceedings of the First ACM SIGSOFT Workshop on Self-Healing Systems (WOSS '02)* (Nov. 2002), pp. 111–113.

[157] SOLE, R. V., BONABEAU, E., DELGADO, J., P., F., AND MARIN, J. Pattern Formation and Optimization in Army Ant Raids. *Artificial Life 6*, 3 (2000), 219–226.

[158] STERRITT, R., PARASHAR, M., TIANFIELD, H., AND UNLAND, R. A Concise Introduction to Autonomic Computing. *Advanced Engineering Informatics 19* (2005), 181–187.

[159] SUN MICROSYSTEMS. Jini™ Architecture Specification. http://www.jini.org/standards/. (May 8, 2006).

[160] SUN MICROSYSTEMS. JavaSpaces™ Service Specification, v1.2.1. http://www.sun.com/software/jini/specs/js1_2_1.pdf, Apr. 2002. (May 8, 2006).

[161] SUZUKI, J., AND SUDA, T. A Middleware Platform for a Biologically-inspired Network Architecture Supporting Autonomous and Adaptive Applications. *IEEE Journal on Selected Areas in Communications 23*, 2 (Feb. 2005), 249–260.

[162] SZYMANIAK, M., PIERRE, G., AND VAN STEEN, M. Latency-Driven Replica Placement. In *Proceedings of the International Symposium on Applications and the Internet (SAINT)* (Trento, Italy, Feb. 2005), pp. 399–405.

[163] TENNENHOUSE, D. Proactive Computing. *Communications of the ACM 43*, 5 (2000), 43–50.

[164] TENZAKHTI, F., DAY, K., OULD-KHAOUA, M., AND OBADIAT, M. S. Placement of Web Proxies with Server Capacity Constraints. In *Proceedings of High Performance Computing Symposium (HPC 2004)* (Apr. 2004), Kluwer Academic Publishers, pp. 101–106.

[165] TERRY, D. B., DEMERS, A. J., PETERSEN, K., SPREITZER, M. J., THEIMER, M. M., AND WELCH, B. B. Session Guarantees for Weakly Consistent Replicated Data. In *Proceedings of the Third International Conference on Parallel and Distributed Information Systems* (1994), IEEE Computer Society Press, pp. 140–150.

[166] TERRY, D. B., THEIMER, M. M., PETERSEN, K., DEMERS, A. J., SPREITZER, M. J., AND HAUSER, C. H. Managing Update Conflicts in Bayou, a Weakly Connected Replicated Storage System. In *Proceedings of the Fifteenth ACM Symposium on Operating Systems Principles* (New York, NY, USA, 1995), ACM Press, pp. 172–182.

[167] TERRY, M., MYNATT, E. D., RYALL, K., AND LEIGH, D. Social Net: Using Patterns of Physical Proximity Over Time to Infer Shared Interests. In *Proceedings of Human Factors in Computing Systems (CHI 2002)* (Minneapolis, MN, 2002).

[168] THE SALUTATION CONSORTIUM. Salutation Architecture Specification – Version 2.0c. http://www.salutation.org/, June 1999. (Mar. 17, 2003).

[169] TONER, J., AND TU., Y. Flocks, Herds, and Schools: A Quantitative Theory of Flocking. *Physical Review E 58*, 4 (1998).

[170] UPNP FORUM. UPnP(TM) Devic Architecture 1.0, Dec. 2003.

[171] UTTAMCHANDANI, S., TALCOTT, C., AND PEASE, D. Eos: An Approach of Using Behavior Implications for Policy-based Self-Management. In *Proceedings of the 14th IFIP/IEEE Workshop on Distributed Systems: Operations and Management (DSOM 2003)* (Oct. 2003).

[172] VALLÉE, M., RAMPARANY, F., AND VERCOUTER, L. A Multi-Agent System for Dynamic Service Composition in Ambient Intelligence Environments. In *Advances in Pervasive Computing, Adjunct Proceedings of the Third International Conference on Pervasive Computing (Pervasive 2005)* (May 2005).

[173] VDE, ITG, G. Organic Computing: Computer- und Systemarchitektur im Jahr 2010, VDE/ITG/GI Positionspapier. URL: *http : //www.gi − ev.de/fileadmin/redaktion/Presse/VDE − ITG − GI − Positionspapier_20Organic_20Computing.pdf* (2006, January 31) (german), 2003.

[174] VITEK, J., BRYCE, C., AND ORIOL, M. Coordinating Agents with Secure Spaces. In *Proceedings of Coordination '99* (1999), Lecture Notes in Computer Science, Springer-Verlag.

[175] WALKER, B., POPEK, G., ENGLISH, R., KLINE, C., AND THIEL, G. The LOCUS Distributed Operating System. In *Proceedings of the Ninth ACM Symposium on Operating Systems Principles* (New York, NY, USA, 1983), ACM Press, pp. 49–70.

[176] WANG, F. Self-Organising Communities Formed by Middle Agents. In *Proceedings of the First International Joint Conference on Autonomous Agents and Multiagent Systems* (2002).

[177] WANG, M., AND SUDA, T. The Bio-Networking Architecture: A Biologically Inspired Approach to the Design of Scalable, Adaptive, and Survivable / Available Network Applications. Technical Report TR00-03, Department of Information and Computer Science, University of California, Irvine, Feb. 2000.

[178] WANG, T., AND ZHANG, H. Collective Sorting With Multiple Robots. In *Proceedings of the 2004 IEEE International Conference on Robotics and Biomimetics* (Aug. 2004), pp. 716–720.

[179] WANT, R., PERING, T., AND TENNENHOUSE, D. Comparing Autonomic and Proactive Computing. *IBM Systems Journal 42*, 1 (2003), 129–135.

[180] WATTS, D., AND STROGATZ, S. Collective Dynamics of 'Small-World' Networks. *Nature 393* (1998), 440–442.

[181] WHITE, T. Swarm Intelligence and Problem Solving in Telecommunications. *Canadian Artificial Intelligence Magazine* (Spring 1997).

[182] WHITE, T., AND PAGUREK, B. Distributed Fault Location in Networks Using Learning Mobile Agents. In *Approaches to Intelligent Agents, Second Pacific Rim International Workshop on Multi-Agents, PRIMA'99, Kyoto, Japan* (Dec. 1999).

[183] WONG, D., PACIOREK, N., AND WALSH, T. Concordia: An Infrastructure for Collaborating Mobile Agents. In *Proceedings of the First International Workshop on Mobile Agents* (1997), vol. 1219 of *LNCS*, Springer-Verlag, pp. 86–97.

[184] WRIGHT, W. A., SMITH, R. E., DANEK, M., AND GREENWAY, P. A Generalisable Measure of Self-Organisation and Emergence. In *Proceedings of the International Conference on Artificial Neural Networks – ICANN 2001* (Aug. 2001), vol. 2130 of *Lecture Notes in Computer Science*, Springer-Verlag, pp. 857–864.

[185] ZADEH, L. On the Definition of Adaptivity. *Proceedings of the IEEE 51* (Mar. 1963), 469.

[186] ZADEH, L. What is Soft Computing? *Soft Computing 1*, 1 (1997), 1.

[187] ZAPF, M., HERRMANN, K., AND GEIHS, K. Decentralized SNMP Management with Mobile Agents. In *International Symposium on Integrated Network Management (IM)* (Boston, USA, 1999).

[188] ZHANG, H., GOEL, A., AND GOVINDAN, R. Using the Small World Model to Improve Freenet Performance. In *Proceedings of IEEE Infocom* (June 2002).

[189] ZHOU, G., HE, T., KRISHNAMURTHY, S., AND STANKOVIC, J. A. Impact of Radio Irregularity on Wireless Sensor Networks. In *Proceedings of the Second International Conference on Mobile Systems, Applications, and Services* (June 2004).

Index

www.ingramcontent.com/pod-product-compliance
Lightning Source LLC
LaVergne TN
LVHW022304060326
832902LV00020B/3266